More Praise for *Smarter, Faster, Better*

"Karlin is without peer among business leaders. Using no jargon or clichés but wisdom and fresh insight, she tells all of us in business, from new recruits to CEOs, how to be the most effective leaders we can be. Her book is as inspiring as it is practical."

—Barbara Johnson, president, Rowland Reading Foundation

"A must-read for anyone who influences people and seeks to be more effective. Karlin Sloan captures her audience with realistic scenarios demonstrating her breadth of experience and keen insights into the human mind."

—Lorri Zelman, president, Human Resources Association of New York

"I am casting an appreciative eye toward Karlin Sloan for her thoughtful work in building smarter, faster, and better leaders. As we emerge from the dark days of corruption in corporate leadership, it is nice to be reminded that there is someone who wants to help leaders be ethical as well as profitable."

—Karen Bloom, principal, Bloom, Gross & Associates, Inc.

"This book is the best thing next to having customized executive coaching sessions with Karlin Sloan. She's truly the master coach, providing practical tactics that have immediate positive impact on the way you lead yourself and your organization."

—Sidney Chapon, vice president, leadership and organizational development, Leo Burnett Worldwide, Inc.

"Sloan has taken not only what she knows but what she intuits, and shares her wisdom with the rest of the business world in *Smarter, Faster, Better*. Through her stories, we recognize ourselves and the challenges we face; through her insight, we see what we couldn't see before."

—M. Nora Klaver, author, *Ask & Receive: The Virtues of Asking for Help*

"*Smarter, Faster, Better* is a courageous book. It reminds us of what we know intuitively to be true but often don't practice in reality. Leadership is a great responsibility, and it's not just about leading from our head, but bringing our whole selves, heart, and passion to inspire others around us."

—Elizabeth Moran, director of global learning, Getty Images, Inc.

Smarter, Faster, Better

Strategies for Effective, Enduring, and Fulfilled Leadership

Karlin Sloan

with Lindsey Pollak

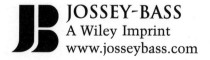

JOSSEY-BASS
A Wiley Imprint
www.josseybass.com

Published by Jossey-Bass
A Wiley Imprint
989 Market Street, San Francisco, CA 94103-1741   www.josseybass.com

Jossey-Bass books and products are available through most bookstores. To contact Jossey-Bass directly call our Customer Care Department within the U.S. at 800-956-7739, outside the U.S. at 317-572-3986, or fax 317-572-4002.

Jossey-Bass also publishes its books in a variety of electronic formats. Some content that appears in print may not be available in electronic books.

Library of Congress Cataloging-in-Publication Data

Sloan, Karlin, date.
  Smarter, faster, better : strategies for effective, enduring, and fulfilled leadership / Karlin Sloan with Lindsey Pollak.
    p. cm.
  Includes bibliographical references and index.
  ISBN-13: 978-0-7879-8268-3 (cloth)
  ISBN-10: 0-7879-8268-7 (cloth)
    1. Leadership—Handbooks, manuals, etc. I. Pollak, Lindsey. II. Title.
  HD57.7.S59 2006
  658.4'092—dc22   2006009301

Printed in the United States of America
FIRST EDITION
HB Printing   10 9 8 7 6 5 4 3 2 1

Contents

INTRODUCTION

Laura is a hard worker, a long-time leader, and a well-compensated executive. She is also a friend, sister, mentor, and avid swimmer. She does laps every morning before work and raises money for an inner-city high school arts program. Once a month, she hosts an all-staff breakfast where she invites employees of all levels to share any ideas they have for the company, and she asks provocative questions of the group, like "What are new ideas for great customer service?" or "Who in our industry has a great employee development program that we can learn from?" She has a committed team that works hard and believes in the value of the organization—and in their role in its success. She also serves on the board of an industry association, where she networks with colleagues from competing companies, and they design ways to work together to create industry awareness. Once a year she takes a ten-day vacation to an "undisclosed location," where she turns off her cell phone and BlackBerry and reads as many novels as she can. Sometimes the stories even give her business ideas.

Lee is also a hard worker, a long-time leader, and a well-compensated executive. Lee used to swim as well, but she recently switched to walking on a treadmill so she can return calls on her cell phone while she exercises. She doesn't have time to take part in any volunteer projects except for writing the occasional check to charity. Lee has found that much of her time is spent covering for other people who are not doing their jobs well. She is afraid of delegating anything for fear the ball will be dropped. Lee has recently become very worried about a competitor that recruited several staff members from her sales team. She avoids any event where she might see any of them. Lee admits she is completely stressed out and seems to have lost her passion for her job. She travels constantly and has two cell phones in addition to her Black-Berry. She has begun to suffer from migraine headaches that debilitate her for days at a time, forcing her to stay in bed and not turn on any lights. On the bad migraine days, Lee says she can't even think.

You don't have to be a leadership expert to guess which of these executives is a more effective, enduring, and fulfilled leader. The first, Laura, is achieving excellent results for herself and her team, and she seems to be enjoying herself in the process. The second, Lee, is clearly missing something.

These leadership profiles, like many you will read in this book, come from my experience as a coach to organizational leaders, and from the experiences of my executive coaching team, who have provided many of the stories housed here. As executive coaches, our goal is to help people gain perspective and self-knowledge, seize opportunities they may not have seen before, achieve their highest potential, and resolve the issues that threaten to hold them back from the success they desire for themselves and their organizations.

Like all my coaching clients, both Laura and Lee are smart, knowledgeable about what they do, and hold positions of power in their organizations. They are both *good*. But, like many leaders, they both want to be more than just good. They want to reach beyond: to be more productive, more satisfied, more valuable.

Organizations and the individuals that populate them often won't call a coach when everything is going along smoothly. People generally come to coaching when they, or their organization, are facing a challenge, an opportunity, a struggle, or a crossroads. If this is the case with you today, I have good news: it is in moments of greatest challenge and greatest opportunity for change that we have the greatest incentive to grow and to cultivate and use our strengths. In fact, I find that the most compelling, life-changing moments I observe in leaders come at the moment when they realize that they are not just striving to compete and begin to think about sustainable greatness—about transcending the everyday struggles and successes of the business world and reaching a stage of real impact.

The good news is that we have all experienced moments like this—moments when it all seems to come together, when we are really doing our best, performing at our peak and feeling pride in our accomplishments. And so, when people ask me, "How can I be smarter, faster, and better as a leader?" I respond right back with a question: "When have you previously been most effective, most powerful, most influential, and most satisfied?" Your own stories hold the key to the best there is in you.

In other words, to figure out how to become smarter, faster, and better, begin to inquire about the times when you are at your smartest, your fastest, and your best already.

THE PATTERN OF PARADOX: LEADERSHIP AND PARADOXICAL THINKING

As a student of leadership, I'm fascinated with how leaders think, grow, and learn. I spend most of my professional life observing the patterns and paradoxes that make up the challenge of leading teams and companies to change, to get things done, to adapt and evolve.

I was fortunate to start my first company during California's Silicon Valley technology boom, surrounded by rule-breakers, innovators, and expansive thinkers. I learned from these clients that I should never take anything at face value. One of the greatest lessons of leadership, I believe, is accepting the need to contemplate paradox. Things are not always what they seem, and when we look at becoming smarter, faster, and better, there are three paradoxical truths to explore.

Traditional (or should I call it "twentieth-century"?) business thinking holds that being *smarter* means gathering knowledge, learning more and more, and becoming a certified expert. It used to be that being a smart leader meant that you simply knew more than anyone else.

But now, information is managed in entirely different ways. Information, thanks in large part to the Internet, is accessible by all. So, in the twenty-first century, being smart often means knowing how to *manage and distribute* information, not knowing the information itself. The idea that the leader is the authority on all things no longer holds.

So if information itself does not make a leader smarter, then what does? Herein lies the paradox. Today, it is the ability to ask powerful questions that really makes a leader smarter. It is a tolerance of ambiguity and an ability to see the big picture—to see the impact of decision making on a complex system. Contemporary leaders must know how to get the information they seek, how to inspire others to action based on that information, and how to surround themselves with a network of intellectual capacity that extends far beyond their own.

The *smarter* paradox is this: To be smarter, we need to stop being the expert and start asking more questions.

On the same theme, what if we altered our definition of *faster*? What if we changed our relationship to time and decided that we will not let time rule us? In 1890, Frederick W. Taylor, a former engineer at Midvale Steel Works, began as one of the first management consultants, performing studies of the time required to complete manufacturing tasks. The discipline of management consulting started with—literally—stopwatches. In some ways, this was very useful: you could optimize your production based on, say, how many shovelfuls of dirt someone could handle in a given time before becoming unproductive. And in some organizations—say, dirt-shoveling companies—that strategy may still be useful. But in most business leadership today, stopwatch logic no longer works.

We now rely on innovation, intelligence, and a big-picture perspective. These things all depend on stopping the tyranny of time. Why? As outlined in Part Two, innovation often happens when your brain is in the alpha or theta states—when you feel relaxed and lose track of time. It is okay for implementers in your organization to be required to accomplish X task in X time. But as a leader, sometimes you have to let go of time pressure in order to achieve great things. As leadership guru Warren Bennis says, "The manager asks how and when; the leader asks what and why."

Slowing down is not so easy to do these days. It is certainly no secret that we live in a culture in which we are expected to be constantly available and constantly "on." Think about this for a moment: What if we weren't? What if good leadership meant setting different boundaries with our time so that creativity and deep thinking would be possible?

The *faster* paradox is this: To be faster, we need to slow down.

I suspect I know what you are thinking at this point, because I have heard countless executives express the same concern: How can I ask more questions when the competition is already proposing answers? How can I slow down when others are moving at laser speed? Here is where the third paradox of leadership becomes so important. It is the paradox of being *better.*

To be better, we need to stop focusing on our own personal competitive advantage. Instead, we should focus on others and on giving back to our company, our community, and our world. I think it's perfectly okay, in fact necessary, to want to keep personally improving and evolving. In fact, I think that to stay vital and alive we should always keep learning and growing. My argument is not really with the word *better.* It's with the word *than.* When you strive to be better *than* someone or something else, you are always defining your success against a force outside yourself. Effective, enduring, and fulfilled leadership comes from a desire not to be better *than,* but to be better *with:* to be better *with* the current market forces, to be better *with* current challenges, to be better *with* your team members, to be better *with* your stakeholders, your customers, and ultimately *with* the external world.

The *better* paradox is this: To be better, we need to stop focusing on our personal gain and start focusing on giving back—to our organization, to our community, and to the world as a whole.

Great leaders do not do things the way everyone expects. They do not follow all the rules. They know the organizational world contains a complex and ever-shifting set of variables, as does the world outside the organization. The smartest, fastest, and best leaders are the most curious and inquisitive; they set boundaries with their time so they have room to be creative and improve themselves and their organizations by accepting and maximizing opportunities at every moment. They focus on their team members, their organizations, their industries, their customers, and their communities. In other words, the ultimate paradox of great individual leadership is that it is really about the success of the whole group. It's about *we,* not just *me.*

FOUR ASSUMPTIONS TO SET THE STAGE

Here is the bottom line: You can kill yourself to get to the top (and crash and burn when you reach the peak), or you can create sustainability in your life and in your company. If you don't want to experience early burnout, stress-related illness, turnover of valuable staff, and daily financial pyrotechnics, then you have to change your mind-set from the daily game of competition to the daily practice of sustainability for your career and your organization. Adopt the following mind-set and I know it will change your life: You are not just leading your organization; you are *leading your legacy*. Every day you are creating the future for your stakeholders—including your shareholders, employees, and customers, and your children and the world.

While you are reading this book, keep your focus on your impact, not just on your company but on the greater world outside your organization as I explore in detail the paradoxes of smarter, faster, and better. To give you some guiding principles, the following assumptions set the stage for the transformational work ahead:

1.   *Your responsibility as a leader is to grow the bottom line of your organization,* and *to contribute to your stakeholders and the world in a positive way.*

Those of us in positions of leadership all have moments of wondering, Who am I and what am I really contributing to? All of us, at times, contribute to both good and bad results for ourselves and the world. But when you begin to look for a greater purpose—through social service, mentoring, designing more environmentally friendly products, improving the lifestyles of employees, developing your community, and so on—the meaning of leadership shifts to a more enduring, effective, and fulfilling responsibility. This is not always an easy endeavor, but it is essential.

2.   *The most effective way to improve your performance is to focus on what happens when you are at your best: to look in depth at your own successes, to look at what is working and how you can augment that, build on it, and keep it going.*

Based on years of study, research, observation, and personal experience, I have learned that successful people focus on what works. Why? Quite simply, what you put your attention on grows. When you focus on the negative (what is not working), what you are doing is becoming an expert in failure. As we study our problems and our weaknesses, we become more and more sophisticated at understanding what our problems stem from, who reminds us of them, how we repeat them, and what they consist of. We become masters of problems. That is not the goal of this book. The goal of this book is to help you become a master of successes, to understand clearly what makes you uniquely successful, and to repeat, expand on, and refine those qualities.

Focusing on the positive also means being without fear—keeping out of the deadly, paralyzing state of fear-based, reactive behaviors and decisions. When we are in a state of fear, we are at a heightened level of anxiety, and our primitive brain stops our smartest, fastest, best thinking.

Creating positive outcomes requires leaders to build on past learning and envision solutions for the future. When we start focusing on positive outcomes, we base more decisions on what would happen in the "best-case scenario," and often that is exactly what we create. Once we begin a careful study of what we do well, we can begin aligning the elements that have helped us succeed in the past. Understanding what we're doing when we succeed is the key to more success.

3. *The first two assumptions are possible to act upon only if you are willing to acknowledge the real.*

You can be amazingly positive and forward-thinking, but it won't mean a thing if you live in La-La Land. You must acknowledge reality. The world, especially the business world, is full of natural disasters, political changes, people with health problems, product recalls, and every other challenge and opportunity under the sun. Bad stuff happens. The *true*—reality—is constantly changing, but it is the foundation for every decision. The good news? In every challenge lies an opportunity, and in every heartbreak there is the possibility of growth. I am not asking you to always like the truth, but as a leader, you must always be willing to acknowledge it. Leadership is fundamentally about truth. We expect our leaders to be honest with us—about the good, the bad, the ugly. We want to know we can trust those people who represent us.

4. *People have a genuine desire to contribute in a positive way.*

There is a tendency in the corporate world in particular to think that people—employees, shareholders, vendors, and all the rest—are motivated by greed. But the opposite is true. Most people are genuinely motivated by a desire to contribute to something larger than themselves, something greater than their own success or bank account. Sometimes people are motivated by greed and attention and many other factors that are based on their fears, but in general, human beings want to know that they are valuable—and not just to themselves.

This is an extremely important assumption to keep in mind, because you cannot become smarter, faster, and better alone. And, as an effective, enduring, and fulfilled leader, part of your success will be based on helping others become more effective, enduring, and fulfilled.

HOW TO READ *SMARTER, FASTER, BETTER*

If you look back to the opening stories of Laura and Lee, who would you rather be? There is tremendous pressure to be as *together* as Laura, but we can't be Laura all the time. We all experience phases of both situations. In fact, the secret is that Laura and Lee are actually stories about the same executive at different stages of her career. And I would argue that we are *all* both Laura and Lee.

So what is the ultimate goal of this book? The goal is to have many more Laura moments than Lee moments. And when you are experiencing one of those frustrating Lee moments, when you are most tempted to gather more and more and more data to support a decision, work later and later and later until you're ill to solve a problem, or when you are paralyzed by competitive envy or the feeling that you are inadequate to cope with the daily challenge of leadership, that is when you need the strategies, lessons, and success stories in this book the most.

The structure of *Smarter, Faster, Better* begins and ends with powerful questions. What impact am I having? When am I having the most impact? Is it the impact I want to have? You may need to reflect on any or all three sections at a given moment, for a specific time frame, for a long-term or short-term challenge. Or it may be that you just need a story of someone who has dealt with the same things you have. Use this book as reflective think time, to help you stop, reevaluate, and think about *why* you are in this position of power. So many business books have a sense of urgency, but this book, true to Part Two: The *Faster* Paradox—is meant to give you the opportunity to stop, reflect, and create new possibilities for yourself as a leader.

I know these strategies work because of the transformations I have seen with hundreds of senior executives who have gone through this process. As the manager of the team of coaches from whom many of the book's stories derive, I am privy to the patterns and results that recur among successful coaching clients. Unfailingly, the busiest senior executives who take the time to work with a coach say that this reflection time—even just a few hours—can be the most important time in their month. And in my life and career as an entrepreneur, I know that when I am struggling with something, the rules and tactics of *Smarter, Faster, Better* apply to me as well.

So get ready to ask questions, focus on your unique strengths, adopt valuable tools, stop multitasking, and create a sustainable way of working that enables you to truly contribute to your world. The path to more effective, enduring, fulfilled leadership is at your fingertips.

I know you are already smart, fast, and good. Now it's time to become smarter, faster, and better. It's time to ask questions, slow down, and start focusing not on just your own self-development but on your contribution to your team, your organization, and the greater good.

April 2006   KARLIN SLOAN
Chicago, Illinois

PART ONE

THE *SMARTER* PARADOX

To be smarter, we need to stop being the expert and start asking more questions.

CHAPTER ONE

IT'S YOU, NOT THEM

Several years ago I was having a crisis of faith. As an entrepreneur, I had just seen my first company crash and burn at the burst of the dot-com bubble. One by one our clients had lost their budgets and ultimately closed their doors. I had recently picked up and moved my life across the country from San Francisco to New York City, and I started to feel like I was missing out on my destiny as a leader. I had few clients, no support group, and a vision of a thriving consultancy that had gone south.

Every day I was working hard to put together a new business plan, establish a new brand on the East Coast, and develop new relationships, but I was uninspired. The ease and creative dynamism with which my first company started just wasn't there. I was struggling. I was convinced I was no longer smart enough, I wasn't fast enough, and I wasn't good enough. I was angry at "them"—the outside forces that were conspiring against me. The economy. The clients who never paid their outstanding bills. The consultant who left. Argh! There had to be a better way. . . .

So I hired an executive coach.

It was the second time I had hired my own private thinking partner. The first was when I started out as an entrepreneur and needed to work with someone who had been there, who could offer support and guidance, who could help me turn an idea into a reality. But this time I needed someone to shake up my thinking, to get me moving again.

The first time I talked to Cynthia, my coach, I was angry at my situation, whining and difficult. I couldn't think my way out of a paper bag. My creative, impassioned, powerful leader self was hidden under a blanket of disappointment. Through Cynthia's pointed questions, her acknowledgment, and her genuine belief that I could change the way I was doing things, after a few months of coaching I was able to successfully launch a new company and grow and develop that new practice rapidly into a firm vastly more successful than the first. That is the power of coaching: to transform—not just a frustrating situation into a better one, but the very concept of what it means to lead.

As a coach and leader of an executive coaching company, I am passionate about the power of the coaching relationship. I have worked with many types of leaders: CEOs of global companies, engineers who didn't trust anything without an off switch, young managers who hadn't had to get anything done through other people before, and HR leaders who ran leadership programs. Through all those experiences, the one common thread that exists in every case is that the *leaders* themselves—the coachees—are the ones who do the work and transform themselves. The coach serves as a facilitator, sounding board, and consistent supporter.

The great executive coaches are the ones who see the big picture and pay close attention to how the leader, as a unique human being, fits into that picture. We coaches are in the business of *attending*—not like students attending a class, but as professionals who are paid to attend—to pay close and careful attention to our clients and their betterment. We are engaged to question people like you, listen to you, and attend to your responses and thought patterns, all with the goal of forwarding you and your organization. We are enlightened witnesses to the perils and triumphs of leadership. It is that attention that enables magic to happen. And it is with a coaching mind-set that I've written this book.

As your coach, I begin with only one assumption: that you are a leader who wants to be smarter, faster, and better than you are today. Every executive who approaches my consultancy cares about doing a great job. They know that great leaders are always pushing the boundaries of what they know, questioning themselves, trying to do ever-greater things. I believe that self-betterment is part of our human spirit, and that it expands when we take on leadership roles. Sometimes the desire for betterment comes from inside ourselves, and sometimes it comes from others, but either way, it drives us to continuously improve.

What Makes You Smarter?

When you think about it, the hierarchical leader of the Industrial Age had it easy. There were fixed, clear structures for being in charge. Leaders gave orders and employees took them. (At least that was how it was supposed to work.) The job of the intelligent head of an organization was clear: set the vision and the strategy, and define a clear plan of action for others to execute. But as we enter and move beyond the Information Age, the definition of smart leadership is rapidly transforming. The Information Age has been about accessing, sharing, and manipulating data. Leadership has been about making decisions based on technology and data shifts. Now, we are entering a new age where we need skills and intelligence related to connectedness. We've enacted a huge shift into a globalized, diverse world with greater and greater levels of complexity to address as leaders.

We've begun the shift beyond the Information Age into an Age of Interdependence. It becomes more apparent every day that our personal decisions impact not just our immediate sphere but our entire world. This requires a huge shift in leadership. We can no longer assume that the people we lead are going to be from our same culture. We can no longer assume that our purview involves creating value from a set of products or services. Leaders are expected to see the interwoven strands that make up the webs of our companies and their interaction with markets, consumers, and resources.

Quite simply, being a smarter leader today is no longer about being the one with the MBA or the background in nuclear physics (which makes for a smart business administrator or nuclear physicist, not necessarily a smart leader). With the rapid growth of technology, it is often the case that college interns with great Internet search skills can access key information faster than the most experienced CEOs.

Organizations are requiring new and different skills and talents in their leaders. Leaders need to create and adapt to new levels of complexity. We who lead are now coordinators of complex systems made up of people, technology, economics, communications, and regulations. We need to be flexible and adaptable, to listen carefully to stakeholder needs and demands, and to respond decisively.

We need to be innovative, thoughtful, strategic, and influential. We need to set the vision and strategy for our companies, and define plans of action that can shift and adapt to new scenarios.

We leaders may not even be at the top of an organization any more. In less hierarchical workplaces, leadership is part of many employees' daily lives. We set visions for our teams at every level of the company. We inspire others each day. We make strategic decisions and are empowered to make changes and embrace opportunities as they arise. Leadership is no longer just for CEOs.

As defined in the Introduction, being smarter in today's world involves a paradox: to become smarter, you have to admit what you don't know. Asking questions and tolerating ambiguity are more important than knowing more and more. The more we develop our flexibility and ability to inquire and make connections, the better prepared we are to deal with an ever-more-complex global business environment. As management theorist Peter Drucker said, "The leader of the past was a person who *told;* the leader of the future will be a person who *asks.*" That future is now.

Now let's get specific. What exactly can you do to become a smarter leader in today's business environment, which is full of change, populated by diverse people from diverse cultures, and affected by market forces that can change direction on a dime?

- First, cultivate an appreciative personal attitude and mind-set as a leader, which is the focus of this chapter.
- Second, as you will explore in Chapter Two, look at your leadership in the context of your organization, or system.
- Third, apply your leadership knowledge to others and develop smarter people around you. This will be the goal of Chapter Three.

And so we begin by focusing on you as a leader. This first section involves four major concepts: applying the "appreciative eye" to work from the positive, letting go of being the expert, embracing curiosity, and practicing the art of inquiry.

THE APPRECIATIVE EYE

It is no secret that every leader is different. This is why we do not need to become experts on great leadership as much as we each need to become expert at knowing what makes us each great leaders in our own way.

Therefore, the first step to becoming a smarter leader is to look for the smartest aspects of your existing performance as a leader—what's working—and then build on them to make you even smarter. This is not about studying what *should* work; it is about becoming expert at what *does* work for you and expanding upon it to become as smart a leader as you can be.

This concept can be summarized as applying the "appreciative eye." It is a simple and powerful perspective to adopt: look to the good first, and build on it. The rule is to first seek answers about what is effective and successful and then work from that point forward. In essence, this is the foundation of an overall positive attitude—seeing the glass half-full, and then looking for opportunities to fill the glass higher.

Let's look at the full definition of *appreciate:*[1]

Ap-pre'ci-ate, v.

1. Valuing; the act of recognizing the best in people or the world around us; affirming past and present strengths, successes and potentials; to perceive those things that give life (health, vitality, excellence) to living systems.
2. To increase in value, e.g. the antique vase has appreciated in value.
    Synonyms: Valuing, Prizing, Esteeming, Honoring, Increasing in Value

The appreciative eye involves the perspective of *valuing*—of looking for the awe and inspiration in everything. When we visit a museum we often appreciate a set of paintings for their beauty, for their meaning, or for the value that they can bring us. This is quite different from the way we might, say, look at our overflowing inbox of unprocessed paperwork. But the inbox really can be looked at from the same positive viewpoint. It's better to have a full inbox than to be unemployed, right?

Really think about this concept and the power it has. What if each day you were assured that you would experience satisfaction, discover a new opportunity, and leave your workplace feeling inspired? It is 100 percent possible. This is the gift of using the appreciative eye as a daily practice.

TRY THIS

Activating the Appreciative Eye

To activate the appreciative eye in your own career as a leader, ask yourself these two simple questions whenever you need inspiration:

1. When have I been inspired, excited, or amazed by my work? What are the details of that story? How did I feel physically and mentally? What was the impact on me? What effect did I have on other people around me?
2. What opportunities for inspiration are available to me today?

You can use this exercise whenever you are feeling stuck. Take time to appreciate yourself and you will be much more able to see the positive in other people and situations.

If I answer the questions in this exercise for myself, I am often inspired, excited, or amazed by my work. When I think back to those moments when I've really met a challenge or collaborated with someone in a position of great power to address his or her leadership issues effectively, I remember why I love what I do. When I focus on that feeling's impact on me, I start experiencing it again. It's as if someone has just given me an inspiration shot in the arm, and I remember my own sense of motivation and excitement. I also remember that I have an opportunity today, right now—and that feeling is directly related to what has inspired me in the past.

The concept of applying the appreciative eye to business is borrowed from organizational change gurus David Cooperrider, Ron Fry, and Survesh Shrivashta, along with their colleagues from Case Western Reserve University's Weatherhead School of Management. They are some of the key thinkers behind a profound new discipline called "Appreciative Inquiry," a discipline that has been used to help whole organizations become inspired, and a concept I explore in detail later in this chapter. The exercises in this section flow out of their body of work on how organizations can address three areas of strategic advantage: engaging people at every level, increasing the speed of innovation, and creating a magnetic setting for the attraction and retention of exceptional talent.

Throughout this book you will find applications of the appreciative eye, because one of the jobs of a leader is to look at things for their value and to increase their value. As you will see, it is both a perspective and an active leadership tool.

Letting Go of the Expert

> *Many senior managers can't bring themselves to say "I don't know," because it seems to undercut the very reason they hold their position. This unease prevents them from discussing the simple fundamental questions of their business. Asking a basic question like, "Who are our customers?" can seem naive, in fact it is essential. Saying "I don't know" can lead to breakthroughs. Leaders lose their edge and value when they assume too much.*
> —from *Hardball*, by George Stalk and Rob Lachenauer

Today's smart leaders know that they cannot be the expert in everything—there is simply too much to know. And sometimes an overemphasis on expertise can get in the way of effective, enduring, and fulfilled leadership.

The expert model of leadership is easy to fall into. Many of us who are successful leaders have been given our positions because of our ability to do something very, very well. Maybe that something is selling cars; maybe it's designing furniture or fundraising for a political cause. We have demonstrated our ability to be in the trenches, solve complex problems, and survive through challenges. And then we are handed the mantle of leadership based on our expertise. But that is where the usefulness of that expertise generally *ends*. Once we cross over into leading others, we have to adopt new strategies to serve us in our new role.

Think about the best boss you've ever worked with. Good bosses are often people with a deep understanding of human nature. They are consistent, trustworthy, and empowering. They honor their people by trusting them, and by giving them the tools they need to succeed. They may very well be expert in their field, but their expertise is not the top reason why their employees respect them. In fact, it's usually the fact that they believe in accessing the expertise of others that makes them great bosses. This is another aspect of an appreciative approach—valuing the expertise of others in addition to our own.

Executive coach Noah Blumenthal honed his leadership skills as a young manager at a major financial institution. According to Noah, letting go of expertise was critical for his success. "I had to stop being perceived as a know-it-all," he says.

As a manager, Noah was new to the job and became excited about hiring people and managing a team. The group was extremely busy, and Noah admits he was trying to do too many jobs at one time. He got used to being the person with the answers. When people came and asked questions, he would be the one who would solve the problem, spitting out ideas, solutions, and answers. Noah was running himself ragged.

After burning himself out in the first three months in the role, he came to realize that the questions of his staff were actually mostly things they could address on their own. His team members weren't asking questions because they weren't strong but because he had trained them that he had the answers to everything, and they could come to him with anything and everything. They weren't taking the time to think for themselves, to develop their own leadership and management skills. This created an unsustainable model. Noah realized he was limiting their development, and he wasn't taking advantage of their talent and decision-making capacity. Noah says, "It took a tremendous effort of willpower to not be the expert—to not provide the answers I had in my head, and to discover through that process just how often their answers were even better than my own." But he did, and he was a much smarter—and less stressed—leader for it. Noah saw that he had to make changes in the way he defined leadership and in the way he thought of himself and his staff.

Another example of successfully losing the expert involves the familiar situation of an executive making the transition from successful salesperson to manager of other salespeople. Oliver, a coaching client, sold magazine advertising until he was promoted into a sales manager position. He needed to soften his aggressive "sales guy" style to succeed as a leader. With coaching, he learned to ask questions about how other salespeople on the team could be successful rather than forcing his own style on a large group of diverse people. This required a shift from being the expert in selling a product to being a coordinator and elicitor of good thinking in many people.

In another example, Tom, the successful leader of a three-hundred-person company, liked to have ideas in his head before he posed a question to one of his employees. When he sought coaching and realized the importance of losing the expert, he became more open to listening and learning, rather than believing his ideas were always best. Now, if he doesn't hear something new that shifts his thinking, he is still letting his team express themselves, and sometimes that means they think it's all been their idea when really he's known it all along. Tom, a great leader, has learned to become comfortable letting go and not always being right. He is happy to look less smart and ask more questions in the moment so as to help other people find their voice, their ideas, and their footing. Ultimately, of course, this makes him a much smarter—and more respected—leader.

The other temptation of the expert is the temptation of ego. When we are great at something (or when we think we are), we can overwhelm people with our ego—the part of us that takes credit for our successes . . . and the part that makes us arrogant and difficult to be around. No one likes someone who believes everything good is the result of his or her personal input alone, even when it's true. A smart leader knows that *not* taking credit is often the best way to serve the good of the group.

A friend of mine once worked for a very famous corporate executive. She has this to say about working for someone with a great big ego:

> Everyone around me thought, "Oh, wow! You're working for so-and-so. That must be amazing! What's he like?" Well, let me tell you. He had a reputation for being a real pain in the you-know-what. Everything was all about him. Every division leader in the company was a power player, but they were eclipsed by his taking credit for all of their hard work.
>
> I could not believe the kinds of things he would say to me. Once, during one of his famous blow-ups, he told me I was too short to be an effective leader. He was really excited to tell stories about

himself and his famous friends. "The President of the United States and I were talking yesterday and . . ." he would say. And it would have nothing to do with anything! Ultimately, this executive is intensely insecure and anyone close to him knows it. Most of the people who work under him end up either becoming a protector of their teams—not letting [the leader] have access to tear them apart—or, they end up ignoring him and his direction because he's so unpleasant. I think it's despite himself that he succeeds at all.

Are there instances where demonstrating expertise and ego is still acceptable for leaders? Of course. When you are leading a shareholder meeting, you must be an expert. When you are presenting the keynote address at an industry conference, you must be self-confident. But when you are leading and managing others, you often need to let go of expertise in order to make the best decisions, come up with the most innovative ideas, and evolve into an effective, enduring, and fulfilled leader.

EMBRACING CURIOSITY

When you lose your need to be the expert, you gain something magnificent for leaders and deceptively simple: curiosity. Our natural state as human beings is to be curious about the world around us. Think of young children, who constantly ask questions like "Why is the sky blue?" and "Where did Fluffy go when he died?" When we ask more questions, as adults or children, we gather more information, we see things from new perspectives, and we clarify our beliefs and attitudes. Curiosity helps us learn. It makes us smarter.

How can you as a leader see things in a fresh and new way? Remember back to your childhood. We were not put on this planet to be serious, inflexible, and intolerant. Children have what might be referred to in Buddhism as "beginner's mind," a clear, unbiased viewpoint that takes things in without immediate judgment or categorization, a viewpoint that allows them to see things a different way. Beginner's mind is the backbone of curiosity. If we believe we have all the answers and we know everything, our curiosity disappears, and with it our ability to grow.

Executive coach M. Nora Klaver shares this advice:

Unfortunately, most adults have lost curiosity. Years ago, during an improvisation class, my acting instructor peppered me with a series of questions: What makes me happy? Sad? How do I meet challenges? What do I like about improv? What am I most afraid of? I answered these easily, but then he stumped me with his last question, "When were you last surprised?" I couldn't remember being surprised by anything or anyone—at least not recently. I was shocked and suddenly curious. Why hadn't I been surprised?

I think that element of surprise is needed for curiosity. We are so accustomed to believing that we know how things—and people— work. We don't even bother being curious. We've convinced our- selves that people are predictable, that they never change, that a simple methodology is all we need to make things work. We are so wrong.

Great leaders cultivate their curiosity. Why? Curiosity breeds excitement, ideas, and innovation. It is naturally appreciative. When we think we know everything, we lose the most exciting part of ourselves—our curiosity. We become coarse and jaded, and we believe that we are always right. Once our thought pat- terns are inflexible, we don't enable ourselves to see clearly and without bias.

When we nurture our curiosity, when we are engaged in see- ing all sides of an issue and in gathering new information that will illuminate previously dark corners, we are cultivating a specific quality of mind and humility in our thinking. We begin to question our set viewpoint and to see things outside our narrow band of ref- erence. Lee Bollinger, president of Columbia University, brought words to this concept in his speech to the graduating class of 2005:

It's easy in this polarized climate to pick a side and become clois- tered in one worldview, to the exclusion of all others. You listen to left-wing or right-wing talk radio—not both. You buy a book on Amazon.com and it instantly suggests five books just like it; the interest is not in broadening your tastes, but in reinforcing them. . . . Over the past several years you have been encouraged not to take refuge in your own opinions. We have urged you to see issues from competing perspectives—to question, to doubt, to resist the allure of certitude.

These words are critical to the curious leader. We must, as part of our discipline of smart thinking, *resist the allure of certitude,* and rely not on our own expertise but on our capacity for reflecting, responding, and questioning.

THE ART OF INQUIRY

Once you have found a comfort level with letting go of the need to be the expert in the room and embracing curiosity, the next step toward smarter leadership is putting your curiosity into action by asking more questions. The act of questioning to gain knowledge is certainly not new. It goes back all the way to ancient Greece and the great teacher Socrates. Socrates used dialectic reasoning—thinking by means of dialogue, debate, argument, and questioning—to uncover the beliefs and best thinking of the people he taught.

Socratic questioning is a method of evoking the knowledge that is already resident in us. It's a method of teaching and learning that depends on a basic faith that people have all the answers within themselves. Socrates also believed that genuine knowledge comes from acknowledging what we *do not* know, that we are not experts, that we must question the dominant thinking of our time and attempt to discover simple truth through asking questions.

Great leaders use this same discipline to learn, to teach, to mobilize, and to shift the mind-set of their organizations. For leaders, asking questions achieves all the following benefits, which contribute to smarter leadership in three ways:

Enabling Better Thinking

- Helps us gather information, including perspectives that are different from our own
- Gives us time to think, by avoiding a jump to rash conclusions
- Focuses us on what is really important
- Defines a powerful platform for decision making, by allowing several angles to be explored

Cultivating Rapport and Relationships

- Develops trust and rapport by showing respect for other people's opinions and ideas
- Demonstrates our willingness to listen and understand
- Empowers employees to achieve

Creating a Smarter Organizational Culture

- Shows us what assumptions we are making as individuals, and as an organization, that might be holding us back from innovation and achievement
- Teaches us to think creatively in all situations, not just during brainstorming sessions
- Creates a feedback-rich culture, which limits hidden agendas, bad morale, and group frustration

I believe that asking questions, or "the art of inquiry," is among the most powerful tools available to leaders. General Peter Pace, current Chairman of the Joint Chiefs of Staff, says, "If you are looking for answers, ask the question." What could be simpler?

But as a leader it is not always easy to ask questions, particularly if your organization has a culture that favors aggressive, directive communication. Sometimes the only questions tolerated are challenging ones: *What were you thinking? Are you a moron?* These, of course, are not the kinds of questions it's useful to cultivate.

You will not become a more enduring, effective, and fulfilled leader by asking any old questions, or negative questions like the ones just mentioned. You must be strategic in your use of inquiry, in the questions you ask of those around you, and even more important, in the questions you ask yourself. Again, the best approach is appreciative.

Appreciative Inquiry is the use of solution-focused questioning to create dialogue and learning in individuals and groups. It is a way of looking at an individual, a team, or an organization not as a problem to be solved or a patient to be diagnosed but as a strong, capable whole individual or group with capacities that you do not yet know. In traditional organizational and leadership development, the approach is to look for problems and then solve them.

In Appreciative Inquiry, you look for strengths, for opportunities to grow, and for the creation of what's next.

While this book is not a guide to implementing a formal Appreciative Inquiry initiative in your organization, the wisdom of Appreciative Inquiry is something you can take into your everyday leadership. As an overview, from *The Appreciative Inquiry Handbook* by David L. Cooperrider, Diana Whitney, and Jacqueline M. Stavros, consider this definition of the technique as a method for large-scale change:

> Appreciative Inquiry (AI) is the cooperative, co-evolutionary search for the best in people, their organizations, and the world around them. It involves the discovery of what gives "life" to a living system when it is most effective, alive, and constructively capable in economic, ecological, and human terms. AI involves the art and practice of asking questions that strengthen a system's capacity to apprehend, anticipate, and heighten positive potential. The inquiry is mobilized through the crafting of the "unconditional positive question," often involving hundreds or even thousands of people. AI interventions focus on the speed of imagination and innovation—instead of the negative, critical and spiraling diagnoses commonly used on organizations.[2]

A formal Appreciative Inquiry can take many forms, from long-term change initiatives to an "AI Summit"—a convergence of people from across an organization, as many as possible, to collectively approach the following questions around a single topic: What gives life? (Discovery) What might be? (Dream) How can it be? (Design) And What will it be? (Destiny). This four-stage process is called the "4-D Cycle."

If Appreciative Inquiry is an approach to developing the best in your organization, what are the key differences between AI and the more traditional mode of thinking?

Traditional Problem-Solving Approach	*Appreciative Inquiry Approach*
Identify problems	Appreciate "what is"
Conduct root cause analysis	Imagine "what might be"
Brainstorm solutions and analyze	Determine the structure that supports "what should be"
Develop action plans	Create "what will be"

It is important to realize that Appreciative Inquiry is a way of thinking and increasing the value of organizations that is the *opposite* of the standard process of focus and analysis in organizational life—problem solving. When we focus on problems, we become masters of problems. When we focus on appreciating the best of what is, leveraging strengths, and looking for opportunities, we become masters of strengths, masters of growth, and masters of opportunity.

For instance, take the question, "How can we gain strategic advantage by attracting and retaining exceptional talent?" Often the first run at this question is to investigate what the blocks are to achievement of this goal. We ask another series of questions: "Why don't we have the best already? What stops great people from joining us? What are we missing?" The assumption behind those questions is that they will help us focus on a problem and then solve that problem. What this is actually doing is focusing our attention on what is not working.

Appreciative Inquiry is driven by an important assumption: that focusing on what works propels us toward a more positive future state. It is about eliciting great performance rather than demanding it. Questions that might be asked in an Appreciative Inquiry might start with:

- When have we been successful, energized, and engaged as a group?
- What would we like to have happen?
- What would a bright and positive future look like?
- What strengths can we build on?
- How have the organizations we look to as having the best people attracted and retained them?
- How have we attracted our best and brightest in the past?
- What are some big ideas our most successful and satisfied employees have about recruiting and retaining top talent?

Always remember that the key to focusing on the right issue as a leader is beginning with the right question. On a frustrating day, you might be tempted to ask yourself, "How can I survive another day of this?" Instead, start asking, "What can I gain from today? How can I hold on to my appreciative eye?"

The results can not only make you a smarter leader, they can also make a profound difference in your outlook on life and work. Robyn Stratton-Berkessel, founder of LIT Global, says:

> In my leadership, Appreciative Inquiry has changed me personally and professionally in ways that I certainly like and that produce results I am proud of. I pay attention to language and choose positive ways of expression over negative ways. I look for the good and what is working, and that comes through with my clients. It gives me great joy in my work, because I see behaviors change and I see beliefs changing. I hear values being identified and articulated. Seeing the world through an appreciative lens allows for greater compassion, and speaking from the heart becomes the norm.

WHAT QUESTIONS DO I NEED TO ASK MYSELF?

Great leaders have the courage to ask the simple questions:

- What does my company need right now?
- What is the biggest value we can create for our customers?
- What steps can I take today toward efficiency, effectiveness, fulfillment?
- What are the opportunities we've got to face tough issues that, if resolved, would change our business for the better?
- What is the truth about our industry?
- How can I be physically, personally connected to my customers, my suppliers, my employees?

One of the most important areas in which leaders can use Appreciative Inquiry is by questioning themselves. Asking questions of yourself does a number of things: it helps you recall information (and goodness knows we all have a lot of things going on at any given moment in our busy minds) and it helps you gain clarity on your ideas, your position, your intentions, and your strengths.

Let's look at an example of Appreciative Inquiry in practice on an individual scale, and see how questions can change a leader's effectiveness. Sarah, a former coaching client, is a PR executive who was feeling frustrated. When we started our coaching together, she said she felt like there was a time limit on her work with her current

TRY THIS

Strengths List

To get in the habit of asking appreciative questions, start by brainstorming your own greatest assets: the attributes, skills, talents, relationships, and resources you possess.

Instructions:

Step 1. Set a timer for five minutes.

Step 2. Write as many strengths as you can in five minutes, with a minimum of twenty-five.

Step 3. When you are finished, ask yourself the following questions:

- What might my best friend or significant other say I should add to my list?
- What is so obvious about me that I forgot to include it?
- What would my coworkers say I should add?
- Are there three more strengths I could add?

Step 4. Review your strengths and answer the following questions:

- How often have you been asked to do this in the past?
- How did it feel to write your strengths?
- Would you be comfortable sharing this list with others?
- How can you use these strengths more this week?
- Is this something you could assign to your direct reports?

organization. Her performance reviews kept getting pushed off. She was supposed to had have one in January, then November and beyond. In general, she felt she was not progressing the way she wanted to in the organization. She felt she was at a crossroads—would she stay at her company or look for a new job elsewhere?

I asked her a series of simple, appreciative questions:

- When was she at her best?
- What accomplishments was she proud of?
- Why did she value her contribution?

In addition to answering these questions during coaching, for homework she wrote a list of the accomplishments she was proudest of every day. The act of focusing on positive experiences changed her entire outlook. Her attitude was more positive, and that made a difference to her team. She ended up getting a job offer in the middle of the coaching experience, but she decided because of the coaching to call off her job search.

When Sarah finally got her performance review, she was criticized for her attitude and not portraying a positive view of her work. Her supervisor said that when she was frustrated, it was very apparent. But, thanks to her new appreciative outlook, her review also mentioned significant improvement on these issues. Her team members had communicated that Sarah was now motivating them and inspiring them in a way they had not experienced before.

Over a short period of time, Sarah's new attitude was showing up in her behavior and in her results with the team. She was motivating people to perform better, and to stick it out through a transition in the company. She was more satisfied with her job, and the frustration that she had been expressing had dissipated.

In addition to the questions I asked Sarah, here are some other appreciative questions to think about when you are facing challenges in your leadership:

- Am I showing by example how to lead well?
- What do I need to change about my behavior to get the best from those around me?
- Where can I go to learn what I need to know?
- What are we doing right and how can we do more of it?
- What does my team need from me?
- What opportunities are we not taking advantage of?

HOLDING A POSITIVE FUTURE VISION

Every leadership book talks about having a vision, which is why we don't need to linger here, but this notion is everywhere for a simple reason: it is of primary importance to establishing not just how you lead but where you're leading your organization to. It's hard to reach the summit of Mt. Everest if you start out saying, "Let's take a walk and see where we end up."

TRY THIS

Appreciation Practice

1. Group Appreciation
   Make a list of your team (or department or company) strengths and the most significant successes you have achieved with that group. Now imagine what you could achieve if the same people developed twice their intellectual, physical, or strategic resources. What power exists in your group that didn't exist before? What could you do if you had that much power? Imagine how good your people can be if you appreciate and develop them. Let your expectations go as high as they possibly can. The higher your expectations, the higher the likelihood your team will meet them.

2. Team Appreciation
   Ask each member of your team to list five positive qualities of each team member. Ask each person to write a few sentences about how your team could be more successful by using those positive qualities more frequently or efficiently.

3. Vendor Appreciation
   What are the strengths of your vendors? Are there some who are better than others? What makes them special? How can you use those relationships to your advantage? How can you teach the vendors you choose to work with how to be as good as the best example?

4. Systems Appreciation
   Where are you most efficient? What systems are in place? Are there procedures, technologies, and systems you can replicate in other areas?

5. Customer Appreciation
   Who gives you the best feedback? Who loves your product or service? What's common about that group? What are they responding to? How can you do more to expand your best relationships?

When it comes to envisioning a positive future, think of this appreciative question: "What is the best our future could be?" or "What are we capable of that may sound impossible?"

Herman Sloane is a man who spends his life dealing with vision . . . literally. A renowned eye surgeon, Herman Sloane heads up the Sloane Vision Center, his own vision-correction practice in Oakbrook, Illinois.

What is Dr. Sloane's leadership vision? When evaluating the possibilities of his own practice, Sloane asked himself two important appreciative questions: What are we doing right? How can we do more of it? His answers: We're doing a great job in patient care and service, and we have excellent technologies that allow us to focus on patient care and reduce distractions.

Sloane then looked at two specific goals: to establish a completely paperless office and use technology to make the office more efficient, and to keep focusing on the patients and making them feel comfortable and well-cared-for. He says,

> As for the reduction in paper, it's helped both in the front and the back. It helps me take more time talking to a patient. When I want to refer to previous visits, I have a clean, quick way to get to the information that I want. Nothing replaces face-to-face contact. I have to connect to people, and give them confidence that they can trust me. Fumbling with papers doesn't help that at all. Also, a clear record eliminates transcription errors. There are no scribbles that need to be decoded. After the information is in the client file on the computer, it is not changed or rewritten. It also saves time. On the back side, it also saves me 1.5 full-time-employee equivalents. Doctors can be very slow to change to electronic records— "What if the server crashes? What if it's hacked?"—I think as long as there's redundancy we're safer than if our office burned and our paper records went up in flames.

> When I set up my practice, I also wanted to set up a place that is all about the patient. From the first time a patient contacts us, from the Web site or a referral, it's important that they feel like they're valued from the beginning. They're important. Today in medicine, customer and patient service is sadly neglected. Because of the third-party system, the relationship between physician and patient has been clouded. Because I'm not in that model, when patients come to me they understand we're going to listen

to them, execute as accurately as possible, and take good care of them.

What is your future vision for your organization? How bright could your future be? What are you capable of that may sound impossible? The possibilities are endless, particularly when you begin to embrace an appreciative approach.

When Your Team Seems to Have No Appreciative Eye

Sometimes it's challenging to hold on to the appreciative approach, particularly when you're working with a team that is, perhaps, cynical, divided, or uncommunicative. Many teams have a long history of doing things a different way and resist any sort of change. What can you do if you are dealing with a difficult team?

TRY THIS

Leading from the Future

Here's a way to let go of the past and begin a dialogue about leading from the future. A simple step is to define what is and isn't working with your team, then make a commitment to tell the truth about what has been, and to lead based on the positives, and toward the vision of the future, rather than the past.

This exercise is adapted from the work of Miles Kierson, a Midwest consultant who has been doing alignment work with executive teams for more than twenty years. Unlike many of the exercises in this book, this one will work best if you use an outside facilitator for it—either a trusted internal organization development resource or an external consultant. It's most powerful when you, the leader, can participate fully rather than work the room.

(Continued)

Step 1. Set aside time for your entire team to focus, and then introduce this exercise as a step toward leading from the future rather than reacting to the past. Make sure the group has the shared desire to focus on teamwork. The session could be a failure if the group doesn't have some commitment to telling the truth.

Step 2. Take the pulse of the team as it is now: What is your current reality? Set up two flip charts: one is for recording the positive, and one is for the negative. The positive chart lists what you will want to keep and leverage for the future. The negative lists what you will want to transcend, deal with.

Brainstorm with the group and write down some key words on each chart. For example "lack of trust, historically working in silos, making lots of money, nervous about the future, too many initiatives, not enough successors in the pipeline, wary of each other, not communicating everything we're thinking." The group may or may not be honest about the present state, but here are some magic questions. "What is the best thing about our organization?" "What are we avoiding talking about?" "What would you say if I weren't in the room?"

Step 3. When all of the individuals have expressed themselves, you'll have a good snapshot of the present. Draw the following model:

Past	*Present*	*Future*
Two flipcharts:	The commitment we're	Shared
+ (what works) /	making right now to let	future
Δ (what we need	the past be, but to start	vision.
to change)	leading from the future	
	we want to create.	

Step 4. Ask the group, "Does everyone agree that leading from the past doesn't work? Are we all willing to say that this is our past and not our future?"

What your team will come to realize based on this exercise is that patterns based on the past are addictive. Like giving up chocolate, giving up behavioral or thought patterns can be a challenge. These patterns continue because something about them works. It's as if you are caught in a current, based on the culture that was. Remember that unless the whole group shifts focus and commits to keeping each other accountable, you'll get caught in the patterns of the past. And if you're coming from the past, then your team will keep getting what you've always been getting. But once you can let go, there's nothing stopping you from actualizing your positive future.

The first step is encouraging your team to let go of past patterns and outlooks that don't support a positive future vision.

Using this exercise, even a splintered team can benefit from appreciative inquiry. Know that it takes constant practice. Results may take a long time, but I know from experience that positive change is always possible.

In this chapter we have laid the groundwork for leadership transformation by using Appreciative Inquiry to change our own perceptions and behavior to a smarter, more positive approach. We have also observed the positive effects of losing the need to be the expert and embracing the open-mindedness of curiosity. In the next chapter, we will start to put these skills in the context of our organizations. Get ready to become even smarter. Here is an appreciative question to get you started: In the context of your organization, what has helped you lead smarter?

Summary

- The more we develop our flexibility and ability to inquire and make connections, the better prepared we are to deal with an ever-more-complex global business environment.
- Engage your appreciative eye: look to the good first, and build on it.
- When you are leading other human beings—your stakeholders—you often need to let go of expertise so as to develop and cultivate leadership in others.
- Embrace curiosity. When we ask more questions, as adults or children, we gather more information, we see things from new perspectives, and we clarify our beliefs and attitudes.
- Ask the right questions, of yourself and others, by engaging in Appreciative Inquiry. This is the use of solution-focused questioning to create dialogue and learning in individuals and groups.

CHAPTER TWO

ARE YOU ASKING THE RIGHT QUESTIONS?

Chapter One set the foundation for becoming a smarter leader: using an appreciative eye, letting go of your need to be the expert, embracing curiosity, and developing the tool of Appreciative Inquiry. The next step is to put these concepts to work in the context of your leadership style and your organization. First, we will assess the organizational system in which you operate and then we will explore a variety of smart tactics you can employ to lead your organization effectively.

WHAT METAPHOR OF LEADERSHIP DO I ADOPT?

Leaders in the Age of Interdependence are required to play many roles. On any given day you may be a visionary, a strategist, a diplomat, a negotiator, a learner, a motivator, a disciplinarian, a champion, a questioner, a problem solver, a systems thinker, and a communicator.

Despite the myriad types of leaders and leadership styles, exploring our basic metaphors for leadership is a great start to getting smarter.

Many contemporary leaders base their people management style on one of two dominant metaphors: the military general and the coach. This is a simplistic view, but there is strength in simplicity, so I'll work with these two as they represent opposite ends of the leadership spectrum.

As I'm sure you can guess, I am a fan of the coach metaphor for leadership, which I will explore in detail later in this chapter. But I know that there are times when the general is absolutely necessary, so it's important for leaders to understand and be able to call upon aspects of both metaphors.

THE GENERAL

In 2005, a one-engine Cessna was seen flying into the restricted airspace above the White House. Rapidly, the leaders inside made decisions about how to respond. Orders were given. People were evacuated. This was not a time to ask questions. It was a time to respond with clear, direct orders designed to get people moving in a single direction. That is the only smart way to work in a crisis.

The military style of leadership is exactly what it sounds like. It is authoritative, hierarchical, and based on making fast decisions that can be acted upon immediately. A great military leader needs to be adamant, demanding, and to tell people what to do. Generals are supposed to think, make decisions, and deploy the troops when necessary. When you're at war, you don't want your leader *asking* you if you think it's a good idea to take that hill! We need this style in a disaster, when there is safety at stake. But what happens when you're not at war but in business? Creative leaders are both coaches and generals . . . depending on the needs of their organization at any given time.

A successful technology entrepreneur I know likes to say that he's in his "Captain Kirk" or his "Captain Picard" mode. At the risk of offending *Star Trek* aficionados everywhere, the beloved Captain Kirk of Gene Roddenberry's original *Star Trek* was a general—someone who gave fast orders, who wasn't questioned (well, sometimes by Dr. McCoy), and was ultimately the hero of the show. The enemy mostly came from outside the starship *Enterprise:* marauding aliens, strange species taking over the ship, and other various bad guys. Kirk was unafraid of getting dirty (or taking off his shirt) and fighting with the enemy. He cultivated respect through his bravery and his directive decision-making style.

Captain Picard, the USS *Enterprise* captain for *Star Trek: The Next Generation,* was different. A more modern leader, Picard worked in a diverse environment with numerous cultures represented, and he needed to build buy-in, to ask questions, and to determine the ethics around various decisions. He worked to develop his team and to build morale. He was more strategist than warrior, and would try to find ways *not* to get into a fight. He cultivated respect through diplomacy and intellect. (And, yes, there are two opposing fan Web sites: "Top One Hundred Reasons Why Captain Kirk Is Better Than Captain Picard" and "101 Reasons Picard Is Better Than Kirk," for those of you who wish to do further research on the topic . . . but I digress!)

As in the Cessna example, military leadership is excellent in a crisis, when people need clear directions and a confident captain. It can also be an appropriate style for leading a new team (like military recruits) that needs to ramp up fast. However, be aware that people won't buy into your military-style directions unless you can demonstrate that you've been there in the trenches with them and you understand and acknowledge their needs.

The military model also carries some risks. By its nature, it tends to encourage dependence on the leader. This may be good business for new employees who need a great deal of direction, but it's not best for the organization or individual hoping to acquire unique expertise. Again, this is important to remember regarding your own leadership. When you lead by telling people what to do, they develop reliance on you and cannot function efficiently if you are not available.

THE COACH

What do you think of when you think of a great coach? A coach is someone who is there for the team, who focuses energy on developing the greatness in others. Coaches are committed, tough, and passionate lovers of the game—whatever game their team is playing. They are strategists and influencers, and when they have to, they lay down the law. The best coaches are the ones who create fierce loyalty and excellence in others through their support and service. They are the ones who elicit the best in others.

In a modern, team-based work context, the coach is the predominant day-to-day leadership style, rather than the five-star general. Coaches in a business environment are adept at asking the right questions, evoking great thinking, and cultivating cultures of success.

Unlike the general, the coach style of leadership allows you to fully access the smarts in your team. When you lead as a coach, respect for the expertise of your team is your starting place. You are using your natural curiosity and cultivating an appreciative approach. This means trusting that those on the receiving end of your management have their own answers and that those answers are not only important in their own right but the very foundation for productive work in the organization. The job of the coach is to help people be the best they can be, which is what we all want, and need, from our teams. Coaches are the ones who make us successful.

Leading in the coaching style and leveraging your team's strengths begins with the appreciative eye and with asking appreciative questions.[1] Look for what's working with your employees and build on that success.

Consider these two scenarios:

• Sue, a high-potential middle manager for a large technology company, said: "I would ask my boss over and over again

TRY THIS

More Great Coaching Questions

Here are some questions to add to your tool kit of Appreciative Inquiry. Try asking these questions to your employees and see what results you achieve:

• Is there a different way to approach it?
• What are the opportunities?
• What would an amazing breakthrough look, smell, sound, and feel like?
• What resources do you need?
• How would this work in an ideal world?
• What's a new way to think about it?
• How could you tap into your creative brain about this?

what she thought. Her answer was usually, 'What do *you* think?' Or, 'I'll tell you after you give me your own answer.' The effect was that I began to notice how much I second-guessed myself in front of the rest of our team. I started remembering to check that behavior and be more confident in my opinions in the room with my colleagues."

• Peter, a very talented sales manager at a Fortune 500 company, knew he needed to work on his communication skills. He was known as a harsh critic of his sales staff and had, on more than one occasion, cut someone down in front of the whole team. Peter's boss, the VP of sales, told him that he was not demonstrating leadership and needed to change his behavior if he hoped to receive a promotion. Peter was insulted and defensive and started to look for a new job elsewhere.

If Peter's boss had used a more appreciative, coaching style, he might have asked Peter, "Is your approach getting you the performance you want?" The outcome might have been very different.

Coaching, because it is not an "expert" style, shares power with employees. You are respectful of the smarts they bring to the conversation. Using inquiry helps people use what they're innately good it. It helps them build on their strengths, develop flexibility and change-readiness, create awareness of shortcomings, and build commitment to self-development and achievement. Remember, it is about *starting with what works.*

As you build your Appreciative Inquiry skills throughout this book, you will see these positive results in yourself and in the people you lead:

• Developing self-awareness and awareness of one's effect on people, process, and strategy
• Cultivating stronger performance, confidence, or presence and flexibility in the face of change
• Developing problem-solving and decision-making skills
• Encouraging responsibility and accountability for results
• Sustaining motivation
• Integrating new material, assimilating feedback, and developing core competencies after training

Leadership Coaching Skills Inventory

DIRECTIONS:

Respond to each statement by circling a number from 1 to 5 (1 = Least Like Me; 5 = Most Like Me). Remember, to benefit from this inventory, be honest with yourself when you respond.

Self-knowledge

I am well aware of my strengths as an individual and a leader.	1 2 3 4 5
I know what my skill set is for the tasks that I have.	1 2 3 4 5
I know that I do not have all the answers.	1 2 3 4 5
I am aware of my emotional state and why I am feeling the way I am at all moments of the day.	1 2 3 4 5
I am very clear about my own guiding values.	1 2 3 4 5

Inquiry (the ability to ask powerful questions)

I know what distinguishes between a powerful question and an ordinary question.	1 2 3 4 5
Questions that I ask of others challenge their thinking.	1 2 3 4 5
My questions originate from my curiosity.	1 2 3 4 5
I ask questions to discover what is possible within my organization.	1 2 3 4 5
My questions challenge others to reveal the real truth about what they think and feel.	1 2 3 4 5

Appreciative mind-set

I believe that, given the proper questions, my team either has or can find the answer.	1 2 3 4 5
I focus on what our organization is doing right.	1 2 3 4 5
I always recognize the contributions of others.	1 2 3 4 5
Appreciating what we have done well will help us do better in the future.	1 2 3 4 5

I know that the only way to realize the goals   1 2 3 4 5
of our organization is through a shared
vision and collaborative action.

Empathy

I often understand the emotional state   1 2 3 4 5
of others.

I am sensitive to the impact that my words   1 2 3 4 5
and actions have on others.

I always listen first, in order to know what   1 2 3 4 5
the other person is thinking and
feeling.

When I make decisions, I take others'   1 2 3 4 5
thoughts and feelings into account.

I take an active interest in the activities   1 2 3 4 5
of others.

Willingness to let go of being "expert"

I am not afraid to pay for brains.   1 2 3 4 5

When I create a team, I look for people   1 2 3 4 5
who complement my skills.

I actively seek counsel from others who have   1 2 3 4 5
more knowledge and experience than I do.

I am constantly aware that there may be an   1 2 3 4 5
idea out there that is superior to mine.

I create an environment around me where   1 2 3 4 5
others feel comfortable about taking risks
without undue fear of making mistakes.

Healthy boundaries and limits

I know what my responsibilities and   1 2 3 4 5
obligations are and am careful not to
take on too much.

I am diligent in making sure that I do not   1 2 3 4 5
do the jobs of others.

I know when to say no.   1 2 3 4 5

(Continued)

I have a good sense of how long a job should   1 2 3 4 5
    take and the resources necessary to
    complete the task.

I do not get overly involved on a personal   1 2 3 4 5
    level with others in an organizational
    context and do not allow others to get
    overly involved personally with me.

Clarity of communication

When I speak to my team, they are clear   1 2 3 4 5
    about what I have told them.

My presentations are clear and concise.   1 2 3 4 5

My voice mail and e-mail messages are   1 2 3 4 5
    easily understandable to others.

When I give instructions about a task,   1 2 3 4 5
    they are never misunderstood.

Meetings that I chair have a clear agenda   1 2 3 4 5
    with clear action items to be completed
    by readily identifiable individuals.

Scoring

Add up your score for each section. If you scored twenty
points or higher with no score below a 3, then that coaching
skill is a strength for you.

GET SMART ABOUT YOUR
ORGANIZATION'S SYSTEM

No leader, whether coach or general, operates in a vacuum. We are
all part of living, breathing systems that we call organizations.
These systems all have their own unique cultures that determine
how we need to lead to be effective, enduring, and fulfilled. In the
spirit of curiosity embraced in Chapter One, think about organizational systems and what they can teach us about the kind of leaders we need to be. As a leader, if you don't understand your broader
perspective, you will lose traction with your organization. Being
smart means incorporating the big picture—understanding the

tone, culture, and trends—of your work environment and how that affects your role at the center of it all.

Franklin Jonath, a Boston-based executive coach and consultant, uses this simple model (developed primarily by David Kanter, a renowned family systems expert at Harvard Medical School) for classifying what he sees as the three types of organizational systems: *closed, random,* and *open.* According to Jonath, when you understand what type of organization you currently lead, you can be smarter about the leadership style, attitude, and strategy that will produce the best results.

The three types of systems are each organized around a core purpose:

Closed-system purpose = stability through tradition

Random-system purpose = exploration through intuition

Open-system purpose = consensus through adaptation

See if you can categorize your organization here:

System	*Clues*
Closed	• Power comes from your position. • Physical space enforces the idea of permanence. Offices do not change, people take on new offices upon being promoted to demonstrate rising in the hierarchy. • Stability is a primary value. • Employees are encouraged to be loyal above other attributes. • Risk tolerance is low to moderate. • "General" leadership style is commonly seen.
Random	• The 9-to-5 workday is not standard—time is fluid and employees adapt to the situation at hand. • The organization holds originality in high esteem. • Energy seems to fluctuate. • Space is created in the moment—people work at a table one day, outdoors the next. • Risk tolerance is high.

Open
- Values participative decision making.
- Employees are responsive.
- Cooperation is important.
- The organization rewards tolerance and cooperation.
- Space is movable and adaptable.
- Risk tolerance is moderate to high.
- "Coach" leadership style is commonly seen.

No matter how well your company fits into one particular system, it probably shows signs at various points from the other two systems, so I encourage you to understand the nuances of all three. Each system has positives and negatives, and is appropriate for a specific type of organization in a specific time frame. Here's a detailed look at each system:

CLOSED-SYSTEM ORGANIZATIONS

Closed systems focus on stability and tradition. They are inherently conservative and based on hierarchy. Individuals are in place to support those who are on top. Jonath says, "Closed systems worked well during the Industrial Revolution. It was more about a management that required people to leave their brains at the door: you come here, I provide a job, you have loyalty, you get a gold watch and retire. The organization was paternalistic and caretaking."

In a closed system, the worker is rewarded for taking direct orders and for *not* questioning or taking personal responsibility for how something is done. The worker has no control or say over what the job looks like. Workers are task-oriented and all strategy comes from the top. The rate at which change takes place in a closed system is much slower than in random or open ones, so closed-system companies are not as easily adaptive and flexible.

The closed system requires a dominant, hierarchical leader who is comfortable in the mold of the military general who makes decisions and gives orders.

The strengths of a closed system? A closed system is designed to "stay the course." People trust their leaders to know what's best for the group and to define the direction of the organization.

Information is held at the top, and roles and responsibilities are clearly defined at the other levels. When a great leader operates a closed system, tremendous loyalty develops.

Closed systems have some critical problems: they resist creativity and innovation that does not come from the top, they don't embrace change or take advantage of new opportunities in the marketplace, and they tend toward employee dependency through the withholding of knowledge. It is my belief that many closed-system organizations cannot thrive in today's information-based economy. Closed-system organizations can also be managed by fear, which is no fun either!

Random-System Organizations

The random system is about the exploration of individuation and individuality. The random system often happens when a start-up company is forming. It is an exploration through intuitive, rather than linear, means. This is a creative, generative system, but is only useful in the short-term beginnings of a project or organization. If it continues too long, the infrastructure and norms needed to produce great work don't develop. Random systems, such as the dot-com start-ups of the late 1990s, require entrepreneurial leadership—creativity, energy, and the ability to harness chaos and make them into something real and tangible. When random systems evolve successfully, they become open systems.

Open-System Organizations

An open system's core purpose is adaptation and consensus. It is based on collaboration and mutual benefit. A knowledge-based economy, as we live in today, requires an open system, where workers are rewarded for taking responsibility and innovating, and *thinking* is their greatest asset. The accessibility to information is up, down, and across all corporations now because of technology. It used to be that those at the top were the only ones with access to information. But we are now in an age in which information is democratized. As noted in Chapter One, expertise doesn't matter when you're leading, because at any place in the organization people have more or equal access to information.

Employees at most companies today no longer work in hierarchical chains of command, as they did in closed-system organizations. They work in webs of communication, cells of knowledge sharing. An information grapevine exists, and companies now do their best to nurture that grapevine through knowledge sharing and transparency. In open-system organizations, everyone can be smart. Many companies encourage this in small ways, like providing as much information as possible to employees on their intranet communications systems. Others choose open-book management—a more extreme form of open-system communication.

An open-system organization accepts that change is a constant, and the only way to deal with change is to respond to it. Based on my experience working with executives in industries ranging from advertising to aerospace, I believe that most companies today are moving toward open systems, if they are not there already. And I believe that anyone who plans to lead an organization into the future needs to embrace an open-system mentality in order to survive and thrive.

TEN QUESTIONS FOR LEADING IN AN OPEN-SYSTEM WORLD

What kind of smarts does it take to succeed in open business environments that are full of change, populated by diverse people from diverse cultures, and affected by market forces that can turn on a dime? The answer is not surprising: lots of different kinds. In writing this book, I looked to the executives my company coaches every day and sought, with my appreciative eye, what was working for them in their open-system environments, or what was helping them become more open. Repeatedly these executives told me that it is not one unique thing that makes them strong leaders, it is their ability to employ a variety of strategies, or smarts, all at the same time. In other words, they do not rely on just one way of being smart; rather, they appreciate multiple types of intelligence and strategies of execution. They tend to think of it this way: not every job needs a hammer. The hammer is only for when you have a nail to be pounded in.

You have already been introduced to several strategies for becoming smarter. The tools developed in Chapter One—losing the expert, embracing ambiguity, and applying Appreciative Inquiry—are leadership tools that are fluid and adaptive, and thus perfect for open-system leadership. The philosophy behind these tools is that leaders never really get to the place of being perfect. Leadership, to borrow the classic cliché about life, is a journey and not a destination. But sometimes on that journey we need to add specific tools to fix specific problems, or to build bigger and better things. Embracing creativity alone doesn't help fix a flat tire, nor is it necessarily the best strategy to deal with a disgruntled employee or a production delay. And so our next step is to add more smart strategies to your leadership tool kit. You never know what kind of smarts you might need at any given time.

Smart leaders must be able to call upon as many tactics as possible to solve problems, develop new ideas, and sustain the respect of their stakeholders. The rest of this chapter is dedicated to offering you some of the most effective leadership strategies I have observed in my work as a coach. Some of these strategies may be familiar to you and some may seem a bit far out, but in today's ever-changing business environment, you never know what tool you may need at your fingertips. In the spirit of coaching, Socratic learning, and Appreciative Inquiry, each new tactic is presented as a question you as a leader can ask yourself to employ each tool, or more likely a combination of several, in any given leadership situation. Some are likely to resonate with you more than others, as each of us learns and leads in a different way.

These questions can also be thought of in the context of the concept of "multiple intelligences," a theory established by Howard Gardner. Gardner, citing such nontypical geniuses as Albert Einstein and the dancer Martha Graham, argues for value to be placed on many types of intelligence: linguistic, logical-mathematical, spatial, bodily-kinesthetic, musical, interpersonal, and intrapersonal. I believe in multiple intelligences, and believe they have countless combinations and overlaps among them. The questions in this chapter are designed to engage any and all of your intelligences, *holistically*. Rather than categorizing each type of intelligence, I simply ask you to open your mind, engage your curiosity, hold some current challenges in your mind, and consider the following:

QUESTION ONE

What impact am I having, and is it the impact I want to have?

The first question is the one to repeat most often. This question will help you in virtually any leadership situation. When you are looking at a change in the organization, when you are approaching a challenging management conversation, when you are facilitating a team meeting, when you are delivering an inspiring speech to your stakeholders, ask yourself: What impact are you having? Is it the impact you want to have?

To see what message you are sending as a leader, take a close look at the results you are achieving. Your every decision has an impact, a ripple effect. Does your mood engender enthusiasm and commitment? Does your strategy align with trends in the market? Does your team respond to you the way you want them to? Are you speaking powerfully? Are you having the impact you want to have?

On a more global scale, look for the impact your organization is having on your customers and clients, on your community, on the environment. In the Age of Interdependence, understanding our impact isn't as simple as focusing in one direction. Each decision we make or policy we uphold has consequences. Are the consequences of your actions something you can believe in? Are you having the impact you want to have?

QUESTION TWO

How can I use my entire brain?

You are probably familiar with the terms *left-brain* and *right-brain*. Perhaps a colleague refers to herself as a "left-brain kind of person," meaning that she is more logical than artistic. This may be true, but the reality is that *all* of us possess both left-brain and right-brain capabilities and call on them in various combinations at various times. It takes a combination of left- and right-brain skills to solve problems, make decisions, manage people, brainstorm ideas, and deal with a variety of other tasks that are performed on a daily basis by leaders. First, let's define our terms for the purposes of this discussion:

Left-brain thinking: Rational, analytic, linear, factual, data-focused

Right-brain thinking: Nonlinear, conceptual, metaphoric, kinesthetic, emotional, people-focused

In today's world of open-system organizations, right-brain thinking has become more and more important. The attributes of desirable talent in organizations today are different, and the big difference is that right-brain competencies are becoming more highly valued. In *A Whole New Mind,* Daniel Pink proposes this theory and discusses the importance of the right brain. In today's world of technology, globalization, virtual reality, and more, we must see the world in big-picture, broad strokes and not just analyze facts. The right-brain mode is becoming more dominant in our day-to-day work lives.

Ann Herrmann, CEO of Herrmann International, knows a thing or two about left- and right-brain thinking from her father's invention of a unique and globally accepted thinking-styles assessment, which has been taken by more than a million people worldwide, the Herrmann Brain Dominance Instrument. According to Ann Herrmann, "What we do know is that the world is a composite whole brain. We haven't been able to see anything but an inherent balance in the world. Systems that are working well have a whole brain component to them."

How does this apply to leadership? Herrmann says that when it comes to the brain, the whole is truly greater than the sum of the parts.

> We tend to self-limit because we all have comfort zones. When we look at the heart and soul of business, much of what the left brain brings to the table is the bottom line and the process that enables us to achieve those numbers, however if we are only living in that, we're forgetting a fundamental component of business—we're forgetting people, and how they engage their brains. We're forgetting vision and mission, and we shortcut our ability to achieve the numbers we set out to create.
>
> What's happened is that we take the left brain for granted, but it's an essential part of growing your business. It may be that you need to focus more on that sometimes, but sometimes we take people and strategy for granted; we think it will be handled by HR—it's soft stuff—but that's where it's *really* essential to move the big ship. The right-brain piece is so important. Depending on your situation, it may seem one mode is more important, but every great business honors all of those different areas.[2]

Let's look at an example from a coaching situation. Marcus was in a frustrating situation with his boss, Bob, who was acting like a determined micromanager. Bob was calling Marcus several times a day to check in on progress on various projects. Marcus was going crazy, because he felt like he was under a microscope and like his creativity was being shut down. To coach Marcus, I asked him to think about left-brain and right-brain styles.

Marcus determined quickly that he was a right-brain, creative type. He liked freedom and the ability to express himself. The more he talked about his boss, the more we saw that Bob was operating from a left-brain perspective. He needed the safety of understanding the step-by-step progress, and he was concerned about what was happening with their projects because he didn't have an established working relationship with Marcus, and he wanted a linear plan of action.

Based on this assessment we designed a plan for Marcus to communicate with Bob that made Bob feel secure and comfortable with the linear progress of Marcus's projects. Marcus accessed his left-brain thinking and scheduled meetings daily for status checks with Bob. What happened? Bob stopped calling and micromanaging, and Marcus felt free to do the rest of his day's work without interruption. Eventually Bob started giving Marcus more autonomy and authority, and ultimately Marcus became his right-hand man and successor.

QUESTION THREE

What motivates my people? What do they need? What do they want?

As a leader, you will often need to motivate your employees and other stakeholders to achieve the results you desire from them. At the root of motivation is determining people's underlying needs. Why do people do what they do?

How can you possibly understand how to think like someone else? Underlying needs are relatively simple. You may have seen the hierarchy of needs proposed by Abraham Maslow. It depicts a triangle that moves from survival to self-actualization. At the bottom of our motivators is basic survival. People are motivated by simple things: survival in a challenging environment, comfort, looking

TRY THIS

Tapping Into Your Opposite

All of us have thinking preferences. Some are numbers oriented, others emotional, procedural, or artistic. There are hundreds of attributes we might give to either the left- or right-brain modes. What are the ones you don't use? To develop our underutilized capacities, we need to exercise the brain the same way that we would strength-train a muscle group. For left-brainers, here's a simple exercise that will help you step into the right-brain mode.

To exercise your right brain:

Step 1. To get out of your logical mind and into your nonlinear thinking brain, come up with a topic to think about. Maybe it's as simple as "Who am I as a leader?"

Step 2. Take two old magazines that you can rip up, a glue stick, a large sheet of paper, and a pair of scissors. Time yourself for five minutes and cut out all the visual images and words that appeal to you, that might express what you think about the topic.

Step 3. Glue the images or words you chose to your paper, and create a collage that expresses your idea.

Step 4. Congratulate yourself; you just got your right brain working!

To exercise your left brain (if it needs it): If you normally favor your right-brain, nonlinear mode, simply take time to focus and make a list of what you need to accomplish in a month, and plug it into a calendar to create a step-by-step plan. That's a concrete way to start that logical, linear mode of information processing.

good or being perceived well, positive regard or relationship, and by their core values.

Maslow, in speaking about what he called "enlightened management," said, "Assume that everyone prefers to feel important, needed, useful, successful, proud, and respected, rather than unimportant, interchangeable, anonymous, wasted, unused, expendable, and disrespected. Esteem needs and self-esteem needs are universal."[3]

When we start tapping into the idea that everyone has an inner motivation that is related directly to these basic human needs, life gets simpler. Our management skills deepen, and we're able to address specific needs of our employees and colleagues.

Marti, the head of operations of a midsized publishing company, thought everyone was motivated by the same thing—more money. Over her brief three years on the job, Marti had been able to turn operations around, saving the company more than a million dollars a year in costs by moving operations to another state and changing vendors and inventory tracking systems. She was generous with bonuses for her team, and was excellent at giving financial rewards to her people, but she had very high turnover in her group, and she couldn't understand it.

When I came in to consult with her, my first question was, "What motivates your people?"

Marti's immediate response? "Same thing that motivates everyone—a paycheck!"

I questioned the accuracy of that, because she was rewarding everyone in the group financially but still seeing people leave. "Have you actually asked them?"

Marti had a 40 percent attrition rate annually in the operations group. "They just can't cut the changes here. We're expecting them to work harder and the level of excellence might just be too much for them." She continued, "The last person to leave, though, was my right-hand guy. I just can't understand it. He was really fantastic at his job. I brought him in from another company because of what he was able to accomplish there."

We started exploring alternative ideas, and decided to have Marti sit down with her employees individually and ask them about their satisfaction with their work, what would make them happy if they got a reward, and what motivates them to stay and do a great job. Marti was shocked at the results.

Many of the people on her team were parents of young children. They were all far more motivated by time off than by money. They wanted the stability of their work, without working on weekends. Through the comments of some of the team members, Marti started to learn that people were leaving because they were not being acknowledged for their contribution, and they were not being rewarded in ways that were meaningful or motivating. This news meant that she had a great opportunity, and she took it.

Marti's next step was to have a "recognition lunch" with her team of ten direct reports. At the lunch, she stood up and said to the group, "I was really concerned that we started losing so many of our great people, and I want you to know I'm committed to you, the same way you are committed to the company. I used to show this just through bonuses, but I want to understand what each and every one of you wants and needs as an acknowledgment. For each one of you who contributes above and beyond this quarter, you will get a bonus day off to spend with your families. I encourage you to come to me if you have a problem, or if you're frustrated or feel like leaving. Let's make this the best team to work on in the whole company!"

Marti's transformation from clueless to clued-in created an enormous difference, and after that experience, her staff became loyal and engaged.

QUESTION FOUR

Whose viewpoints have I discounted? What additional viewpoints can I adopt?

Again, I cite Lee Bollinger of Columbia University:

> We all speak of "seeing the other sides" of issues, but the question always remains: How deeply into our beings can we imagine or incorporate what it is really like to think another way? This personal quality of empathy and release of our own assumptions is hardest of all to develop, and rare. It is to let others become a part of you, and to do that you have to be prepared to be changed,

to be a somewhat different person in the end—to learn how, to borrow a phrase from the philosopher Hans-Georg Gadamer, to "fuse your horizons with others."[4]

How do we learn to see another person's point of view? It is by no means easy, but it is a tool that leaders can develop over time.

We've all heard the phrase "to walk a mile in another person's shoes." What is the best way to exercise this ability? Imagine yourself as being a person with whom you bitterly disagree. Imagine what you would think in that person's place, how you would feel, what your day looks like, what is informing your stance in a given situation. What worries you? What makes you satisfied? What do you feel optimistic about? This is most challenging when we are angry or frustrated, and we want to hang on to our own viewpoint. It is impossible when we don't activate our empathy. But it is a very powerful exercise.

Another technique for seeing multiple viewpoints is to listen for both process and content in other people's speech. The best listeners don't just listen to what someone says, they listen to how they say it. That's the difference between content and process. Develop your awareness of the difference by listening carefully during your next conversation. Pay attention to what's being said, but at the same time, pay attention to how it's being said; body language, tone, pace. Is your companion rushed? Calm? Leaning in

TRY THIS

Awareness of Pace and Tone

For one day, pay attention to the pace and tone in which people around you are speaking. What new information are you absorbing by listening and observing at that level?

Be aware that seeing an issue from multiple viewpoints does *not* mean multitasking and switching back and forth. It is about holding multiple perspectives and calling on a variety of different ways of thinking, rather than *doing* many things at once. This is an important distinction.

TRY THIS

Empathy Exercise

Step 1. Think about something you believe in deeply. Take the opposite perspective. What new knowledge can you learn? Write down any insights.

Step 2. Who in your world do you not understand? What new insights can you gain from imagining yourself "walking a mile in their shoes"? Write down any insights.

and looking you in the eyes? The *how* is often just as important as the *what,* and some of us miss it.

QUESTION FIVE

How am I, and others, inspired by where we are going and what we will achieve?

Leadership often involves looking at the big picture, seeing broad strokes. Liken it to an impressionist painting, where the painter sees an image in the flash of an eye, a quick overview, and then paints the impression, not the detail. Or to viewing a landscape from above or with the help of a large-scale map instead of with the naked eye. Often we get so mired in process details that we forget to step back and think about big-picture vision. This involves both left- and right-brain thinking: the right brain provides the creative vision and the left brain helps make it happen.

Vision is necessary for powerful leadership. To create momentum and excitement, you need to be able to understand where you're going—and how to align your team with that compelling future. Sometimes we get so mired in the day-to-day that we forget about our vision. But it is crucial to step back regularly and think forward ten, twenty, a hundred years into the future and allow yourself to dream a bit. As Yogi Berra said, "If you don't know where you're going, you'll wind up somewhere else."

Consider President Kennedy's vow to put a man on the moon—we knew we were going to do it, but we didn't yet know the details.

> ## TRY THIS
>
> # A Bird's-Eye View
>
> Here are some questions you can ask about your own 20,000-foot (or 20,000-year) vision for yourself and your organization:
>
> - What is my personal vision? What is my vision for the organization?
> - What are my hopes? Fears? Opportunities?
> - What do the key stakeholders in my organization see as our greatest opportunities?
> - Who are my role models or heroes?
> - What do we do better than anyone else?
> - What is the dream that this organization can become?
> - What do the employees envision for their future? How could that vision be expanded, encouraged, and realized?
> - What would people least expect from us? How can we surprise them and ourselves?
> - What vision will keep me excited and interested, and keep others feeling the same way?

Clearly the scientists at NASA and their mathematics, engineering, and physics backgrounds were crucial. Conceptual thinking is visionary. It is about being able to see a whole system—and then call in the factual and logical tools to realize the vision.

QUESTION SIX

What does my intuition advise?

> *Intuition does not always appear as the ingenious breakthrough or something grandiose. Intuitive thoughts, feelings, and solutions often manifest themselves as good old common sense. Common sense is efficient.*
> —DOC CHILDRE AND BRUCE CRYER, *FROM CHAOS TO COHERENCE*

As head of Twentieth Century Fox Productions, Alan Ladd Jr. followed his intuition in the face of massive opposition. His colleagues thought he was crazy at his choice of green-lighting a space flick conceived of by a young director with only one theatrical release under his belt. "Everybody chased a certain model, instead of going after their own instincts," Ladd says. The other execs at Twentieth Century Fox were stunned when Alan Ladd's choice, *Star Wars,* became the highest-grossing film in North American history by the end of its first run.

The word *intuition* comes from the Latin "to look within." Humans are equipped with sight, hearing, taste, touch, and smell. We are not always conscious of the information that is being absorbed by our senses in every situation, but we get important data from our surroundings every moment. When we stop and look within ourselves for answers, rather than to our external world of the senses, we have knowledge that's ready to tap. Think about it: the moment we walk into a strange place, a new city, a new job, or a new relationship we begin processing information through our senses and through our experience. Our brain analyzes what's in front of us and gives us a "gut response" to our new surroundings. We feel comfortable or fearful, excited or relaxed, depending on the intuitive response we feel inside our body.

Intuition, like other right-brain functions, is something that is being acknowledged more clearly as a necessary skill in business. "Intuition is one of the most important abilities we can cultivate," says Jagdish Parikh, a Harvard researcher. "It is becoming necessary for a comprehensive personal and global perspective." He should know; he conducted a study of thirteen thousand business executives, and 80 percent of the respondents credited their business success to relying on their intuition.[5]

Intuition, or gut feeling, is when your body picks up on subtle cues from your environment and gives you clues to what's right and what's wrong. Great leaders through history have used this inner voice to guide them, and when we trust our intuition it's a great source of information.

Intuition is a loaded word, however. It conjures up images of impressionistic thoughts that are not fueled by experience or information. When I use the word you may look at it one of two ways: you may think I'm tapped into something important about our innate abilities, or you may think I'm searching for otherworldly phenomena. I want to challenge your perception of the word *intuition*. Intuition is not magic, although it may seem magical. It is one of the primary ways we make decisions, and one of the most important aspects of leadership. I challenge you to find a great leader, from Albert Einstein to Barry Diller to Winston Churchill to Meg Whitman, who has not relied on intuition at some point.

Intuition works only when you can separate your past experience from what's happening in the present moment. If your past is interfering and you're feeling a gut response based on a previous experience, then fear or habit may be getting in the way.

Here is an example. Lauriann's past was a problem at work. As the survivor of a difficult, abusive childhood, she had triumphed over great odds to become a successful IT manager. Her team was intensely loyal, and she was able to build an IT department from three to thirteen in a few months. Normally, Lauriann was excellent at listening for process and content. She could hear the tone in someone's voice and really understand what they needed or wanted. This ability to connect to her people was her greatest asset. She was also an excellent decision maker who often said, "I rely on my gut." Every so often, though, Lauriann's gut betrayed her, and it was directly connected to her past.

When I began working with her, she was becoming more and more afraid of her boss, Ravi. Ravi, COO of the fast-growing com-

TRY THIS

Intuiting Emotional States

When you are walking through your workplace, your gym, your city, or your town, take time to play a guessing game. What are the people around you *feeling*?

Intuiting the Right Thing to Do

Act on your gut response for one day. Make choices based on intuition, not logic. Whom should you talk to? What do you feel you should do? The more you exercise this "muscle" of intuition, the better information you'll get from it.

pany, was constantly stressed, agitated, and angry. It manifested in a surly disposition, but it didn't come out directly with Lauriann. Her antenna for emotional states was so fine-tuned, however, that she found it difficult to be around him. She began feeling afraid that he was going to explode. She was not acting like herself. It was as if this strong woman had disappeared, and in her place was a quivering child. "Sometimes I really think he's going to hit me," she admitted. I asked her for evidence. "I don't have any, it's just a gut feeling." At first I wondered if Lauriann was right. Was Ravi really that far off-balance? I realized after speaking with her and observing her in action that she was somehow "misfiring" when she saw him. Everything he said, no matter how innocuous, evoked a fearful or defensive response.

My sense was that if Lauriann didn't start distinguishing between her real, healthy intuition and the feelings of fear that were left over from her past, that she would end up damaging her career by avoiding her boss and not communicating with him.

We went through a series of exercises in which she asked herself:

- "Is this feeling from the present or the past?"
- "Is this feeling familiar?"
- "What evidence do I have to back up this feeling?"
- "Is this my intuition, or is this a memory?"

Lauriann began to use her natural intelligence to differentiate between the two. She learned to trust her ability to check in with herself, and to balance her physical "gut feelings" and her logical mind. Through these exercises, her signals became clearer and she began to see Ravi as a frustrated guy rather than a threat. Her interactions with him started being less about fear, avoidance, and defensiveness, and more about partnering with him to reduce his anxiety and aggravation. They became great coworkers, and Lauriann got her intuition back.

Accessing your intuition can be as basic as sensing something is wrong when you are interviewing a potential new employee, or it can be as serious as sensing that a loved one has become injured. Intuition is perception that is not from your conscious mind, which makes it difficult to learn. The only real way to develop your intuition is to begin to listen to it and see what results you get.

The more you get used to it and practice it, the more in tune you can be.

QUESTION SEVEN

What is my mood? Is this the best mood for what I want to accomplish?

> *Human beings, by changing the inner attitude of their*
> *minds, can change the outer aspect of their lives.*
> —WILLIAM JAMES

Your attitude as a leader has far-reaching implications, well beyond your own office. An illustrative article on leadership appeared in *Harvard Business Review* in 2001, featuring an excerpt of the book, *Primal Leadership: The Hidden Driver of Great Performance,* by Daniel Goleman, Richard Boyatzis, and Annie McKee.[6] According to the article, the hidden driver to great performance is nothing other than a leader's *mood.*

That's right; you read that correctly: mood. According to Goleman and his colleagues, leaders' emotions and emotional style affect not only their own mood but also the moods and behaviors of everyone they manage. The authors call this phenomenon *mood contagion:* "Emotional intelligence travels through an organization like electricity over telephone wires. Depressed, ruthless bosses create toxic organizations filled with negative underachievers. But if you're an upbeat, inspirational leader, you cultivate positive employees who embrace and surmount even the toughest challenges."

If you understand the effect your mood can have on employees and other stakeholders in your organization, you can proactively manage and improve this element of your leadership. According to Goleman's group, "An emotionally intelligent leader can monitor his or her moods through self-awareness, change them for the better through self-management, understand their impact through empathy, and act in ways that boost others' moods through relationship management."[7]

I once worked with a CEO—call him "John"—whose team gave him the nickname "Hydekel," a cynical synthesis of the famous Jekyll and Hyde. John's mood swings were legendary. A powerful entertainment company executive, John was a superstar in his field and the brains behind award-winning artists for the company's record label. He was also, some said, crazy—particularly when interacting with people inside his organization. However, with the musical talent, John was fantastic. He was pleasant, caring, thoughtful, and patient. With his staff, he was an ogre. Needless to say, John thought that the talent was more important than his staff, and he acted accordingly.

The problem, of course, was that John's bad mood was contagious among his team members. Over time, his own team started quitting one by one. John started to recognize this as a problem. On the personal front, John became a new father. A single, powerful question turned his thinking around. "All of your team members are someone's kid. How would you want your daughter to be treated by her boss?"

The lesson? Smart leaders are smart about their moods and the effect those moods can have.

Positive moods and positive emotions are also activators of our social consciousness. Positive emotions draw us out of our preoccupation with our own well-being and self-gratification, and they increase our sense of community and relationship to others. Positive moods activate altruism and help make organizational life more collaborative.[8]

A 1998 study by Barbara L. Fredrickson, published in the *Review of General Psychology,* states that "positive affect" broadens both the scope of thinking in an organization and the scope of action. That is, people with a positive attitude not only think positively, they also achieve better results with their actions. Fredrickson's research also shows the healthy ratio of positive to negative "watercooler conversations" in the workplace. For every negative statement, the organization needs two positives to maintain a thriving culture. (In a marriage, this number shoots up to 5:1—wouldn't you know it.)

Fredrickson concludes that positive emotions—such as joy, interest, contentment, and love—also broaden the scope of attention and cognition and spark creative thinking. They build physical, intellectual, and social resources, undo the aftereffects of negative emotions, and even may protect your health.[9]

QUESTION EIGHT

How am I attuned to synchronicity?

I cannot resist looking at the concept of synchronicity through the lenses of three very different thinkers who all describe this same phenomenon. The rock group The Police have a song titled "Synchronicity" that begins "A connecting principle / Linked to the invisible. . . ." Carl Gustav Jung describes it as "a meaningful coincidence of two or more events, where something other than the probability of chance is involved." And Joe Jaworski, founder of the Centre for Generative Leadership and former head of Global Scenario planning for Royal Dutch/Shell Group in London, writes:

> My quest to understand synchronicity arose out of a series of events in my life that led me into a process of inner transformation. As a result of this transformation I decided to follow a dream that I had held close to my heart for a number of years. It was the most difficult decision I had ever made, but the day I made it, I crossed a threshold. From that moment on, what happened to me had the most mysterious quality about it. Things began falling into place almost effortlessly, and I began to discover remarkable people who were to provide crucial assistance to me.[10]

Each of these thinkers talks about universal connectedness. In the Age of Interdependence, synchronicity becomes even more important. It's a meaningful connection that, to the naked eye, is improbable or coincidental. What does this mean? Jung defined synchronicity as a connecting principle that was "a-causal": a "meaningful coincidence" that occurs because all living things are related through our "collective unconscious." As a result, all we need to do is stop exercising our will and start exercising our receptivity to change. Once we stop trying to force things to happen the way we think they should and start being receptive to the ongoing unfolding of things, synchronicity begins to take hold. And then accessing our connectedness is effortless. Let's look at this in practice and see how an understanding of synchronicity and the collective unconscious can make leaders smarter.

Dante is a creative director in an advertising agency. His unique style of creative thinking taps into synchronicity. When he has a new project to think about, he pays attention to seemingly random events. He takes time to observe whatever patterns reveal themselves to him. As that happens, he says,

> It's like the ideas just come through me. I'm not responsible for the information I'm getting. I just tap into this "zone" and everything around me is telling me what to pay attention to. One example was I was doing a car commercial, and I was struggling to do something different from the same-old, same-old. The craziest things kept happening. I saw a big newspaper come flying right out of the sky. I'm sure someone dropped it from their roof, and it landed not two feet away from me. I was really paranoid so for three days I just kept looking up.
>
> Then I was watching television and there was an ad I really liked that had angels flying in the clouds. I kept getting that message to look at the clouds, look up. I kept looking up at the sky in the morning and the evening when I would walk to and from work. I kept seeing little things in the clouds, and then finally as I was looking up I saw this military helicopter that had these incredible patterns in it, and I just knew how I wanted to visually present my new idea. I had a real career success when that happened.

In another example, a successful entrepreneur named Kevin told me a story about his unique way of doing his best thinking. This story illustrates just how different we are in our ways of drawing on our "smarts" and realizing synchronicity in our lives. According to Kevin,

> The best thinking I've ever done has been in a classroom full of people during a boring lecture. I will always remember in graduate school that when I was disengaged from the content of what I was supposed to be listening to, and I would write "notes"—they would be all sorts of creative ideas for my business in them. I always knew I wanted to be an entrepreneur, but my business plan would just not come out when I sat down and tried to put it together, but when I was in class not paying attention, well *that* was when my mind went wild and I knew just what I had to do!
>
> Every twenty minutes or so my mind would wake up, hear a word or phrase that had to do with what I was thinking about, and I would be on a new roll. The words might be completely out of context—

like the lecture was on a quality assurance processes and my mind went to something about how to find quality employees. In one weekend seminar I think I wrote twenty pages of my business plan.

Whenever I got stuck I knew that I needed to either sit in a class and write "notes" or sit in front of the television or the radio and let it blare on while I wrote about something different. I realize this sounds crazy, but it works for me.

When it comes to synchronicity, remember the famous proverb: "Luck is when opportunity meets preparation." Watch for opportunities and use that appreciative eye and they will come to you.

QUESTION NINE

How am I using visual images in my planning and decision making?
One of the most striking elements of our society today is the amount of visual stimulation and communication we have. Think of advertising, video games, the Internet, cell phones, BlackBerrys,

---

TRY THIS

Seeing Meaning in Random Events

Jung believed that all of our collective consciousness is available to us to dip our thoughts into at any given moment.

For three days, notice and write down words and themes you hear as you go about your day that catch your attention. Turn on the radio and notice what song is playing. Notice what happens when you decide to observe "signs" in everyday activities. That napkin looks like a snowflake! The piano truck wasn't there this morning, so I got the parking space that allowed me to run into the store quickly and just make my flight!

Take a moment to imagine that these things are meaningful—that you should be learning something from them about your work. What lessons can you glean from what you're observing randomly?

PowerPoint presentations. Our thinking has become highly visual, not only equating products or ideas with their names but also with their visual symbols.

Graphic facilitation is becoming an increasingly popular form of idea-capture for corporate meetings. The facilitator or graphic recorder is responsible for taking the process and the content of a meeting and translating it into visual symbols. This process is intensely valuable, because it works differently on our memory—many of us find it easier to recall the information shared when there is a visual map (see Sample Visual Metaphor on next page). For example:

- In a team conflict, the graphic facilitator may document the conflict, the perspectives, and the issues on the page, and thus put the participants on the same side of the table as they look at the images.
- In a visioning exercise, the graphic facilitator or recorder may guide the group through visual metaphor creation. They will document where they are visually, and create a visual for where they want to go. This frees up their right brains to dream and envision metaphorically versus just linearly.

Daniel Pink uses the example of how high-end design is getting into every part of our society: Target discount stores now have products from Isaac Mizrahi and Phillipe Starck. Pink calls this the "Democratization of Design." We are all getting much more attuned and sophisticated about aesthetics.

Leaders need to be attuned to the design of their products, to the aesthetics in their offices. Aesthetics have an impact on productivity. They help people, both inside and outside the organization, connect to the brand. This can affect any range of interfaces with the world—the design of a reception area or the packaging of a particular product. Think of Mini Cooper cars, for example: How can you look at one and not smile?

I believe we are only becoming *more* attuned to visual communication in our environments. As a leader, you can learn to use this language to communicate what you care about. It's one way of using your right brain to address the whole of how you operate.

Here's an example with some irony to it. Lionel, a publishing industry executive who had worked in a visually creative environment

SAMPLE VISUAL METAPHOR.

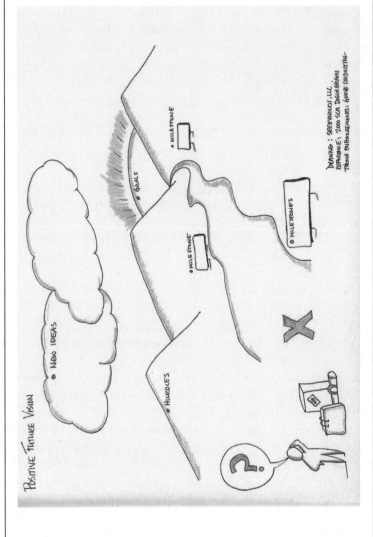

Source: Serevnolds, LLC.

for more than fifteen years, kept his old office when he was promoted from publisher of one magazine to overseer of a large group of publications. His identity for many years had been completely aligned with one visual entity, and his entire office was decorated in the colors of his former magazine, with cover posters from the magazine all over his walls and awards he won while at the magazine displayed prominently. This environment reflected his past—and not his present and future as a representative not of the magazine but of the company as a whole. It may not have been intended to make a direct statement that he is still identified with his old role, but it did so nonetheless.

When his new direct reports talked about him, they said things like, "He sounds excited about the new job, but he's really hanging on to the old one." The day he took down the posters and put up some different artwork was a major shift.

We all need to start observing our communication from a visual perspective. What are you communicating through the environment you create?

Question Ten

How am I living and working from my values?
This final question is often the most important of all. Good leaders not only ask the right questions and apply different strategies to different situations, they also understand that answers are not always clear, and that every decision cannot be right. Many of our decisions as leaders require that we tolerate both positive and negative outcomes in different areas. We must tolerate this for the greater good of competing stakeholders—stockholders, employees, and community on both local and global levels. Developmentally, as we grow and evolve as people, we see the world in varying shades of gray rather than in black and white. So how do we make decisions? Enter personal and organization values—guiding principles that round out our leadership tool kits.

To behave ethically, we must understand the difference between right and wrong in our own minds. We must have empathy and compassion for others, we must have the self-awareness to know how our behavior affects others, and we must have the self-control to make decisions based on the greater good rather than on immediate personal gain, and we must have the social skills to influence others to follow our lead.

To become smarter leaders, we must ask questions about our ethical philosophy. While we have already addressed values-based questions in some of the exercises you have completed, it is important to delve further into your own ethical framework. Why? When we answer basic questions about our personal philosophy, we work toward developing a simple model for the complex process of ethical decision making in leadership.

Here is a closer look at values:

- Values are our primary motivators.
- Values help us make decisions.
- Knowing our values is basic to self-knowledge, and therefore basic to empathy, understanding, communication, and influence— our emotional intelligence.

JETBLUE: VALUES-BASED DECISIONS

I've been fascinated by JetBlue ever since my first flight on the airline from New York to Long Beach, California. I was seated next to a venture capitalist whose group had invested in the airline, and he was delighted to see so many happy faces flying "his" airline. That's one of the things JetBlue seems to succeed in across the board: people feel that this company is theirs, and that they have an investment in making it work. JetBlue is a casual, friendly brand, which is reflected in how its CEO, David Neeleman, interacts with the customers and the employees, including traveling on the airline and talking to the passengers and really asking questions and listening: "What do you like about JetBlue? What could we change to be even better?"

Sound familiar? It's Appreciative Inquiry in action. Another important thing about JetBlue is the energy created in the culture through slowing down, really listening, engaging with values, and focusing on people. What's the result of that slowing down? A dedication to customer service, for one. Being named best U.S. airline in *Condé Nast Traveler*'s 2002, 2003, and 2004 Reader's Choice Awards is another. A high on-time rate is another.

Allison Weir, a leadership facilitator in JetBlue Airways' Learning and Development department, talked with me about how they use their values in every aspect of their organization:

> There's an enormous amount of pride working with JetBlue. There's pride in believing in what you're doing and in our leadership's vision. It stems from David Neeleman and Dave Barger [respectively the president and the COO]. We call them David and Dave. When they send out messages it's always signed casually, "from David and Dave." They're part of the team, not separate from it. They're friendly and down-to-earth. I really see it as humility above all. They care. They want to be there, and they're thankful for all the crewmembers do.

> It's important to them to preserve our foundation as a close-knit family unit while undergoing massive growth and change. They're at orientations welcoming new crewmembers to the JetBlue family; they're at "pocket session" meetings to share and discuss what's happening at JetBlue and the industry with everyone in their JetBlue family. It's not a lecture, it's a shared dialogue with questions and answers, which encourages people to say what they think, question things, and engage in free-flowing conversations about getting better. Even when entering a room, David and Dave make a point to greet each person warmly and always conclude their discussions with a sincere "Thank you for your commitment and dedication to the company."

> We also have a no-layoffs policy. People get worried, gas prices are rising, and other airlines are going bankrupt. Many people here have had lifelong careers in the industry and there is some concern during this volatile time. It speaks volumes to the commitment our senior leaders have to our people that we have that policy. It sends out a strong, positive message that they care about creating an environment where people are always our number one priority.

> We have five JetBlue Values: Safety, Caring, Integrity, Fun, and Passion. Those values are integrated into everything that we do. They're part of our hiring process; we look for them in candidates. They are part of our decision-making process. As an airline, we already have a large set of federal rules to abide by. Senior leadership didn't want to create a bigger rule book, but instead wanted crewmembers to have the freedom to make decisions based on

these simple JetBlue Values. Is it Safe? Is it Caring? Does it have Integrity? Is it Fun? Does it have Passion? Freedom and trust come from using the values. If you make a decision based on the values, it's supported.

I've worked for a variety of places, such as a nonprofit where values were very important, but they never played out quite the same way. The values are integrated into the way we do everything here. We live and breathe them so that they become baked into our cultural DNA.

One story is about the blackout in New York in August 2003. My peers and I manage the "Principles of Leadership" series, our leadership development training. We were in the middle of a class with leaders from across the operation when the lights went out that day. When many people at other companies were asking "When can I go home?" the only question we heard was, "How can I help?"

My manager gathered up our team and we ended up going over to JFK [airport]. We got there and jumped in with fellow crewmembers and crew leaders to do anything and everything to help our customers get through this experience: handing out food and water, lending our cell phones, inviting stranded passengers at the airport to stay in our terminal for the night. There was a lot of confusion and concern because people had no way to communicate with their families. It was so soon after 9/11, and people were unsure of what was happening. We just knew we had to go out of our way to make them feel more at home. David was helping, even procuring an ice-cream truck to feed people who were stuck waiting.

It was truly an amazing experience. We all saw firsthand how closely aligned we were as a group, and how we've been taught to be flexible thinkers by not having that rule book, but by working under the banner of the values. We were able to immediately mobilize to help. The flexibility, the JetBlue Values, the people—we were definitely set up to do the right thing in the moment.

David Neeleman has nine children. He's a family guy. He's someone who is incredibly inspiring. What makes him that way? The humility is a huge part of it. He speaks without ego. We are part of a JetBlue University led by a chief learning officer and we all know that training and development is valued here. In the "Principles of Leadership" series, we partner with internal and external coaches and facilitators to deliver leadership development training. We teach all leaders feedback and coaching skills so they can incorporate them into their leadership style—asking great questions and letting the crewmember solve the problem are at the core. The initial event in our series includes small breakout and panel discussions with our senior leadership team, including David and Dave. It's a big commitment on their part and one which they all fully embrace. We continue to strive to do the best we can. It's never about arriving somewhere; it's about continuous learning, continuous improvement, and growth as individuals, as a family, and as a company.

To rally smarter thinking among those you lead, which will be the focus of Chapter Three, you need to be able to understand where you yourself are going and how to get people to come with you. Just as individuals have personal values that support their own visions, an organization like JetBlue has values that support *its* vision. Once your organization's values are established *and expressed* by you and your leadership team, these values become behavioral guides for every employee and stakeholder. Values significantly influence the corporate culture, and they show employees how to move, on a daily basis, toward the company's vision.

How do personal values and organizational values intersect? To be fulfilled or satisfied on the job, individuals must be able to live their own values in the context of the organization. Ellen, a former entertainment executive, faced this issue head-on. She says,

> My life was empty, because it was all about making a ton of money. I love to work, but I turned forty this year and I want to make a difference on this planet. I was disheartened by the way I was treated. I was feeling like I didn't belong there. I'm a down-to-earth person, what was I doing in a flashy entertainment environment? What am I doing at all these parties and glamour-fests? I just knew I was not serving the world through this work, and I wasn't making the people around me on my team better because of my attitude.

> In working with my coach, I discovered that I have a lot to give to the world. She helped me clarify my values. Before I left my job, I was able to clean up all the relationships that had been messy or uncomfortable. I was able to identify a successor. I was able to think clearly about my work again, and help the person who was taking over to do an even better job than I did. I've been brave and I've changed my life for the better.

I'm not at my flashy entertainment job where I was driving myself and everyone else crazy. I'm really happy and today I run operations in a whole country for the Peace Corps.

Although you may not make quite as radical a change as Ellen, what could a values clarification do for your leadership?

TRY THIS

Values Clarification

The objective of this exercise is to elicit your personal driving values. You can complete this exercise on your own or, better yet, work with a partner (coach, friend, trusted colleague) and have them verbally ask you the following questions.

1. Exploring your personal values:
   - What was a peak experience in your life?
   - If you were to see twenty years in the future to a party in your honor, what would you like the keynote speaker to say about you?
   - If you could do anything in the world, what would it be?
   - What are your top three priorities?
   - What do you love about your job?
   - What values do you see in your responses to these questions?
2. Exploring the link between your personal values and your work and organizational values:
   - How do you feel you are living up to your personal values at work?
   - What corporate values do you particularly relate to?
   - How do your personal values link to the values of your organization?
   - How do your personal and organizational values motivate you at work?
   - How do the values of the organization influence your leadership?
   - What insights do you have into the link between your personal values and those of your organization?

When you more clearly understand your values, you can make decisions based on them and influence people based on where your values intersect. You can also inspire people based on where your values intersect with theirs, with your organization's, and with those of your community and world.

I would argue that often the *toughest* decisions we make as leaders are related in some way to values. Such decisions are the least clear-cut.

Think of the following values-related dilemmas you may face as a leader:

- Establishing new manufacturing sites while shutting down others.
- Moving aspects of your business to another country while laying off local workers.
- Firing or laying off people near a holiday or after a disaster.
- Making decisions based on quality or expense. Will you take the cheap option and sacrifice quality or safety?
- Breaking policy when you think it's important.
- Maintaining corporate social responsibility programs. What do you support?
- Promoting employees who do their work in an unhealthy way (for example, pulling all-nighters or never taking vacation) above employees with more work-life balance.
- Using PR spin-doctoring techniques to change public perception.
- Insert your own here. . . .

Everyone has ethical dilemmas, and these dilemmas are always unique to each specific situation. The key is to come back to your values and the values of your organization. Remember Johnson & Johnson's Tylenol scare in 1982? In Chicago, seven people died when someone unrelated to the company laced bottles of Tylenol with cyanide. J&J's leadership looked to their values in the form of their corporate credo when they decided to recall all the Tylenol in the United States and launch a large campaign to alert the public after the tampering incident, at a cost to the company of $100 million. People still talk about how this action maintained their trust, and many years later the outcome is loyal customers who believe in the brand. Remember that you can look to your values to solve ethical dilemmas for yourself. At the end of the day, you are the one who must look at yourself in the mirror.

THE BUY-IN CYCLE

When you lead with the desire to inspire and motivate others to work with you, one of the most important actions you need to take is securing buy-in for your positive future vision. Asking questions, listening carefully, letting go of your need to be an expert, and maintaining a positive outlook are all critical skills in getting other people on board with your leadership—but remember that all of this is a process, not a single event.

Often, people don't like change, and when you propose a new vision, a new future, there is no guarantee that everyone will be as excited about that future vision as you are.

Most resistance to organizational change is based on one of two things, or a combination thereof:

- *Fear:* Fear of consequences, by-products, outcomes, or the unknown.
- *Logic:* Understanding the positives behind a different course of action from the change you propose.

Keeping in mind that with every change you will come across both valid and invalid fear and logic, I propose a five-phase process that I have used successfully with leaders in a variety of change situations:

1. *Share that positive future vision (you do not have to be the sole owner).*

The biggest question leaders ask me when they have to lead a change is "How do I make my team feel like they own this idea?" The answer: it takes sharing the positive vision in a way people can relate to it. If your team doesn't care about the bottom line, it's useless to say how much impact you will have on it. Think about speaking to both the analytical and emotional sides of the issue.

2. *Listen (gather information).*

Sound simple? It is. Just take the time to sit down one-to-one or in small groups to ask questions and listen. Say what's important to you about the change you propose. Listen to others and see what they think. You might just learn something that will cause you to change direction in a way crucial to the success of the idea. And even if not, your stakeholders will still feel acknowledged, and you've started the process of creating ownership, not just buy-in.

3. *Feed back what you've heard (acknowledge).*

Take a moment to paraphrase what you're hearing, both the content of what's being said and the emotion or tone behind what's being said. For example, "I've just heard that the IT department is going to have an enormous integration task on their hands because of this change, and I hear the frustration in your voice when you're telling me."

4. *Listen for resistance and for buy-in rather than ownership.*

When you are expressing a new or updated vision for a project or for your whole company, listen carefully for signs of resignation or resentment in your conversations. Be sure to address any feelings you notice by asking questions about why people might not be signing on to your vision. Don't let dissent fester. Also listen carefully for those who think it's a fine idea, but take no personal responsibility for making it real.

5. *Connect individuals to the vision.*

When you have the alignment and ownership of your stakeholders, you can achieve your greatest goals as an effective, enduring, and fulfilled leader. Connecting individuals to your vision means finding what's in it for them. It could be adopting a new process that will make the organization more efficient, in which case in the long term things will work better and with more cost-effectiveness. It could be that the change will allow the company to survive, in which case the stakeholders will still have their jobs. It could also be that they will have some difficulties in the transition. What's in it for them? The company will be stronger and more viable in the marketplace if change X occurs. Don't withhold the *why*. Trust your people; they will often be more amenable to change when they understand the reasons behind a decision.

Accessing multiple leadership tools and being familiar with your deepest-held values means that you can simplify and streamline your leadership. You can make decisions, solve challenges, and connect with people on many different levels, using many different techniques. Smart leaders are always learning and applying that learning in the real world. In today's world of open-system environments, having an extensive leadership tool kit is more important than ever. Beyond surrounding themselves with smart ideas, smart leaders must also surround themselves with smart people—and take time to appreciate and develop smarts and values in others. This is the focus of Chapter Three: When is your team at its smartest?

Summary

- Many companies today function best as open systems, attributes of which are adaptation, consensus, collaboration, and mutual benefit.
- To see what messages you are sending as a leader, take a close look at the results you are achieving. Think about your impact.
- Access both your left-brain and right-brain abilities.
- Understand that people are generally motivated by simple things: survival in a challenging environment, comfort, looking good or being perceived well, positive regard or relationship, and by their core values.
- Vision is necessary for powerful leadership. To create momentum and excitement, you need to be able to understand where you're going—and how to get people to come with you.
- Trust your intuition.
- Be aware of mood contagion: leaders' emotions and emotional style affect not only their own mood but also the moods and behavior of everyone they manage.
- Clarify your values. When we answer basic questions about our personal philosophy, we work toward developing a simple model for the complex process of ethical decision making in leadership.
- Engage in a multiphase ownership development process to help create and sustain changes you want to make in your organization.

CHAPTER THREE

SURROUNDED BY SMARTS

Perhaps at this point you are thinking along these lines: It's all well and good to know myself and be smarter and have an overflowing tool kit of smart leadership strategies, but does this make any difference to the people I lead? In other words, if I am smarter in an empty forest, will anyone know? The next necessary step in becoming the smartest leader you can be involves assessing your leadership smarts in the context of other people, and then helping those people become smarter—perhaps even smarter than you are.

First, we will look to ways for you to continually maintain the strategies from Chapter One and Chapter Two by cultivating a smart support network around you. Leadership coaching, as you will see, is most effective when it is an ongoing process and not a one-off device for crisis management. Next, we will look at several ways to cultivate the smartest team of employees around you. Strategies include mood contagion, accessing multiple leadership styles, delivering appreciative feedback, and investing in key performers.

YOUR PERSONAL LEADERSHIP TEAM

Never forget that you are a member of the team you lead. Therefore, when you think about training, development, assessment, and motivation, it's important to think about all these issues for yourself as well as your employees. As a leader, you need to cultivate the same support network around you that employees can access at companies. This is crucial to your development as a smart leader—and to your sanity. We can't do it all alone.

We all have allies, colleagues, and coaches who help us achieve effective, enduring, and fulfilling work. These are people we have chosen to have in our lives as leaders. They are people who don't just blindly support us; they tell us the truth, good or bad. Who is on your personal leadership team? Here are some useful categories to brainstorm:

- *Colleagues:* Peer relationships at your own level.
- *Coaches:* Professionals who help you think by asking you great questions and provide you focused attention and insight.
- *Mentors:* Those who have succeeded at what you're trying to do and can provide guidance, wisdom, and direction.
- *Experts:* People who know something about a specific topic in depth.
- *Friends:* Your personal support network.

Let's look at one smart leader's story of surrounding herself with the support she needs:

"Part of the leadership journey started for me when I realized my true strength was in recognizing what my blind spots were— not only recognizing those blind spots, but seeking out an input environment and support that I'd need to deal with them."

Thus says Ann Herrmann, CEO of Herrmann International. (As a reminder, this is the company behind the well-known thinking-styles assessment, the Herrmann Brain Dominance Instrument, which was developed by Ann Herrmann's father.) She explains,

> I started by joining a CEO group. I was the classic CEO who doesn't want to reach down for that support, so I was more open to work-ing with a group of peers. I had tried to start a group like this, but found that the industry focus got in the way of the breadth of thinking I was looking for. I went to someone I respect, Marjorie Blanchard. I know her from being in our industry. I'd watched what they did with their business and their family business to boot.
>
> I said to Marjorie, "Give me the magic bullets, the secret sauce," and she recommended that I set up a board of advisers or join a group of CEOs. I think that was the beginning of my ability to make sure I had people around me who were totally willing to get in my face about what I needed to pay attention to. I had to take the time to *think* before I acted.

I can't believe I wasn't doing this before, but as leaders we are so oriented toward working on the immediate. I'm in the thinking business! It's very easy to get caught up in moving quickly and not reflecting. This group is forcing me one day per month to reflect. It's *excruciating* to get away once a month for my own development. I have a four-hour drive to get there, and I hate taking the time for it. But it adds to my think time! I'm not distracted by anything. I use the time as that ramping down and ramping up, as well as just having a block of time to process information.

I've been doing that since 2001, and we've been growing at a 30 percent growth rate since. What I've realized is that it's really all about my learning, and my helping others in the organization learn. If they don't learn, I won't grow. It forced me to be in a learning mode. Now that I've done this—Why is this such a big leap for me to be devoted to this at least one day per month? We get so caught up in having to have it all figured out that it's almost frightening to publicly declare that you need to focus on your own development— it's putting on public display that you do need to learn. Really, you're teaching everyone else how critical it is for you to learn. That has created a very different way of looking at what's important and I'm modeling it every single month. It's having a big impact on the culture.

It's also allowed me to have the discipline around keeping top of mind some of the core issues that I have been stuck with for years. It's not just about learning, it's also about having people around you who have a different perspective. Learning to ask . . . what a concept! Leadership is all about asking questions of yourself, of your industry, of your people, about what we should be doing or not doing, and about looking in the mirror. It's much more that than it is telling. The learning for me has been that I need to *own* the breadth of the role.

Leadership is not about your doing something; it's about you facilitating something happening. Leadership is about enabling things to happen.

Another leader, Juriaan Kamp, is the founder and editor of *ODE Magazine,* which is dedicated to being a global voice of positive change, be it corporate, cultural, political, or economic. To take on such an ambitious project, Juriaan and his wife, Elaine, have needed the support of family, friends, and colleagues. I was lucky enough to catch Juriaan on his way to The Netherlands one gray San Francisco afternoon in the summer of 2005.

> I am moved so often by seeing people contribute and change. Recently there was a biologist from Chile—Francisco Varela—he's one of the people creating a new way of looking at biology. Varela wrote a book called *The New Biology,* which shows the many different things going on in nature, and that there is really more cooperation than competition.
>
> Hearing leaders in their field looking at things a new way really inspires me. A couple of years ago I traveled to some companies in the Third World, and I met people who were really changing people's lives through micro-loans. That is so inspiring. Change is possible, and it's happening, no matter what you read in the paper.
>
> I've given up many hours of sleep for my work. Elaine, my wife, and I say it's our fifth child—a child is always there, 365 days a year. It's had a positive and negative impact on my life. If you would ask my children how they feel about *ODE,* they may say they hate it. There is a sacrifice of time. I would also say that I would do it all over again. I would do a couple of things differently, but in terms of the mission, I would do the same.
>
> I have been lucky to always have friends and family around as a support system. I would enlarge that—people feel personally connected to the venture that goes beyond us. There are always personal relationships. It's different to talk about our mission versus the mission of a cola company. It makes it much easier to do our work. There have, of course, been dark moments. One of the challenges is that we really started the magazine from a wish to make a positive contribution. We didn't look for the most economical, efficient way. We know that there are zillions of magazines. The business challenge is major.
>
> This means that friends are very important and necessary. We have always found a friendly helping hand when we were in the dark places. Now that we are more stable than we were as a start-up, we don't have the same issues, but we do know we have support.

Your Professional Leadership Team

In addition to personal leadership-advancing relationships like the ones Ann Herrmann and Juriaan Kamp describe, leaders also have key staff members on whom they need to rely. Now that you know from the first two chapters who you are and how smart you need to be as a leader of your organization, you can better assess the areas in which you might need some help from other smart people. Here is an overview of the areas of smarts a leader needs to have in some way. No leader can excel in every single one of these areas, so take note of the areas at which you are best, and the ones where you might need some help.

Look at each category in the following list and make note of which kinds of people you currently have on your team, and which areas might need new staff members or outside experts. Note that even if you excel in one or more of these areas, you need to cultivate people with these smarts around you so you can go about the business of leading. Remember, you don't need to be an expert all the time.

- *Process people:* Those who help keep you organized and get things done. These are generally operations experts.
- *Emotionally intelligent people:* Those who help with people issues and understanding stakeholders' needs. These are generally human resources experts, leadership development specialists, or organizational development people.
- *Analytic people:* Those who are really smart about the numbers and can feed a leader data when it's needed; they help a leader make good financial decisions.
- *Creative people:* Those who think for themselves, come up with new strategies, and take new risks. They always ask, "What can we do next?"
- *Conceptual and intuitive people:* Those who understand the big picture, the concept, the strategy. These people help leaders stay on track with their vision. They look at how everything fits together. Think of chief strategy officers, or the traditional role of the adviser to the king or queen. These people hold the global view.

It's no secret why corporations have the departments they have; successful organizations need each kind of intelligence. When I look at these questions, I know that my client Jain is great at the emotionally intelligent role. She is really good at building and maintaining relationships with her team and making clients feel welcome. But as a leader, she doesn't always have time to chat with

people and make them feel welcome. She needs to bring in someone else who can replicate what she does—and recently she has.
She's good at rapport and relationship building—and enjoys it very
much—but that is not the most important thing she can do for the
company right now. Because she enjoys it she can certainly take
part in the "people" side of her business, but this cannot be her
main function as the leader.

Ultimately, smart leaders are able to differentiate what their
focus needs to be in the moment from what they might prefer
to focus on. You need to prioritize what tool you should be accessing in any given moment, and then delegate the rest to the smartest
people in any particular area. Narrow your focus and give things away.
Ultimately, this makes you and the people around you much smarter
and, as we will explore in Part Two, much faster and more efficient.

MAKING PEOPLE AROUND YOU SMARTER

As we are all aware, you can't always control who is around you. So
one of the keys to fulfilled, enduring, and effective leadership is
managing and developing people—whether you hired them or
inherited them. Here are some overarching themes to keep in
mind when developing a smart team around you:

- *The people you lead will have answers within them.* Your trusted
employees, constituents, clients—whomever you are leading—are
often capable of coming up with the best solutions themselves. You
may need to provide them with feedback or other information to
generate the solution, but they are capable of generating great
solutions if you approach them with encouragement, respect, and
high expectations. Remember that the essence of inquiry is to
reveal the wisdom of the individual.

For instance, ask the manufacturing plant workers to tell you
how to make the line more efficient. They'll know that if you service the machines once a week versus once a month, they'll work
better and have fewer breakdowns. Apply your Appreciative
Inquiry skills to any and all of your team members.

- *Stories offer a wealth of valuable information.* Great solutions to
any leadership challenge draw on, or from, real-life experiences.

They may even be your own stories. Ask employees to tell you stories when they come to you with a problem. You can then build on something that they have tangible familiarity with and emotional connection to. This helps solve the immediate problem and adds to the store of real-world knowledge you can access for future leadership dilemmas.

Susan, a human resources vice president at a nonprofit in California, was in charge of helping the organization shift from a grant-based model to a product sales model. The employees were having trouble getting excited about the shift, and they were disengaging from the process. Susan started asking some simple questions like, "When have you seen a positive change in an organization you've been in? What was it like? How were you a part of it?" When they began telling their stories, their attitudes began to change, and they found a window into how this shift might work for them. As you can see, appreciative questions are open-ended; they allow people to tell informative and creative stories rather than simple yes-or-no responses.

- *Conversations have great power.* Never underestimate the impact of the human connection achieved in a one-to-one dialogue. A seemingly impossible leadership issue you are facing often becomes manageable after you talk it through with another person. Dialogue is a powerful learning tool.

As a coach, I see this principle in action every day. A client of mine, Paulette, is an academic leader who is brilliant but emotionally on the edge. Her relationship with her boss has been very positive, but it's also been challenging. He is constantly expecting her to raise the bar on her performance. He is a committed leader but not a touchy-feely type. In a breakthrough coaching session, Paulette was saying that she just wanted to quit and go somewhere else where she could have a new boss with whom she could connect better. "I don't do well with people who are like Davis," she said. "He's just not a people person. He doesn't give me enough feedback on how I'm doing. I don't know what to assume. I know he's helped me and my career, but I just want to have someone I can relate to."

I knew Paulette pretty well at this point, and asked her, "Is this part of your pattern of thinking that you can't ask for anything in a relationship? You assume that he will never meet your needs and you will never connect, but have you actually tried to connect with him?" Paulette was shocked. It was an emotional moment for her as she realized that she had a responsibility to try to make the relationship work better for her, and that this was part of a lifelong pattern of not asking for what she wants or needs. In the weeks following, she was able to say to Davis that she would like more feedback on her performance, and he was happy to oblige.

Conversations can result in instantaneous change. People transform as they connect and communicate with others. This belief is at the heart of Appreciative Inquiry theory. The "Principle of Simultaneity" recognizes that "inquiry and change are not truly separate moments; they can and should be simultaneous. Inquiry is intervention. The seeds of change are the things people think and talk about, the things people discover and learn, and the things that inform dialogue and inspire images of the future."[1] In other words, we change when we tell our stories, hear them reflected back to us, and hear the insights of others.

- *It's smart to be solution-focused.* One of the keys to leadership is helping your team to lead. Often people will bring challenges and problems to their leaders without having thought of any options or solutions that would help to solve the problem. So teach your team to offer solutions, not just problems. When someone has a problem or challenge, affirm the fact that they need to think creatively about what can be done about it. They may not have the best answer, but they need to have ideas, not just complaints. This will immediately make you feel that the people around you are smarter because they will be bringing you more constructive ideas.

- *Leadership is about truth, and the truth will set you free.* Our old friend Dr. Abraham Maslow writes, "Assume that everyone is to be informed as completely as possible of as many facts and truths as possible, of everything relevant to the situation. There is the clear assumption in enlightened management that people need to know, that knowing is good for them, that the truth, the facts, and honesty tend to be curative and healing."[2]

The open-system leader knows that knowledge isn't for hoarding, it's for sharing. When you tell people why you are making the decisions you are making, when you give people the facts and the truth, you are demonstrating profound respect and trusting that they will use that knowledge wisely. It is not always possible to tell your employees everything, to manage in an open-book style, but it is always possible to tell the truth, and often it is stating the difficult truth that creates the best outcomes.

Delivering Appreciative Feedback

If we take people as we find them, we may make them worse, but if we treat them as though they are what they should be, we help them to become what they are capable of becoming.
—Goethe

Research has shown that when teachers think they are teaching a class of A students, the students (no matter what their prior performance) achieve As. The same is true of Cs and even Fs. Teachers give so-called high-potential students more attention, and the result is better achievement.[3] As leaders, we are no different. Our attitude and expectations set the stage for all that is to come from ourselves and our stakeholders. In fact, expectations *significantly* affect results. When we expect greatness from our direct reports and peers, they rise to the challenge. When we expect less than optimal performance, people usually respond accordingly. So to achieve positive results as a leader, you must begin with a positive attitude about yourself and the people you lead.

To explore this concept further, think about a common situation that leaders face: offering feedback to employees. In many organizations the word *feedback* is synonymous with criticism. Think about the times when you yourself have been on the receiving end of negative feedback. The word itself conjures up distorted guitar sounds and earsplitting headaches. I'm sure you felt discouraged, misunderstood, or unsupported—not a big motivation to work harder, right? There is a better way to deliver feedback—appreciatively.

The appreciative approach to delivering performance messages is a more effective way to enhance performance, motivation, and confidence in your employees. It is also a more enjoyable way for you to work as a leader. What does *appreciative* mean in this context?

When we look at others for their unique strengths, capacities, and opportunities for development, our attitude immediately shifts to a more constructive and positive leadership approach. This is a different mode from looking at others as *problems to be solved,* or as *underlings to be disciplined.* People do not want to feel like problems, so they react poorly to leaders who treat them in such a way.

These are the simple steps to apply appreciative feedback to your smart leadership tool kit:

1. Notice what works and state your observations. Have specific examples in mind.
2. Suggest what can be changed to be even better. Have examples of what didn't work, and how if it had been changed, it would have worked.
3. State the positive result you want to see, rather than the negative problem you want to eliminate.

Here is an illustration of the power of the appreciative approach. Nancy is a talented and enthusiastic employee who is constantly late. She supervises two young interns, and Neil, her director, is concerned that she is too informal with them, and that they are not performing up to par because she tells them "don't worry about it" when they don't complete assigned tasks. The team likes her—and relies on her for comic relief at team meetings, where she helps to defuse tension in the group.

Neil's original approach was to tell Nancy, "You have to change your approach with the interns. Your lateness and informality are setting a bad precedent, and I need you to change it so that they understand their deadlines are solid." Neil's approach was clear and direct, but came in the form of criticism and a focus on what was *not* working in Nancy's management style. Nancy's response was to worry, to get to work early every day, but to shrink from contact with her colleagues and direct reports, taking away her energy from her work. The result of this supposedly straightforward approach was that Nancy turned away from her natural strengths.

After some coaching on appreciative feedback, Neil changed his leadership style. Instead of providing "constructive criticism" to Nancy, he applied appreciative feedback: "Nancy, you are great with your peers, and you are using the same easy, informal style that works with them to manage the interns. That style isn't translating as a manager. I think if you create a more formal relationship with them and if you set the expectation that they perform, then they will work better for you. I'd like to see you succeed in getting them to complete their tasks on time and with respect for you as their leader. If you don't shift, you could sabotage your success. I want to see you succeed not just with your peers but as a manager too."

What was the result of Neil's appreciative feedback? Nancy's motivation increased and her behavior change started with an immediate conversation with the interns setting a new precedent. In her follow-up with Neil, she thanked him for his support and guidance.

If Neil had not focused on the positive attributes that Nancy possesses, he would not have been successful in improving her performance. In the second example, Neil was able to help Nancy focus on the solution rather than the problem.

Appreciative feedback is rooted in the idea that motivation is maintained through positive emotional states. The more common managerial approach of "constructive criticism" creates resistance from employees rather than enthusiasm for growth and challenge. Remember, when people feel defensive they don't listen. Smart leaders know that positive feedback comes from a helping perspective and inspires others to *want* to develop, learn, and grow.

WHEN PEOPLE JUST DON'T FIT

Even the Beatles didn't start with a perfect team; they had to let Stuart Sutcliffe go.

Sometimes no matter how appreciatively you look at an employee, that person is just not a fit for your organization. Don't think in terms of good or bad, just think in terms of fit. This takes the emotion out of firing people. One of the toughest jobs is letting people go. Your job as leader is to hold what's best for the company—and if what's best is that people go, you have to be willing to do that. Ultimately, it makes the fired employees smarter in their own careers as well.

An example is Sasha, who was hired by a financial services organization to fill a very senior role. She gave a great story, and she had a great background and a stellar résumé. Unfortunately, she just didn't have the skills to succeed in the job for which she was hired. But Sasha was such a nice person that her manager didn't want to let her go. Sasha herself was miserable because she knew she was failing. Finally, in her performance review, her manager said that she was great at certain things, but she was not a good fit for this particular job. By using the term *fit,* the manager avoided being overly critical or personal. Sasha ended up leaving the company to take on a more appropriate position elsewhere, and she actually thanked the manager for being honest with her.

With Sasha, the issue was a skills mismatch. In my own company, I experienced a cultural mismatch. A while ago I hired someone to come into my organization and consult to our team about our operations, and how we could streamline our processes. He came with superb recommendations, had the skill set, and was excited to do the job, but his style was far too formal for our group. He wasn't able to merge smoothly into our flexible culture, which is collegial and casual, and where many people work from home offices. He would show up to a meeting in a suit and everyone else was in jeans. Our correspondence is often a casual e-mail message or a phone call, but he would send e-mail in a formal business construct. People felt a disconnect with his formality and ultimately we mutually agreed that he would be able to find a better fit elsewhere.

Sometimes, though it can be very hard to admit, the person who doesn't fit may well be you. If you are experiencing a lot of leadership struggles, ask yourself if you are really the right fit for your organization's culture. Do you look like a good fit with the people at your organization? Do you adapt to its formality or informality in dress and conversational tone? Are you vastly older or younger? Do you make lots of internal phone calls while everyone else uses Instant Messenger? Does everyone else start e-mail messages with "Hey guys!" while you say "To whom it may concern"? Do you provide information visually, in charts or pictures, when everyone else gives numbers? Sometimes being different is a great asset, but unless you are able to connect to those around you, your differences may be blocking you from achieving what you wish to achieve.

Here's a smart practice I've adopted to make sure I fit culturally when I am working with a client: I try to match the pace and tone of the people who work at the organization. If they are quick and rush about, I'll do the same thing. I'll match and demonstrate that I can track with them. If they are more reflective, quiet, and refined, then I will try to match that pace.

In other instances, you may want to lead your organization's culture in a new direction, so you have to be a bit different. I experienced this firsthand when I pitched my company's services to a conservative consulting firm. I knew we were the right provider and they really liked us, but they chose another vendor because of the way I was dressed for our first meeting. Although I was wearing what I perceived to be a conventional gray suit, the person I met with felt that my little black glasses were too funky and I was too edgy. They liked this about me—that the real me was shining through—but they worried that their senior executives would not respond well to my progressive thinking and appearance. They selected another vendor who was more "blue suit" and conservative.

What happened was that the conservative company they chose didn't work for them because the consulting firm realized they wanted to *be* more progressive. In the end, they did hire my firm because we represented where they wanted their company to go. They wanted to be more of an open system, and what we represented was a nontraditional, innovative company—rather than traditional, which is what they are. What they were trying to accomplish was change. We represented that change. But one of the sponsors of the program still took me aside after they brought us in to say, "You might want to buy another pair of glasses."

MAKING SMART PEOPLE SMARTER

> *A manager who wants to build an organization that will last, one in which people are motivated to contribute and to stay, has these three options. The first is to make the objective conditions of the workplace as attractive as possible. The second is to find ways to imbue the job with meaning and value. Third, by selecting and rewarding individuals who find satisfaction in their work, leaders can steer the morale of the organization as a whole in a positive direction.*
> —MIHALY CSIKSZENTMIHALYI, *GOOD BUSINESS*

FOCUS YOUR TIME ON THE SUPERSTARS

Most managers spend the majority of their time dealing with problem employees. Appreciative leaders do the exact opposite. Instead of spending most of your time coaching people who need the most development, the smarter choice is to spend the time with people you think need it less. Everyone knows that your top performers make all the difference in the bottom line, so why do you spend your time with the people who need the most development? The greatest opportunity is with those people who are your best performers. They are the ones who can most benefit from a thinking partner. Invest in a place where you can see the highest return. Your superstars will in turn help develop other people. There is a huge cascade effect to coaching—Capital One demonstrated in a recent study that nine people in their organization benefit when one executive is coached—a wonderful ripple effect where everybody grows and succeeds.

However, to foster this cascade effect, you need to take one more step: Instead of just rewarding your superstars when they succeed, reward the *team* that does the best. When you recognize accomplishment publicly, don't single the stars out; let them know in private. In public, it's all about collaboration. Otherwise, you will create a culture of backstabbing and other terrible behaviors that are antithetical to your group's becoming smarter. Being a smart leader in an open system means understanding—and encouraging your team to understand—that we are a part of a whole system. We're not on our own. All of our ideas, knowledge, and successes are together in one network.

TRY THIS

Tapping Top Talent

Take a moment and think about the most productive conversations you've had with your team members. Who are the people you should invest more time with? Who will give you an exponential return on your investment?

In her wonderful book on healthy organizations, *Creating We*, Judith Glaser says, "We are all connected. . . . When those connections are broken at work, what was a healthy, growth-oriented culture turns unhealthy and every member of the organization, every cell of the human organism suffers."[4]

TEAM SMARTS

> *Build with your team a feeling of oneness, of dependence on one another, and of strength derived from unity in the pursuit of your objective.*
> —VINCE LOMBARDI

Great teamwork occurs when a group of individuals sharing a similar vision but possessing diverse skill sets collaborate effectively to create results that could not be achieved by individuals working alone. When thinking about your team, it's helpful to think about what the best version of your group might look like. Make sure your appreciative eye is working, and try this brief teamwork assessment.

I once sat in on a strategic planning session for the leadership team of a nonprofit organization in New York. The goal of Rachel, the team leader, was for the group to understand each other's motivations and differing perspectives. She decided to try an appreciative approach and created the following inquiry:

- Tell me about a high-point experience when you were part of group growth—part of breaking through a barrier to get to the next level of achievement.
- In telling the story, answer these questions: What is it you value in yourself? What is it that you value about your contribution and your work? and What is it you value in the organization that you're a part of?

When you do this the same thing always happens, and this group proved no exception. Because this is a very respectful act of inquiry, everyone listens to the other team members with great respect. For the people telling the story, they feel that their viewpoint is valued,

TRY THIS

Quick Teamwork Assessment

The following attributes are those of a high-functioning team. Becoming aware of what attributes your team does or doesn't have is the first step. The next step is to cultivate what works and build from there.

Answer the following True or False

Our team . . .

Acknowledges each member as important	T/F
Understands our roles and responsibilities as individuals and as a group	T/F
Respects differences	T/F
Manages conflict effectively by bringing things out in the open	T/F
Tells the truth	T/F
Communicates with clarity	T/F
Understands our role in the organization and how we create value	T/F
Shares a vision or set of goals	T/F
Celebrates accomplishment together	T/F

This brief assessment can focus your attention on the areas you might need to focus on team building. What attribute about your team would you most like to change? A good way to begin is to focus on the team attributes that are working and use that success to build in the areas that are not to your liking. Remember that awareness is always the first step toward positive change.

TRY THIS

Appreciative Interviews:
A Team Discovery Process

Step 1. Inquiry Selection

Choose the topic of your inquiry. (Just one will be your focus.)

Examples:

High-Performance Teamwork

Customer Loyalty

Compelling Communications

Magnetic Culture Building

Inspirational Leadership

Living Our Values

Step 2. Appreciative Interviews

Activate a series of Appreciative Interviews with the following foundational questions of AI. Each team member will be responsible for conducting three interviews with selected participants. These may be colleagues, customers, vendors, leaders, but they must be available to attend a one-day retreat to explore your chosen topic. Here are the points to cover:

Describe a high-point experience in your organization or team, a time when you were most alive and engaged.

Without being modest, what is it that you value most about yourself, your work, and your organization?

What are the core factors that give life to your organization, without which the organization would cease to exist?

What three wishes do you now have to enhance the health and vitality of your organization or team?

(Continued)

Step 3. Group Debrief

Convene with your team members and discuss the following:

What were some "golden innovations" that people came up with that could implemented? What were moments of great emotion, passion, and enthusiasm? How did people respond to your questions? What arose that you would like to carry forward? How can you keep the momentum from this exercise, and thank your interviewees for contributing?

For more information about conducting a formal Appreciative Inquiry see the Resources section at the end of this book.

and thus they feel more open to listening to other people's unique viewpoints.

Asking the right questions begins to give individuals and organizations new focus. Then cultures begin to change: They become more conducive to creativity and innovation. Communication becomes smoother and more effective. A new sense of respect is conveyed not just to those within the organization, but to customers and vendors as well. And your experience and success as a leader can be enhanced exponentially.

TEAM RITUALS

One thing that many smart leaders know is that small rituals create big changes for the better. Whether it's having a lunch as a team after a group success, celebrating birthdays once a month, or using the same meeting opener and closer every week, rituals create a consistent message that a group is cohesive and valued, and that each individual is part of a greater whole.

At Burrell Communications in Chicago, meetings include rewards, not just for those people who do great things, but for those people who make a great "assist." To use a basketball metaphor, someone on the team is setting up the great shots, helping move the ball down the court. Team members are encouraged to write up acknowledgments of other teammates who are then rewarded for "assisting." Calling out the assist is a fantastic way to reward teamwork, and a great ritual to ground those teamwork behaviors.

As you will see in the next parts of the book, team rituals are also essential to making your organization faster and better. Every member of your team can feel fulfilled and successful when you as the leader place importance on your organization's values, your culture of work-life balance, and the legacy you want to leave. Make sure your team rituals are as positive as they can be, starting, as in the exercise below, with the simple stuff, like closing an average meeting.

TRY THIS

Appreciative Meeting Wrap-Up

At times our own light goes out and is rekindled by a spark from another person. Each of us has cause to think with deep gratitude of those who have lighted the flame within us.

—Albert Schweitzer

When finishing a group meeting, create a ritual that will help your team communicate and connect by acknowledging each other. The simple power of this exercise comes through even the first time you try it, and it grows with regular use. This can be used with small to medium-sized groups (three to thirty people).

Step 1. At the end of your meeting, have everyone stand up.

Step 2. Give the instructions, "Every person in the room needs to be appreciated or acknowledged before we leave, and each person should give an appreciative or acknowledging comment. It could be a thank-you for something that person did, or providing an observation about something positive the person brings to the group. I'm going to let someone else start."

Step 3. Watch to make sure everyone is appreciated or acknowledged before you announce, "Thank you—that's a wrap."

Step 4. Notice the impact—pretty positive, eh?

At this point, your leadership tool kit should be overflowing with smart strategies. I encourage you to come back to these chapters when you face a particular leadership challenge, or when you need a boost of smart strategy. If we had all the time in the world, I know that we would all try to use every single leadership tool at our disposal every day. But time is always limited, so smart leaders know that they must prioritize. In the next part of the book you will begin to build your time and energy management tool kit to deal with this eternal challenge. The next step in becoming an effective, enduring, and fulfilled leader is to use your limited time wisely. Begin to think about what is working in your relationship with time, and how you can build on that to feel that time is abundant and always on your side. In what ways is time already on your side, and how can you build on that?

Summary

- You need a *personal* leadership team. Coaches, mentors, colleagues, advocates, and personal support are necessary. Modern leaders don't go this path alone.
- You need a *professional* leadership team with expertise in a variety of areas. Even if you excel in one of these areas, you need to cultivate people with those smarts around you so you can go about the business of leading.
- Trust that the people you lead will have answers within them.
- Never underestimate the impact of the human connection achieved in a one-to-one dialogue; conversations have great power.
- The appreciative approach to delivering performance feedback is an effective way to enhance performance, motivation, and confidence in your employees.
- Spend time with your superstars. Instead of spending most of your time coaching people who need the most development, the smarter choice is to spend the time with people you think need it less.
- Build small team rituals to create big changes for the better.

PART TWO

THE *FASTER* PARADOX

To be faster, we need to slow down.

CHAPTER FOUR

FESTINA LENTE

> Festina lente.
> —ROMAN PROVERB MEANING "MAKE HASTE SLOWLY"

No matter how smart we are, everywhere we look today we are confronted by speed. Faster microprocessors, faster Internet downloads, faster exits from the hospital after treatment, fast-tracked employee development programs, "Fast Pass" lines for rides at amusement parks. Some even say that the high-speed racing of NASCAR is overtaking the slower-paced sport of baseball as America's national pastime.

Why our obsession with constantly going faster?

Many factors obviously contribute to our 24/7, go-go-go world. Technology, globalization, and a rapid onslaught of media imagery with fast edits come easily to mind, but these barely represent the tip of the iceberg. It could be argued that our cultural focus on speed has become something of an addiction. Think of Tom Cruise's character in *Top Gun:* "I feel the need, the need for speed." In this chapter we will focus specifically on three behavior patterns that are common expressions of that need for speed in the business arena: multitasking, fear-based behavior, and perfectionism. Each of these patterns can be damaging to leadership. The good news is that for each addiction, there is an effective course of detox that leaders can adopt.

Why the constant "need for speed," particularly in corporate America? There's a reason they call it a "rush" job. Adrenaline is addictive. We high-achiever leaders get a big reward from constant, productive action, and often fear the moments in which we are not "rushing." What might happen? Will we stop being successful? Will we stop being valued as contributors? Will our employees perceive us to be lazy? Will we lose our edge? Will our energy crash and burn and we'll never return to our former glory?

Many companies and managers believe that speed will give them a competitive advantage, because they will gain market share if they are the fastest to market. This can be true—until, of course, a better product or service comes out, or a more sustainable model is created. One example is a comparison of the iPod versus first-to-market MP3 players. MP3 players arrived first; iPods took over. We are conditioned as early as childhood physical education classes to believe that if we are the fastest we will be the first to reach a stated finish line, and so we will win. But, more often than not, this is untrue in the real world—and can be quite a damaging belief. Just ask the tortoise and the hare.

Before we go any further on this topic, let's pause for a brief check-in. Stop for a moment (your first lesson in slowing down to go faster) and answer this question: What do you really want as a leader? If you are reading along and thinking, "I just want to get in, lead my organization, and get out as fast as I can," then this is not the section for you. This "slow down to go fast" paradox is for those of us who want to achieve and endure for the long haul. This discussion is for those of us who value sustainability—the ability to hit the occasional wall, take a pause, and then keep going. This is not for those of us who use our strength just for short-term wins; it is for those of us who are sometimes willing to sacrifice instant gratification for longevity. If you are interested in creating a sustainable leadership strategy, then slowing down to go faster will have a big impact on your leadership effectiveness—and, almost certainly, your overall happiness and work satisfaction.

WHY GO SLOW?

Slowing down to go faster? Isn't that counterintuitive? Yes and no. We all know that keeping the pace is important when you're running a distance. Organizational life is no different. Pacing is what allows a racer to go the distance. If you are able to slow yourself down, reflect, and think effectively, that slowing down will have its impact on both processes and people. Imagine that you are rushing too fast, not thinking, just fighting fires. Those around you match your pace. Mistakes happen, long-term thinking goes out the window, and time passes while no one looks at the big picture—while no one has the time necessary to ask, "Are we having the impact we want to have as an organization?" and all those other important questions that take thinking, reflection, and calm.

Determining how you personally need to slow down to go faster is another exercise in using the appreciative mind-set from Part One of this book. Think of when you are at your peak performance level. Are you rushing? Are you doing sixteen things at once? Are you obsessed with perfection? Are you exhausted? Stressed out? Skipping lunch every day? Some of these things may work some of the time . . . but I would guess that your peak performance vision is focused, smooth, productive, and, dare I say, joyful or exciting.

Perhaps you are wondering at this point about all of the screaming, rash, kinetic, hundred-miles-a-minute leaders you know. They seem to thrive on that pace of life. There certainly are many of these people, and a significant number of them hold powerful positions and are quite wealthy. What's with that? The reality is that many fast-paced people rise up the ranks to leadership positions. And some of them can produce strong results for their organizations. But are these leaders, the kind you might call "bulldozers," the people you think of as effective, enduring, and fulfilled leaders? Are they role models? Do people like working for them? Do they seem content? Do they seem like they will last over the long haul? Some might, but the likelihood is that they are overstressed, overtaxed, and physically unhealthy. They are also using a skill set that is no longer serving them now that their job has moved from doer to leader.

The goal of this section of *Smarter, Faster, Better* is to help you become a more effective, enduring, and fulfilled leader by bucking conventional wisdom and actually *slowing down* to stay ahead of the curve by *thinking* more effectively, by maintaining working practices that create resilience rather than burnout, and by shedding the fear behind our "need for speed." In other words, going slower can actually help you and your organization to become faster—which, in its best leadership-related definition, means maximizing the return on your time and energy. How? It's all about optimum performance, and in particular, appreciating your "think time" as a leader (yes, faster is also about smarter). This doesn't mean slowing down the critical processes that keep your business functioning; rather, it means slowing down your thinking process as a leader, so that you can be *smarter* (and thus more successful) regarding your processes, product development, and management strategies. Think about it: No one ever says, "I want to be a faster leader," so why do we rush? And what do we give up as leaders when we are going too fast?

At this point I'd like to propose a somewhat controversial idea: Work shouldn't feel *hard*. When we are doing our absolute best work, it *feels* easy, enjoyable, and *right*. It's not painful or paralyzing. We may work diligently and for many hours in total, but our best— most effective, enduring, and fulfilling—work flows out of us easily, without struggle, with grace and simplicity. And it takes place at just the right speed—as fast as it needs to be.

What happens when a leader doesn't do any slowing down? Matt is the president of the European division of a professional services firm. His European colleagues see him as a "typical American," because he is in hyperdrive all the time. When you are in his office, papers are everywhere and he is answering the phone and talking to five people and talking so fast he is talking over everybody else. He is in such a state of panicked intensity that, to put it bluntly, he upsets everyone, and no one wants to be around him. People are immediately stressed by observing his constant, frenetic motion. Another important point is that he is not getting anything done right. Matt's level of anxious running means that he misses out on doing any *one thing* right and getting it off his desk. Instead, he is in a whirlwind of incomplete ideas, projects, and discussions.

Furthermore, Matt is so deeply stressed that he has no concept of what is going on with his physical body—he frequently looks like he hasn't slept in a week. His custom-tailored clothes are picture perfect and "put together," but he doesn't look like it—he looks in the middle of chaos, as if any moment he is going to crumple. He is in a world where everybody looks good, but he is so frantic, he looks bad.

His direct reports go in to talk to him all the time; he never says no. He has what he calls a "constant open-door policy." He always says, "Come on in," but he never pays attention. He is too busy guzzling Diet Coke and offering you one: "Would you like a Diet Coke? How does anyone live without Diet Coke? How are you? I'm a little scattered, I'm going to have to pick up the phone in a second. Don't go anywhere. Marianne, where's my phone charger? Sorry, I lost my phone charger. Nice to see you." It's exhausting just thinking about it.

Matt, as you might gather, is wonderfully likable, but when you get out of a meeting with him you notice that all the energy has drained from your body. You feel like you are now zapped and he took it all out of you . . . and he's still going.

He has not learned that he will get things done faster if he slows down, focuses on one issue at a time, and listens to other people, involving them in the project and using their time as well as his own to solve a problem. He has to slow down to engage them.

Matt won't even take his time for his executive coaching. He waits until the very last second before a meeting, then skims what he was thinking about working on and apologizes profusely, saying all the while, "No, I really need your help. Just wait—I was really on the hook last week. Next time you'll get my prep stuff two days in advance. I swear."

The people around Matt—his direct reports, his boss, and his peers—all comment that Matt is a "crazy American." Not only is Matt making himself look bad, he's also making himself into a stereotype in the minds of his colleagues.

What's wrong with Matt? If he doesn't take time to stop multitasking, relax his brainwave state, and recalibrate and shift his pace, he ultimately will crash and burn. He will fulfill his own fearful prophecy that everything will go wrong. He will multitask to the point where he can't get a single thing done well. A project will fall through the cracks, he will get seriously sick, or he will completely burn out. Matt needs to spend significantly more time recharging, and more time gathering his energy together rather than letting it dissipate.

The first step I took as his coach was to slow Matt down and get him back to his best thinking. Our first discussion about slowing down involved activating Matt's creative mind to address his fast-paced life. We started with activating his creative mind with five minutes of quiet relaxation at the beginning of each session. You can imagine what a challenge this was for speedy Matt.

We'll return to Matt shortly, but first, think about this: Why is it that people often come up with their most brilliant new ideas in the shower, in the middle of a movie, or when they are about to fall asleep? This is because their brain is in the "theta state," with brain waves operating at a slower frequency than when they are active, alert, and engaged in an activity like working. The theta state can be understood as the in-between state, between waking and sleeping. Probably the best-known activity to occur in the theta brain state is the fine art of daydreaming.

Current thinking is that brainwaves can be in any of five states, and every person has a unique combination of brainwave activity that incorporates different levels of all five states over the course of a day. The same five states are common to men, women, and children in all countries, all cultures, and all stages of life. Anyone can access all of them. By developing an awareness of each of the states and their value, you can call upon them in various situations to use them to your advantage as a leader.

Basically, the human brain is full of electrical charges. Brainwaves are electrical signals given off by the brain during different states of consciousness. For our purposes, we will place our attention on the beta, alpha, and theta states, ignoring the lowest frequency delta state, which is seen in deep sleep, and the highest frequency gamma state, which is associated with high-level information processing.

Beta: The beta brainwave state is associated with heightened alertness and focused concentration. When your mind is actively engaged in mental activities, the dominant brainwave state will be beta. A person in active conversation, playing sports, or addressing an immediate threat would be in a beta state.

Alpha: Alpha brainwaves are slower in frequency than beta brainwaves and represent a state of relaxed mental awareness or reflection. Alpha brainwave states are typically associated with contemplation, visualization, problem solving, and accessing deeper levels of creativity.

Theta: Theta brainwaves are even slower in frequency and represent a state of deep relaxation and meditation, enhanced creativity, stress relief, light sleep, and dreaming. Theta brainwave states have been cultivated in meditation for centuries. Research has proven thirty minutes a day of theta meditation can dramatically improve a person's overall health and well-being.[1]

Don't worry if the description of the theta state feels the most foreign to you; many fast-paced leaders would say the same thing, and many people have never experimented with meditation. But the theta state holds the key to the "faster" paradox. We need to slow down our brains to make our thinking faster—to engage our best creative intelligence. How does the theta state help us achieve this? When the brain is in the theta state, we are functioning at optimum *creativity*, which leads to the new ideas that fuel innovation.

Let's go back to Matt, the crazy American. Matt's next step in the coaching process involved scheduling "think time." This resistant leader had to make a commitment: to slow down and make a serious effort to access his best thinking. Matt needed to kick his creative brain into gear. Instead of trying to do everything, Matt needed to *stop* himself from running off the rails; he had to start focusing and cultivating think time. We talked about how Matt could access his most relaxed, creative thinking by accessing the theta state.

Matt first dismissed the idea of slowing down to think. We were facing each other across a low table in the corner of his office. In Matt's left hand was a pen that he had obviously been chewing, as well as a stack of paper. In his right was the ubiquitous can of Diet Coke. "That's meditation—I can't do that, I'm a doer. I need to be active." I asked Matt to bear with me and think about it for a moment. "What if you let go of all the stuff you're juggling—literally—and let your hands be free? You wouldn't be inactive; you'd just be ready for a new action.

"It's not just chanting and staying still that gets us into a creative state, Matt. It's just about changing our mental state for short bursts of time."

Why is there not much talk about the value of the theta state outside the world of meditation? Perhaps it is because being in the theta state doesn't feel like *work*. We tend to discount theta moments or portray "shower inspiration" as dumb luck. Or we only associate the theta state with leisure time, like yoga class, listening to classical music, knitting, or walking in nature. One of the problems with the speed of the world today is that we are all spending less and less time in the theta state in general. This is actually the exact opposite of what we should be doing if we really want to get ahead in any aspect of life. To increase creativity and innovation, we need to spend more time in the theta state—relaxing, renewing, and opening ourselves up to creativity. I urge you, as I urged Matt, to think of the theta state as a necessary component of your leadership.

INDUCING THE THETA STATE

A fellow coach once shared the story of an executive who hung a whiteboard in his shower because that's where he had his best ideas. (Hopefully he had a big enough shower to keep it dry.) While the shower whiteboard is a little extreme, this story raises an important question: If the theta state is the state in which we can cultivate our best, most original thinking, then how do we get into that state more often? The answer: Just keep doing what we already do, but better and more frequently. It's the appreciative approach again: See what already works and build on it. Here are some strategies:

Beginner theta-accessing strategy: The first step to being able to induce the creativity of the theta state at will is first to capture the power of our *existing* theta states. Observe them, appreciate them, and study how they operate. One simple way to do this is to keep a notepad by the bed so that you can capture any late-night or

---

TRY THIS

Mini-Meditation

Instructions: Take an egg timer and set it for five minutes. Sit in a comfortable chair and clear your mind. Activate your "observing" self. Watch all the thoughts that come up, and let them pass out of your mind. Observe the temperature, the texture of the chair, the sounds around you, the feelings in your body, the visual stimuli around you. Watch any judgments, positive or negative, that cross your mind, and let them pass out of your mind. Watch your thoughts. Keep cultivating this "observer" self until the timer goes off. When time is up, take a deep breath, change your physical position, and sit or stand up.

early-morning epiphanies. Keeping a personal tape recorder in the car is another strategy. Leaving yourself a voice mail message after you've had some theta time (such as exercise class, walking after work, or staring out the window of your commuter train) is another favorite. My friend Anna taught me to keep a file on my desktop to store ideas conjured in the theta state. I usually keep a notepad and pen with me so I can jot down my theta musings and then file them. I like to think of these files as a storage container for inspiration.

Intermediate theta-accessing strategy: A more formal way to access the theta state is through the art of meditation, as I've mentioned several times thus far. Meditation has many benefits: it slows down our biological processes, enables us to cultivate peace of mind, and sharpens our clarity and focus. What we don't think about is its application to the theta state. Sometimes the best way to get access to your best thoughts is to stop thinking. If you have never meditated before, or even if you are an old pro, try the mini-meditation exercise.

This exercise has multiple results:

1. If you are in need of a daily pace reset, this mini-meditation will start you off positively.
2. While you are not taking much time, you are getting exponential results for your thinking brain. The same relaxation that happens when you step away from the office can be yours in just five minutes, allowing you to start over with a clear mind.
3. Meditation can shift your brainwave state to one more conducive to creative and strategic thinking—either alpha or theta.
4. This can also enable you to disengage any defensive or threat-based behaviors that might otherwise sabotage your communication and make you less effective. Don't try this while you're driving.

Advanced theta-accessing strategy: Believe it or not, theta induction technology is available on the market. Yes, there is technology that can help us achieve a theta state. Audio CDs and visual "cortical stimulators" have been designed to activate different brainwave states through sound, rhythm, and light sequences. To find such technology, visit http://www.avstim.com, http://www.photosonix.com/about_us.htm, http://www.dynamind.com/ls.htm, or http://www.toolsforwellness.com/48425.html, or explore the Web to find a multitude of new and different theta-inducing ideas. There is even video game technology to assist in your pursuit of the theta state. One example is The Journey to Wild Divine (www.wilddivine.com), a program designed to teach meditative techniques, induce relaxation, and cultivate other energy states using biofeedback.

According to Kurt Smith, CEO of The Wild Divine Project, the video game, which can be downloaded onto a computer desktop, is the first product to offer biofeedback at the consumer level. The game, according to Smith, includes activities and events that "help people slow down and get in touch with their intuition to make better decisions as leaders."

Smith practices what he preaches. "I've always had a mindfulness practice," he says. "It's made me successful. I've had many start-ups and I've been a team leader. I do my meditations throughout the day to be totally present to those around me. I can really hear and listen to what people have to say. As a leader, it's impossible to make wise decisions without input."

Smith says that The Journey to Wild Divine promises to "help people get more in tune. They can take five minutes, tune up, and recognize that they might not have been thinking straight."

Smith's goal is to help people cope with the stress of everyday life and help them interact better with others. The product is positive, scientifically credible, and extremely innovative. Who knew that playing a video game for five minutes could add hours to your patience and effective work time?

Now that you know some ways to get to the theta state, what is the real application of the theta state to the leader of an organization? Do all leaders really need to take thirty minutes out of their workdays to meditate? Well, yes, that wouldn't be a bad idea. Of course, it is not everyone's cup of tea to chant or practice sitting meditation, but really smart companies and leaders schedule space in their day for "think time." Rather than calling it meditation, you might conceptualize this time as moments of reflection when you can get into a creative state and block out that pile of "urgent" work on your desk.

You may be familiar with Steven Covey's time-management model from one of his seven habits, "putting first things first."[2] His concept of managing time revolves around a four-quadrant model, with one axis being "urgency" and the other "importance." Urgent and important issues might be crises or deadline-driven projects. Urgent and unimportant issues may be meetings, phone calls, e-mail messages. Important but not urgent is the quadrant Covey highlighted as the one to shift attention to. In this quadrant come all things critical to building your business that are not immediate. They include planning, building relationships, strategizing, preventing problems, and the like. That quadrant requires think time.

Most people only think about "reflecting" at specific moments, such as when they are gripped by a decision, a transition, a challenge, or an opportunity. These instances, especially when something goes wrong or we feel stuck, are what bring on a sudden realization of the need to access some inspiration or spend some time in thoughtful silence. But part of the "slow down to go faster" philosophy involves taking time to reflect even—or perhaps especially—when things are going well. In fact, it's when work is flowing along at a nice, successful pace that your thoughts are flowing as well. This can be the *best* time to reflect and come up with creative new ideas that will maintain that positive momentum. For me, if I am happily in the flow of writing an article and take time to check in with myself for a few minutes, all of a sudden I have all sorts of ideas about other areas of my business.

Matt's experiments with theta-state thinking proved fruitful. Shortly after we began coaching, Matt was using some of the techniques, including mini-meditation and think time to get himself to stop, focus, and relax. Now he was calmer and able to think more clearly about his priorities.

Matt said, "I can't believe it—even short meditation is really working for me. I'm starting to notice how I upset some of the people around me. I never meant to ignore them; I thought they knew that I'm just a really busy person, but my team members have been commenting to me that I'm paying more attention and listening better. I'm also starting to realize that I haven't been thinking about the long term at all—I've just been fighting fires."

There's a big difference between a passer-by rushing around throwing water on a series of erupting flames and a professional firefighter who is armed with all the tools needed to douse a blaze in minutes.

Think about what kind of preparation it takes to be a professional firefighter. Years of training. Hundreds of pounds of gear. A team of other professionals who work as an organized unit. Is this the way you're thinking about addressing problems, or is it random, chaotic, and stressful?

I asked Matt to start thinking like a real live professional firefighter, someone who is prepared, ready, and organized about addressing issues as they come up. Someone who knows what he needs to do back at the station to take care of business.

If you prefer a sports metaphor, then think about the concept of "bench time." In no professional sport can an athlete compete on the field 100 percent of the time without experiencing exhaustion or injury. Even if it's just for a minute, everyone needs to sit on the bench for a breather in order to win in the end.

Still not convinced? How about this: Even downtime of one minute can have a positive effect for a leader, particularly in a time of challenge, stress, or crisis. Just sixty seconds of slow breathing can help you orient yourself and think before you act. You will get back your executive functioning, the full extent of your experience, wisdom, and intelligence that can become murky in a moment of panic. When you understand the power of the theta state for thinking, focusing, and avoiding disaster, you start to wonder how many problems could have been avoided by a simple time-out.

Great moments of understanding, inspiration, or revelation are often brief. They are the result of some moment of insight, a moment of creative brainpower. It's the time spent crafting, articulating, and translating the "big idea" into reality that requires a different type of energy and drive. Many people in the grip of the creative force, when inspired, will work intensely when the idea is fresh, and will intersperse that intense push for completion with moments of quiet thought—what my writer father called "percolating." There is a need for great ideas to simmer, and to fully form within the thinker.

If you have a bright idea, take time with it. Let it mature before bringing it to light. Some of the greatest books imagined have never been written, because they've been talked out over a beer at the local pub.

And now back to Matt. Matt's next challenge after slowing down a bit involved checking in with his priorities and values.

Prioritization

*There are two things that are most difficult to get people
to do: To think and to get people to do things in order
of importance.*
—John Maxwell

We all know that great leaders are able to regularly prioritize what
is urgent and important. What is the one thing that you should
be focusing your time and energy on—something that, if done
well, could create great results in your working life? How much
time are you spending on that one thing? How do you prioritize?
How often?

Time management gurus have spent decades observing that
leaders and managers address the urgent and unimportant
before they address the important. How many hours have been
wasted and stress levels elevated because of this strategy? We all
know prioritization helps, but we rarely stop to do it. Why not?
Well, because everything seems more important.

Sometimes—often—it takes years to accomplish something
worthwhile and important to an organization, such as the development of a new product. Think about Matt: he wasn't looking at
the big picture—the long-term impact of decisions he was making
in the moment—because he chose to focus himself on the immediate rather than on opportunities that would grow and bloom
over time with the right investment of resources.

If the leadership of an organization launches a new product
too quickly or diverts thinking to a variety of other projects at the
same time, those products may work in the present, but they could
falter one, two, or ten years down the road. This is why companies
generally invest copious resources—people, creativity, money, technology, and time—in projects like research and new product development. They know it is worth their while not to rush because of
the potentially huge long-term gain.

A recent example involves Steve Jobs's May 2005 announcement
that Apple Computer would switch to using Intel chips instead of
Power PC chips. What seemed to the public to be a sudden, earth-
shattering move by Apple in reality resulted from a long history of
secret research and development. OS X, the Apple Mac operating

TRY THIS

Prioritization 101

Step 1. Work to your strengths.

Ask yourself this question: What can I do that would add the most value to the organization this week?

What can I do that leverages my strengths?

Step 2. Delegate.

Ask yourself: What can I give away? What priority items must be addressed by me, and what part of those items can be done by others?

Step 3. Prioritize prioritization.

Put your prioritization time in your calendar, and do it weekly if not more often. The more you train yourself to think in terms of importance, the simpler it will be to make necessary decisions.

Step 4. Be willing to ask yourself tough questions regularly.

What am I spending time on that I shouldn't be?

What is a long-term project that needs my regular attention?

What is going to add to my own energy and time?

What value can I deliver?

Are my priorities in line with those of the organization?

Do I have enough think time?

Am I using my strengths and working according to my values and those of the organization?

system, was originally (and quite purposefully) developed not to be dependent on one type of processor, so it could run on both IBM and Intel chips. So, the seemingly out-of-the-blue move by Apple was really five years in the making. This is a long-term strategy that will not necessarily result in short-term wins: many Apple customers will wait for the next generation of laptops before they make their next purchase. But the positive results—the ability to meet client demand to create smaller and smaller machines, better laptops that run without heating up and causing long-term wear on the battery, and improved processing speeds—could endure for decades.

If Apple's leaders were always running a mile a minute, unconcerned with the future or focused solely on the present success of the iPod and the opportunity to create more personal and home electronics, they probably would not have had time to stop and think about what kind of microprocessors they were using. At some point, a leader at Apple *stopped . . . thought . . . focused on the issue . . .* and set the wheels in motion for a launch five years down the road. How can you apply the Apple example to the more immediate, pressing tasks that you face as a leader every day? How can you turn the need for speed into a focus on efficiency? You can remember to stop and prioritize—and remember to keep room for the long term.

REFLECTING ON VALUES

Think back to the values discussion in Part One. Regularly checking in with yourself and reflecting on your state and the state of your organization means checking in on whether you are acting *on purpose*. Reflection means taking time to make sure that your actions are in line with the values and vision that you have outlined as key to your success now and into the future. If your check-in results in a belief that you are in the flow and your leadership decisions are in line with your values, then you are on the right track and can feel confident and calm about your course of action. If reflection results in a feeling that you are not in line with your values, then you can be pleased to have caught yourself before you went too far in a dangerous direction. The more often you pause to think, the more quickly you will avoid going down dead-end paths. Therefore, the faster and more focused you will become.

Remember, too, that reflection means different things to different leaders. It might involve going on a walk, writing notes, just sitting and thinking, or even drawing a diagram or picture. I work with an amazing woman whose job is in graphic design. When she takes time to think, she likes to draw diagrams, flowcharts, and pictures because she is such a visual thinker. Do whatever works for you. If you struggle with the act of reflecting and need some structure, refer back to the "Try This" segments in Chapter Two to revisit the values clarification exercises.

Multitasking Mistakes

Fact: It is absolutely impossible to multitask and focus at the same time. While managers often reward their employees for the ability to handle multiple tasks at once, this is not a quality that leaders themselves should develop. (And it's not very smart practice to encourage your employees to do this either, but we'll get to that later.) Why not? Because leaders—especially leaders who want to be effective, enduring, and fulfilled—know that their attention is not needed on their present tasks only. Leaders must have long-term vision as well. And to have long-term vision, they have to slow down, think, and *focus* on what is really important to the future of the organization.

Take Matt again: Matt's multitasking was so far out of control that he was unable to stop himself for long enough to focus on prioritizing what was most important. So I gave Matt a simple assignment: Step one in *any* situation should always be to think.

To apply this assignment, Matt started looking at what was happening in a normal day of too many tasks. On an average workday, Matt would get in to the office and open up his e-mail while returning phone calls at the same time. When something in his e-mail could be delegated, he would shoot it off to someone with no instructions, trusting that they would come back to him with any questions. The problem with that idea? People never knew if Matt was sending them something they simply should be aware of or something they should do something about, and many important ideas and issues were dropped.

While on the phone, Matt's lack of focused attention was obvious. People who listen can always tell when someone's not paying attention on the phone . . . and Matt's clients were listening! Complaints started to surface. Matt was perceived as distracted and uncaring.

According to a study published in the journal *NeuroImage,* managing two mental tasks at once actually reduces the total brainpower available for both tasks. In another study, research showed that for all types of tasks, subjects lost time when they had to switch from one task to another, and time costs increased with the complexity of the tasks, so it took significantly longer to switch between more complex tasks.[3] Is this just employees trying to get their work done faster and leave early? Not exactly. A study by the Families and Work Institute found that 45 percent of U.S. workers feel they are asked or expected to work on too many tasks at once. Multitasking, it seems, may waste more time and energy than it saves.

When it comes to leadership, multitasking has an even bigger problem. When you do too many things at once, information goes only into your short-term memory and not into your long-term memory. This is fine, as long as you are in a situation in which you don't have to retain any information, such as when you are packing your luggage and watching television at the same time. (But beware! You just may pack your Hawaiian shirt for that business meeting in Zurich.)

Fear

In business, when things go too fast, it's often due to our own self-consciousness or need to get through our work in a rush. Interesting, isn't it, that a phrase like "rash decision" has negative connotations in our culture. Rash decisions are rarely considered good decisions, so why do we insist on praising speed? Faster often means fighting, fleeing, defensiveness. It is a time when you are not thinking; you are *reacting.* The instinct to go faster almost always stems from a state of panic or fear. And our employees, clients, and other stakeholders absolutely sense this.

Perhaps you are familiar with the extreme of the fear-based type of leader: the frenetic worrier. Consider these two examples of fear-based, anxious leaders:

Joan is an executive whose top value is hard work. She is a self-made entrepreneur whose company has grown significantly as she has worked harder and harder. She has a phenomenal success story, starting in rural poverty and ending up at the top of her game as CEO of a privately held U.S. company of which she is the 100 percent owner. There is nothing wrong with her story so far, right? Her story—her *myth* at this point—is that because she worked harder than anyone else, she was able to achieve the American dream of rising out of poverty into success and wealth.

Her belief supports her experience; it validates the struggle she went through to get where she is. The only problem is that her original belief—the ethic of hard work above all else—no longer supports the success of the organization as it has grown. She has achieved true mastery in her discipline, but still expects her organization to conform to the idea that everything must be difficult or be a struggle in order to be worthwhile. She is afraid to change her work style. When she works with her executive team her expectation is that they will be working 24/7 on any challenge given to them. She expects them to care just as much about the business as she does, and she expects that care to be reflected through struggle and self-sacrifice.

Joan's unfortunate reality is that her belief now creates intense stress and fear in her staff members, who are paid to be creative and to produce new, innovative ideas for her product line. The stressful environment keeps people away from that easy, flowing state that is responsible for the best, most relaxed thinking. Joan has created what the employees call a "culture of fear." Instead of feeling free to express ideas or thoughts about what could be changed to be better, employees spend time thinking about how not to change anything, how to keep things quiet, how to mask their stress and put on a happy face—an inauthentic one, I might add.

In starting work with Joan, the first thing we did was a short, informal 360-degree assessment—basically interviewing people all around her. We came up with a set of questions about Joan's strengths and challenges, and what people wanted to see more of from Joan, and asked customers, board members, and direct reports what they thought. The result? Joan started seeing a pattern. People were frustrated with the idea that struggle was rewarded, not eased. They were frustrated with what they thought was a creativity-stifling management style. Joan had no idea! She thought her passion and generosity—financially and with trips and gifts—were more than enough to keep everyone excited and motivated. Not so. Joan was shocked when she got her feedback, but it opened her eyes to what she was unconscious of. When she stepped back, she was able to question her assumptions of what would motivate others, and to come up with new ideas, plans, and attitudes.

Another leader, Tim, has worked for twenty-five years at an exclusive boarding school. He is head of admissions, which carries some interesting challenges—irate parents, disappointed kids, heartbreaking stories of poverty and tenacity among scholarship applicants.

Tim had an intensely stressful relationship with two members of the administration. One, the headmaster of the school, was so focused on test scores that he would not tolerate recommendations from Tim to waive certain requirements based on other kinds of merit. The other was Tim's ex-wife, who was a department head at the school. Between those two relationships, Tim's life seemed like a constant stream of conflict: Arguments about funding. Arguments about public relations for the departments. Arguments about admissions and about students. Arguments about fundraising. Arguments about requirements for tenured faculty. Anxiety, anxiety, anxiety.

For the past five years, Tim had been completing a book, an academic text that would be a culmination of many years of research and hard work, and the pressure was on. Tim's anxiety levels grew higher and higher. He was eating out every night at his favorite restaurant—steak frites was his nightly meal—and he was spending very little time either at home or with friends. His anxiety was palpable. His colleagues avoided him, believing that he didn't have the time for chit-chat. He seemed to retreat into a shell of work. He looked forward to writing, to working with the students, but not much else. At a routine visit to the doctor, Tim was diagnosed with hypertension and told that if he did not lower his stress level, he did not have long to live. That wake-up call drove Tim to quit his job altogether and to let go of his urgency about the writing. If he hadn't, he might not have survived.

Tim's decision was drastic, but he knew he had to change. He took two weeks to stop and think, and sat down with a coach to talk out his life path. What was most important to him? Was it teaching?

Was it the book? What meant the most? He realized that he had been prioritizing things that were not the most important to him, and changed his priority list, starting with his health. Tim started a strict diet. Tim decided that his favorite exercise was walking along the waterfront near his home. He adopted a four-year-old Labrador retriever named Rupert at an animal shelter, and walked the dog every morning and evening. He decided that his book, while it was something he wanted to finish later, needed to be put on hold. He wanted to teach, and his focus needed to be on finding a job where he could interact with students, teach classes, and get home at a reasonable hour to spend time with Rupert, who was a source of pure joy, unconditional love, and relaxation for Tim.

Perhaps Tim's story appears dramatic, but it's all too common. Intense fear, anxiety, and stress can have dangerous, even fatal, results. Too often we need to be hit over the head before we will change the unhealthy habits (such as all-nighters and screaming sessions) that give us short-term wins. Catastrophes like a heart attack, a stress-related illness, or a crisis can be the only notice that it's time to slow down. But there are many ways to avoid an unhappy fate before it's too late.

One thing we too often forget—to slow down means to savor our moments. Slowing down allows us to be more fully absorbed in we're doing in the moment. Time expands. When we enjoy good food, when we relax into a walk in which we are not focused on just getting somewhere, when we align ourselves with our natural rhythms, we are slowing down enough to really enjoy this precious life we've been given. Productivity and health both depend on these moments of rejuvenation and joy.

LEARN TO RELAX . . . REALLY

> *People need to learn how to relax under pressure. The first step to being able to achieve this is to learn how to relax in the first place.*
> —KEN KESSLIN, LEADERSHIP COACH

Let's look for a moment at what happens to the body during fear. The good part is the message to watch out, to protect yourself. The physical parts, the fight-or-flight mechanisms, are triggered and a series of chemicals are released into the bloodstream: cortisol, adrenaline, and noradrenaline. Nerve cells fire differently from normal, respiratory rate increases, and breathing becomes shallower. (Note that this is the opposite of the meditative theta state.) Our awareness sharpens to detect threat. Our perception of pain diminishes. We begin scanning our environment for threats to our survival, and we begin to believe that anything might be a threat.

This fight-or-flight response overrides rational thought process, and distorts our thinking. The rational brain is in the background, and the foreground is filled with detection of the enemy. When we stay too long in this state, the stress response begins to taint our thinking. It becomes a self-perpetuating state. We lose our optimism, our clarity, and our best thinking. We lose our capacity to connect fully with others, to listen and to strategize outside the context of survival. We lose our ability to maintain an appreciative perspective and to find great opportunities. This fight-or-flight mechanism, of course, is designed to help us when we are in true danger. It's the healthy response in a true emergency: when we need to run for our lives or to take on a terrifying enemy. But this is not often the case in a work environment.

While most fight-or-flight responses at work may seem far out of place, let's remember what we take to work with us. We depend on work to maintain our survival, our self-concept, our lifestyle, and our status. We come to work with all our human capacities for love, joy, collaboration, and creativity, and we also come to work with all our fears and past experiences of hurt, betrayal, and threat. And if your fear comes from anxiety about losing your footing as a leader, keep in mind that manic action is generally looked down upon. Remember that to slow down will actually help you to *endure*.

What can we do to stop the natural fight-or-flight response? As with any disease or virus, we need an antidote. So, to counter the fear response, we need to trigger a relaxation response. To successfully interrupt the fight-or-flight reaction, we need to send out chemicals that counteract the "speedy" chemicals released under stress. To refer back to brainwave language, we must move into the alpha-wave state of the brain, where we are filled with a sense of calm. One strategy is the five-minute mini-meditation and time-out already discussed. Here are some additional antidotes to the fight-or-flight response in the workplace:

- *Take a series of deep breaths.* This is the simplest and one of the most effective ways to stop the rush of adrenaline into the bloodstream. It is your physiological reset button.
- *Change your physical stance and posture.* This may mean taking a moment to stretch, to loosen up tight shoulders, neck, ribcage, or joints.
- *Create a calm retreat space in your office.* When in doubt, have a place that triggers a relaxation response rather than a stress response. This may be a comfortable chair, a fish tank, a photo of your family, or an outdoor space away from your office.
- *Perform some sort of aerobic exercise.* Even five minutes of aerobic exercise, while it won't help you lose fifty pounds, will certainly help you negate stress. A quick set of jumping jacks, pushups, sit-ups, or a swift walk around the block will stimulate your endorphins and calm your anxiety.
- *Pray, meditate, or ground yourself in your spiritual beliefs.* Our personal spiritual beliefs, our connection to God, nature, or community, can sustain us greatly in times of stress or fear. Fear is isolating. Reach out and connect to your spiritual life.
- *Play music or sing.* The natural rhythms in music, particularly repetitive chanting or drumming, are wonderful ways to cultivate the more calming brainwave states.
- *Use fear as an opportunity.* Fear offers an incredible opportunity for change. If, instead of attempting to rid yourself of fear, you embrace and move toward it, what happens? Often that is the moment of breakthrough. When we focus on our fears long enough, without repressing, denying, or avoiding them, we deplete their power. Take a look at your fear. When you are fearful, ready to fight or flee, notice the physical sensations in your body. Focus on the stimulus. What is true in this situation? Are you truly threatened? Is this a shadow of some previous pain? When you have to make a presentation and your knees are knocking, what is at the root? Will you be humiliated? Probably not. What's the worst that could happen? You could die of embarrassment in front of the whole crowd. Now how likely is that? The truth is, no one ever died just from making a speech.
- *Anchor yourself to relaxation.* Once you become relaxed, anchor that feeling with a physical movement. It could be holding your fingers together, putting your palm on your knee, or any other simple physical touch point.

- *Cultivate your optimism.* Remember that appreciative eye. A final, more long-term strategy to combat the fight-or-flight response is to change your inherent beliefs about what is threatening. This is where the appreciative mode of thinking comes in to ward off stress. When we cultivate our optimism, when we look for what is working well, we automatically engage a relaxation response. Think of the biggest challenge you have at work right now. What are the opportunities inherent in that challenge? What positives can come of that challenge? What does your intuition tell you? What strengths do you have personally or organizationally to address that challenge? You do have power. You do make an impact every day whether it feels like it or not. Remember that life is a series of possibilities, of opportunities to enjoy.

TAKING CARE OF BUSINESS STARTS WITH YOU

It's clear that thinking is important and that everyone needs to cultivate energy, but why focus on the physical? We're not manual laborers, so why should we care? Because your body and mind are all part of a single system: you. If your goal is longevity and endurance, remember that you've only got one body. Don't forget to care for it while you can.

Your body is your instrument of endurance. Remember that in the old saying, healthy is inseparable from wealthy and wise. If you need additional incentive to practice self-care as a leader, here are some points you probably already know to keep top of mind:

Results of Stress

- Premature aging
- Chronic health problems
- Anxiety and increased fight-or-flight response
- Poor decision making
- Exhaustion

Results of Relaxation and Good Health

- Sustainable, renewable energy
- Longevity
- Resistance to disease and illness

- Flexibility, both physical and mental
- Effective strategic thinking
- Resonance with others and ability to connect

ZAINAB SALBI'S STORY

Zainab Salbi is an inspiring nonprofit leader.[4] Her organization, Women for Women International, helps refugee women across the world to escape poverty and loneliness through connection to other women. It takes incredible devotion and energy to run, and through hard effort, Zainab discovered that she needed to take care of herself first. She says,

> I put 100 percent of my time toward Women for Women in Bosnia— it changed my whole life. All our personal plans, not even big things like having children but basic normalcy, doing things like going to restaurants, what other couples do—we completely put that on hold. The price was high. There were three years of significant financial suffering, and I was mentally and physically exhausted. I was giving anything and everything to my work. I was overwhelmed with fatigue.

> What I've learned is that it has all been worth it, but that fatigue isn't something you can live with for long. The organization has helped over forty thousand women connect with job training and sponsorship, and it would never have gotten to this point without that hard work and sacrifice. When you act on your passion, things work out. Different doors opened from different directions, different people. Everything happened in ways that worked amazingly well to get us where we are now.

> I also learned the hard way about taking care of yourself. There was actually one time in 1996 when I had to be hospitalized for mental and physical exhaustion. The doctor asked me, "When was the last time you took a vacation?" and my answer was, "Never." He asked, "When was the last time you did something for you?" and I said, "Never." I knew that was not going to last—I had to start focusing on taking care of myself. . . .

> If I am impoverished, fatigued, if I don't have the basic things I need to be healthy I can't help others. The goal here is not to have others pull me down, but to have me pull them up.

> I grew up in a very privileged family in Iraq, and I had access to whatever I wanted. I was the only daughter with two brothers. I was

more or less my parents' princess. I didn't want for anything. We traveled the world, went to good schools, had fine clothes, I was very privileged. I found myself at nineteen with one suitcase in the U.S. when Iraq invaded Kuwait, within a two-month period I found myself stuck in the States away from home and family, one suitcase with summer clothes and $400 in my pocket.

It's in the back of my mind that I can never relax, I may lose what I have. Because of my own experience I understand the fear that these women have. There is a part of me that I see in them, the concept of loss and dispossession. I can't tell you how important their resilience is for me. It reenergizes me. It keeps me positive.

On a personal level, I am now thirty-three, and I look younger than I did at twenty-three years old when I started the organization. Back then I took myself so seriously. Now I believe we must dive into the beauty of life. . . . I enjoy myself now. Now I like shopping and dancing and doing fun things. I don't feel guilty about it just because others don't have access to those things. I see it as a way to reenergize me so I can keep going. Sometimes people thank me just for smiling at them. I would not be able to smile if I didn't have joy and peace somewhere in my own life.

The Relentless Pursuit of Perfection

We all know leaders who are both workaholics and their own worst critics: people who are always overprepared, hyperfocused, and captivated by getting things exactly right. In other words, perfectionists.

Here is the story of another coaching client. Bob is a guy who was in charge of a marketing team, and he was told he would not get promoted if he didn't lighten up on the perfectionism. He had two project teams starting up in Europe. One day he called me (his coach at the time) from Berlin, saying that in the morning he was starting with a new team and he didn't want to suffer the same mistakes he had made in the past with perfectionism and high anxiety. To begin, I asked him what he had done to prepare for the project team kickoff. He recounted for me that he determined the objectives and the agenda for the meeting, he had made a match between the participants and their future roles, he had identified responsibilities for each person on the team, he had set deadlines, and he had identified performance measures.

Then I simply asked him, "Why are you in Berlin? Why didn't you just e-mail everyone this information and tell them what they were doing?"

He got very quiet and said, "Well I have to make sure the team does the work."

I said, "Do you actually have a team? My guess is that you don't have a team. You have a group of people who are being told what to do. That doesn't sound like a team." Then I asked him to delete everything he had prepared and to stop to listen, observe, and bring out the best in the group. He was so nervous that he was giggling. What I suggested he do was walk into the meeting and write up a partial agenda on a flip chart, and then ask other people to contribute items to be covered that day. I challenged him to trust these professionals—to trust that they would know what needed to be done. He called me the next day, laughing. He said it was the best meeting he'd ever had. By letting go of his perfectionism and do-it-all tendencies, he'd discovered how to be a more effective and fulfilled leader.

Perfectionism certainly has its benefits—any perfectionist will be more than happy to rattle them off. Clearly, the perfectionist cares deeply about excellence. Work product delivered by a perfectionist is virtually always clean, clear, and without error. A managing director at a large financial institution once said to me, "It's either A or not A, and if it's not the right thing, then it's nothing." I absolutely appreciate that. When I want something done, I want it done right.

Another plus is that there is a laserlike focus that results from perfectionism. That focus is valuable within organizations. It means excellence and a sense of protection of the good of themselves, their team, and their company by being on top of the details. The image a perfectionist gives is one of safety, security, and control. Perfectionists are people to be counted on because they will deliver something complete and high-quality. You can trust that they have reviewed their work with a fine-tooth comb. Perfectionists also can be inspirational, particularly for direct reports who look at the high standards and quality of the leader. They contribute to the persona of the organization.

But—and you knew there was a big *but* coming—perfectionism is *enormously* consuming of time and energy. Perfectionism slows you down.

If everything were to be absolutely perfect, forget about going faster—nothing would ever be completed at all. Perfectionism results in that dreadful analysis-paralysis that is the enemy of decision making. Remember, the worst decision is none at all, and that is the risk if you are concerned with a perfect outcome.

An executive friend of mine, when she heard I was writing this book, asked me, "So how do I stop being so anal about everything? I just don't see what I can *do* about this, even though I know it's a problem. There are moments when it's great and moments when it's not serving me, and I hate to watch my team making mistakes. I always want to jump in and take over, but I know deep down I'm not helping them improve. I know I can't just give up and watch things fall apart and not work. I'm the one responsible. So what do I do?"

My immediate answer is to find out where the perfectionism is coming from first, then work to change what's not working for you. For many people, perfectionism comes from "catastrophic thinking": figuring out the worst thing that can happen, and doing everything in your power to make sure it doesn't. This is, of course, a completely fear-based attitude, and often is completely baseless.

I'll prove it to you. Take a moment to think about any current fear you might have. Think about the worst-case scenario of what will happen if your deliverable, project, task, conversation, or whatever is not perfect. And now ask yourself the following questions:

- How likely is that outcome?
- What will happen if that happens?
- What will happen next?
- What is the worst thing that could happen then?
- What is the catastrophic fear underneath this perfectionism?

It may take you many layers of "what could possibly happen next" to reach a basic fear. Maybe it goes something like this:

If I don't get this Web site launch right, our client will leave the organization. (Possible, but not likely.)

If our client leaves the organization, it will be my fault and I'll be fired. (Possible, but not likely.)

If I'm fired I'll be humiliated and destitute. (Not likely.)

If I'm humiliated and destitute no one will ever hire me again. (Not likely.)

If no one ever hires me again I'll be homeless. (Not likely.)

If I'm homeless I'll die broken and alone. (Not likely.)

Absurd! By the end of your catastrophic thinking, I hope you realize your fear is probably unwarranted.

Sometimes this exercise doesn't work. Why? When worry is actually valid. Listen to this executive, Ivan:

"What will happen if we don't get the Web site launched? It will be unacceptable. This is the culmination of all of our hard work as a team. I will not accept less than the right way. I don't care if I have to stay up three nights in a row. I need this to work."

Sometimes perfectionism is a valid choice, as long as it does not lead to incapacitation or the catastrophic thinking I just described. In essence, I am very accepting of perfectionism in moderation.

Perfectionism isn't all that bad. It's really an overuse of strengths. We all have strengths, and when we rely on them too much they can sabotage our effectiveness. When you're friendly, it can do fantastic things for your career. What if you were overly friendly, all the time, even to people you hated, to your own detriment? If you're excellent at getting the job done, perfectionism just takes that excellence beyond where that strength is helpful. The key question for perfectionists to add to their leadership tool kit is, When is it better to let go? Here are some good reasons to let go of perfectionism:

- When something is not a priority to the immediate needs of your company, your personal values, or your long-term goals
- When perfectionism will cause you to damage someone's learning because you take over for them
- When perfectionism sabotages your ability to get other things done
- When something sets up outrageous expectations in others, for example, staying up all night to deliver a proposal in twelve hours.

Perfectionism is great as long as you set clear priorities. Sometimes perfectionism is necessary and expected. An airline's repair checklist must be perfect before every plane takes off. Surgery must be perfect. But there are some things, many things, that don't need to be perfect. For example, ideas don't need to be perfect; indeed, creating new ideas depends upon the space and time for complete imperfection, for strange or absurd thinking. And, as we all know, relationships, whether personal and professional, are always imperfect.

Let's look at an example of perfectionism at work. Victoria and Carla are partners in a small entrepreneurial company. Victoria is a complete perfectionist and Carla is a self-professed C student. The two business partners have completely opposite styles. Carla believes that if a potential client wants a proposal, the partners should dash it off and get it to client the next day, even if it is not their best work. Victoria, on the other hand, will tweak a proposal for a month before sending it out, just to be sure it is comprehensive, error-free, and captures every possible idea she can present to the prospect. The result of these opposing styles is that neither succeeded. Carla's too-fast method led to proposals that clients couldn't understand or use. Victoria's too-perfect method meant that prospects went with another company while she was busy tweaking the proposal to death.

As with so many things in life, the solution was compromise. When they did succeed with a pitch, it turned out to be when each partner nagged the other, advocating for her own style. Carla slowed down, Victoria was smarter about letting go of absolute expertise—and the result was a better, more successful process and end result: more clients. Their collaboration made both of them much better. Carla also learned to set better boundaries with potential clients, saying, "We'll deliver the proposal next week so we can do a good job." Victoria needed to break out of putting all of her energy into the process of this proposal and reflect on the fact that it was better to do something slightly imperfect that still captured the main ideas, rather than producing a totally perfect proposal that actually lost the opportunity. Carla and Victoria found the "just right" model for them.

If you have perfectionist tendencies, then perhaps you are thinking: "I know perfectionism isn't great, but it's gotten me very far." It's true; there is something about having become a leader that requires perfectionism in some part of your life. In other words, to achieve as much as you have, you are getting something right. But consider this: perfectionism (unless, as earlier discussed, you are a surgeon or in a similar life-and-death role) gets you to a point, and then it hurts you. Once you become the leader and not the doer, perfectionism is harmful.

Remember back to Part One and the concept that to be smarter, you must let go of being the smartest one in the room. You have to ask questions. You have to be comfortable not being the expert. When it comes to perfectionism, you have to let go of it to lead. Why? Because people are imperfect. The people you lead will, I guarantee, be imperfect. People will like your humanness. Personal vulnerability inspires people. Think of the public disdain expressed for such perfectionist people as Martha Stewart prior to the missteps that landed her in prison. Perfection equals robot, in many people's minds. And robots do not make the best leaders.

GET OVER THE PERFECT

Perfectionism is a hard addiction to overcome, because it is often so rewarding to the perfectionist. What beats an A+?

Remember this; often, creative (and lucrative) ideas result from mistakes. Teflon, for example, was a mistake. On April 6, 1938, a scientist at DuPont, Dr. Roy Plunkett, was working on coming up with a better type of coolant gas. He left a container of experimental gas in his lab overnight, and in the morning, lo and behold, a slippery, waxy solid had appeared. Ten years later the first nonstick pans were manufactured in France, and the rest is cooking history. If Dr. Plunkett had been perfect, there would be no Teflon, and no nonstick cookware. I know at least my mother would be sorely disappointed.

I promise you that leaders who set limits to their perfectionist tendencies are ultimately faster and more effective in their decision making and achievement of important goals. To restate what was mentioned earlier, one of the main reasons that limiting perfectionism is so effective is that most people don't want to work for a perfectionist leader.

Another coaching client who comes to mind was a perfectionist whose attention to being the best was sabotaging her success. Her coach has this to say:

I decided to assign her the "homework assignment" of being imperfect. We used the idea that for a week that she would be a B student instead of an A student. After a few days, she realized that people were able to better connect with her when they were not intimidated by the perfectionist persona she had always adopted. After this exercise, she tried very hard to accept mistakes within herself and show her team that if she could accept her own mistakes and humanity, then she could accept theirs. She wasn't always successful, but that was the point.

The perfectionist is always successful and this was her opportunity to make mistakes. If you are trying to get over your perfectionism, you might try to make one mistake a day. Be five minutes late for a meeting. Cross the line to a point where it's still okay, but it makes you uncomfortable. Note that the world does not fall apart. It sounds simplistic, but it works. Just push a little bit and you may notice that you get a *positive* response where you were expecting a negative. For instance, most employees will be extra worried about work they are delivering to a perfectionist boss. Sounds like a good thing, right? The work will be more carefully prepared? Not really. What most often happens is that employees are *afraid* of a perfectionist boss's reactions, so they produce their work in a state of fear. As we discussed earlier, fear is not a good place from which to produce positive work. An employee who is too scared to offer work that may be creative but imperfect is bound to produce a worse end product.

As a friend said to me once,

Sometimes you just have to look at people and see that they're perfect in all their imperfection. Your friends, your kids, your spouse— they all have faults, but those faults are part of who they are, and you've got to love that. When I taught my son to use a knife to cut vegetables, his first attempt was with a big red bell pepper. I showed him how to do it, and let him cut the pepper on his own. Of course it wasn't perfect—the pieces were thin and thick and uneven, but did I care? No way! My son just cut his first pepper! That one was going in the sauce and everyone else was gonna like it, because he succeeded. Now he's a fantastic chef, and it's because he didn't get squashed by perfectionism and told his peppers were too thick or too thin—he was encouraged to try and to experiment, so now he's a pro.

TRY THIS

Perfectionist Writing Exercise

Take a blank piece of paper and write answers to the following questions:

What does perfectionism do to me in my personal and professional life?

How am I rewarded for my perfectionism?

What happens when I am imperfect or make mistakes?

What needs to be in place for me to let go?

How does perfectionism stop me from moving faster?

Now take on this challenge: for one week, be open to your own humanity. Be imperfect. Don't worry about failure. Live free of judgment. When you notice a judgmental thought, observe it and let it go. Don't agonize over what's gone wrong, what could go wrong, or whose fault it might be. Trust that all will be well, no matter what. Once your week is complete, come back and review your list. Have your answers changed? Were you willing to be imperfect?

———————

As you have seen in this chapter, even hyperfast leaders like Matt can learn to slow down, take time to think, and improve their effectiveness. The first step in this process has involved acknowledging where you personally are going too fast. Now that we have addressed various needs or addictions to speed—multitasking, fear, and perfectionism—and some helpful solutions, the next step is to delve into the nitty-gritty details of time management. No matter how much you slow down, you still need a strategy for completing all the tasks in your role as a leader. The next chapter assesses your current time-management skills and helps you to develop a more effective, enduring, and fulfilling relationship with time.

Summary

- Multitasking is a mistake—stop to focus, and you'll retain more information.
- Take time to think, and to get your brain into a creative, theta state.
- Calm your fear—anxiety drives up the pressure, not the performance.
- Learn to relax . . . really! Just minutes a day makes a world of difference.
- Embrace your imperfection—not everything holds the same importance.

CHAPTER FIVE

DO YOU WEAR THE WATCH OR DOES THE WATCH WEAR YOU?

In *The Highest Goal,* the wonderful Michael Ray, Stanford professor of creativity and innovation, says this about time: "If you are conscious about your relationship with time and stress . . . you will be in self-time, creating your own way of experiencing life without the restrictions of time. As you get into more situations of resonance with your highest goal, you'll be surprised how easy, effortless and enjoyable the flow of life will become."[1]

WHAT IS YOUR PERSONAL TIME STYLE?

What is time, anyway? Do all leaders think of time in the same way?

The short answer is no. Many factors affect our own personal relationships with time. Gender, for instance, may affect our feelings about time. Dr. Bob Deutsch, a cognitive neuroscientist and anthropologist, says that across cultures, particularly with primitive tribes, men relate to linear time and women see time as cyclical. In other words, men generally feel that they are in a straight trajectory toward death(!), while women see life as many beginnings, middles, and endings. Do you see time as linear or cyclical? Do you see the organization you lead as being on a straight trajectory or in terms of cycles?

For children, time stretches out. A three-minute time-out is an eternity to an angry two-year-old. A year is unfathomable—how many vast and incomprehensible changes can happen in a year when you are twelve? As we get older, our relationship to time changes. Time seems to fly by faster. Months and years seem shorter. All of a sudden, we've been working for twenty years. Our children grow up before our eyes. That old business plan from three years ago has nothing to do with what we're working on—but wasn't that just moments ago that we defined our strategy?

Our feelings about time also link to our values. Many people change their lives when they realize they are not spending time with the people or activities they value most.

We don't even have to look back into the past for a different view of time. Time is also affected by culture. I see this when I visit South America to work with my clients in Peru. The minute I arrive at the airport, I can feel that things are slower (although the cab ride to the hotel is usually way too fast). Dinner in Peru, even a business dinner, is a wonderful, timeless experience, where everyone talks about family, kids, hobbies, and other personal topics. There is so much time for the personal. Nothing feels rushed. The food does not reach the table quickly. When I'm facilitating a workshop in Peru, the issues we discuss are quite personal—leadership, coaching, and values. In Peru, it appears easier for people to talk about such emotional topics and not be concerned about the timekeeping of the workshop. They would much rather go deeper into one topic than quickly cover everything on the agenda.

A colleague who has worked in Australia explains how she adapted to their different time clock:

> In Australia, the general vacation benefit, or "holiday" as they say, is four weeks a year, so many employees, even leaders, take all four weeks together, usually in the month of January. This means that it might be a month before you can do business with someone. I found this shocking when I began working in Australia: In America I found that people would occasionally complain when someone went on vacation or took a long weekend, but Australians cherish their vacation time and value this for others. I eventually got used to the value Australians place on vacation time, and of course came to love it—it's a great way to maintain a balance between work and relaxation.

Beyond gender, age, and cultural issues, many different attitudes influence the nature of time and our relationship to it.

Think about your own relationship with time: Do you see time as fleeting? In your opinion is there never enough time to accomplish all your daily tasks, all your life goals? What are some common beliefs in our culture about time? Are these affecting your role as a leader?

The irony, of course, is that medical advances are leading us all to live longer lives than our ancestors ever imagined. Because of what's happening with longevity, we might be unhappy that we have a finite amount of time, but we are the generation that may have the opportunity to prolong our lives by decades and more.

TRY THIS

Time Style Assessment

The following questionnaire is a quick way to see where you fall on a variety of "time style" continuums. (Important note: there is no "perfect" score, this is just information gathering, and if we engage our appreciative mind-set, every score has its advantages.)

On a scale of 1 to 5, rank the following statements as follows:

1—always; 2—sometimes; 3—neutral; 4—rarely; 5—never

☐ I believe I have enough time.

☐ I am always aware of the time when I am at work.

☐ I set firm boundaries around my time.

☐ I respond well to deadlines.

☐ Everything must be perfect, or we can't release it.

☐ I rely on my technology to store my schedule, to-do list and priorities.

1	2	3	4	5
Infinite Abundance of Time				Scarcity of Time

What are the benefits to seeing time as infinite?

What are the benefits to seeing time as scarce?

1	2	3	4	5
Clock Watcher				Clock Avoider

What are the benefits of watching the clock and being constantly aware of time?

What are the benefits of avoiding the clock and staying away from knowing the time?

1	2	3	4	5
Set Firm Boundaries			No Boundaries Around My Time	

What are the benefits of allowing people easy access to your time?

What are the benefits of holding time for your own deliverables?

1	2	3	4	5
Deadline Driven				Deadline Dread

What are the benefits of being deadline driven?

What are the benefits of dreading a deadline?

1	2	3	4	5
Perfectionism			Tolerance of Imperfection	

What are the benefits of perfectionism? (Refer back to Chapter Four if necessary.)

How does this affect my time management?

What are the benefits of tolerating imperfection?

1	2	3	4	5
Reserve Computer Brain			It's All up Here	

What are the benefits of storing knowledge in technology?

What are the benefits of retaining information in your mind?

We have prolonged our lifespan amazingly in the past few generations. For us, time is not diminishing; it is expanding.

By becoming aware of your personal relationship with time, you can start to shift your beliefs to what you want them to be. If you notice you don't set firm boundaries around your time, you can follow the directives given in the next section for setting stronger boundaries. As with any assessment, becoming aware of your attitudes about time is the first step toward changing your behavior.

ENOUGH IS ENOUGH

A common complaint in the contemporary workplace is that everyone is busy and no one has enough time to get everything done. Demands on every individual contributor are increasing as companies look to cut costs and increase productivity. Consider this: *There is plenty of time.* Time is infinite; it never stops. At the same time, there's a paradox here: There's never going to be enough time to do *everything*.

Yes, we as humans have a finite life span, but we don't know how long that is going to last. It is ironic that we are living longer lives today, but the world is ever more focused on the short term: We see the ad and we want to buy the thing. We see the food and want to eat. We want the quick fix. Perhaps it is because we have been conditioned to want everything now. We have also been conditioned to think that productivity is enhanced by longer workdays and faster paces. That is a fallacy.

According to Evan Robinson's article, "Why Crunch Mode Doesn't Work":

> More than a century of studies show that long-term useful worker output is maximized near a five-day, 40-hour workweek. Productivity drops immediately upon starting overtime and continues to drop until, at approximately eight 60-hour weeks, the total work done is the same as what would have been done in eight 40-hour weeks.
>
> In the short term, working over 21 hours continuously is equivalent to being legally drunk. Longer periods of continuous work drastically reduce cognitive function and increase the chance of catastrophic error. In both the short- and long-term, reducing

sleep hours as little as one hour nightly can result in a severe decrease in cognitive ability, sometimes without workers perceiving the decrease.[2]

Do we really not have enough time to complete the work necessary to stay ahead in the modern world? To answer that question, my instinct is actually to look back into history. Thomas Edison once said, "There is time for everything." He lived in a time with shorter life spans and far less technology—and look how much he accomplished. It took him ten thousand tries to get the incandescent light bulb to work. *What if he'd been in too much of a hurry?*

There is time. You just have to do some work to find it, and use it to your advantage as a leader.

Your Personal Time Clock

Now let's get personal. What is the maximum amount of work you can perform and still be an effective, enduring, and fulfilled leader? If you are exhausted and stressed, you are not functioning at your peak brain power and peak energy level. When you slow down and focus you can make decisions much more effectively, and it is more likely you will make *smarter* and *better* decisions. It isn't always easy to stay perfectly calm and creative and centered, but you will come to know your own ideal speed. How late can you really stay up without burning yourself up? What are your best hours for working? When do you have the feeling of being "in the zone" while you work?

Take the time now, while you are in the relaxed state of reading this book, to answer the following questions to explore your time management strategy in depth. Note that some of these questions relate to themes I discussed in Part One, and many will recur throughout this part of the book in greater detail.

1. Who are my thinking partners?
2. How am I leveraging the skills and talents of others?
3. How am I using technology to augment my personal thinking?
4. Am I ready to change direction on a dime?
5. What stops me from being flexible?
6. What enables me to be flexible and creative?

7. What can I delegate?
8. What time can I take for thinking?
9. How do I optimize my own thinking through physical means?
10. What attitude will help me to become faster?

You may not like the answers to some of these questions. If so, then ask yourself why you are doing things the way you are. Is it because "that's just the way it is"? We exist in punitive cultures. We think that because our culture says to stay until 10 o'clock, we have to stay late every night—no matter what we are working on. Remember: *The only way to change a system is to do something differently.* We tend to choose to go along to get along and do what the culture says is normal and good (such as staying constantly connected to our BlackBerrys and cell phones), or we choose to complain, but we usually don't choose to set a strong boundary.

Ken Kesslin, a leadership and team development coach on my team, shares this story of companies not getting it when it comes to work-life balance, boundary setting, and slowing down to go faster. Ken says:

> I had been asked by a former coaching client to work with his regional team. They worked for a big pharmaceuticals company and they were the Western region of the team. The group would get together once a quarter. Because the employees were all pretty stressed, my client told them our work and they invited me to work with the group. They turned over an evening and the entire following day to me to lead a workshop on balance. Over the course of dinner and the following day, we looked at their lives, talked about setting boundaries and saying no to unreasonable demands, and did a long visualization process about the life they hoped to have and how different their current life was from that vision. We talked about how they could move closer to a balanced life.
>
> It was a wonderful day and the Western regional group raved about it so much that the rest of the team, 150 people total around the country, wanted their own workshops. I got a call from their training department and the person who called me said, "We heard great stuff and we want you to come meet with all the groups—do a session for each—in six regions." I said, "Great!" But then she said, "We know you did a day plus, but we

want you to come and do the same topic with less time—we'd like it to be a two-hour session."

I replied, "And what will they be doing the rest of the time?"

She said, "There will be two sessions before yours. They will get up at 7 A.M. and go nonstop until 10 P.M. with a two-hour 'balance' session in the middle that you will lead."

I said, "Do you hear what you're asking? Do you know why the day and dinner that we did for the Western regional team was so successful? It was because we had a whole day devoted to them."

She said, "Yeah, yeah, yeah, I know. But we only have two hours this time."

I said, "Well, then you'll need to find someone else to do it. I won't do bad work. You're shooting yourself in the foot! You'll get people really mad at a two-hour session because you're speaking the words, but demonstrating in every other way possible that you have no regard for work-life balance."

This was a big step for me, and it meant turning down about $60,000 in work. I've done the same thing since with other kinds of things, where people have tried to shorten sessions that require time—you just can't force them into less time. You can't help people relax and think about bringing relaxation into their lives in a frenetic schedule!

So, what is the right way for a company to address balance and give this topic the time it needs? According to Ken,

> Most companies need to recognize there is an investment required to really develop amazing people and an amazing workforce. Most companies are too distracted by short-term crises and whatever is immediately going on. They run around like chickens with their heads cut off rather than thinking intelligently.

> Companies need to design a program that allows people to reflect and make intelligent choices about their work, leadership, careers, and visions for the company. They have to think about what structures they need to set up to do that. Often this type of thinking requires a day of "luxury" thinking time. Companies say they can't justify the cost for this, but in my opinion they waste many more hours at conferences that feature information you could have read in an e-mail note!

The only reason to bring a group of people together is to let them deepen their relationships with each other and to talk about critical, challenging issues where you need facial expressions, voice tone, and things like that. Most conferences are a total waste of money and time and could be done without bringing people together. In my opinion, the most benefit people get from conferences is in the conversations they have with other attendees between sessions. They get some information from the speakers, but the most value is from the colleague network they form when they chat or play golf or have a spa day together. That is real. The real ideas can take place because people are more relaxed and have time to think.

As the leader of a company, you can't just *say* balance is important. You have to have it yourself in your own life to some degree and understand what resources you need to provide. A two-hour session doesn't cut it. It is *so* much worse than not doing anything at all. If you don't have real time to discuss work-life balance issues, then my advice is to schedule longer breaks at your conferences and meetings so people have more time to interact. That's where the real team building takes place. Don't squeeze a development opportunity into a silly little time slot. It doesn't work that way.

How to Have More Time

Yes, you read that correctly. You can not only change your attitude about time, you can also change the amount of time you have. How? It's a paradox, of course. You can have more time in your day by flipping your thinking about what a leader needs to spend time doing. By slowing down, doing less, and focusing on what's in front of you in this moment, you can achieve infinitely more.

You really can make a positive difference in your own relationship with time. Here are some strategies you can implement immediately to begin adding precious minutes—and eventually hours—to your day.

• *Practice present-moment time.* A significant time-expansion strategy is to feel better about the long-term, grand scheme of time by focusing on a tiny amount of time—this exact second of time right now, in fact. Executive coach Steve Goldberg calls this "going into present-moment time." Here are some strategies to use present-moment time as a leadership effectiveness tool:

1. *Breathe.* Take a deep breath. Remember the simple power of the breath, and slow it down.
2. *Focus on the person you're speaking with and to.* Stop your awareness of every other thing you are responsible for, and pay attention to this individual interaction. Listen carefully for the insight, assistance, or knowledge that others have to offer.
3. *Focus on the process of the communication as well as the content.* Instead of listening just for *what* is being said, listen to *how* it is being said.
4. *Keep a touchstone or physical reminder to center your mind and focus on the present.* This physical reminder can be as simple as a rubber band in your pocket or a shell you picked up on the beach when you felt calm, centered, or fully present.
5. *Pay attention to your heart and not just your head.* Use self-inquiry to determine your immediate feeling state. What are your emotions telling you? What is your gut feeling telling you? What can you do to stay present with your emotions?
6. *Scan your body for tension.* Recognize any tension you are holding, and let your body relax. Check your posture—are you slumped, crunched, or otherwise knotted up? Take a moment to lengthen your spine, push your shoulders out of your ears, put your feet on the ground, and lift your head straight up.
7. *Take a big-picture snapshot.* Take just a moment to think of how this day is part of a larger picture. How is your work today assisting your company, your employees, your investors? What pace do you need to set to fulfill your role as a leader?

Present-moment thinking is one tool in a large box. Of course, if we were always in the present we would never analyze past experiences for their valuable lessons, and we would never envision future possibilities.

- *Listen.* In my training programs, I use an exercise where executives partner up and one person must be totally silent for one minute while the other person speaks. Sounds easy, right? You would be amazed at the resistance to this activity. People cannot believe they have to be quiet for a full sixty seconds. It feels like a lifetime. But the reality, as they soon learn, is that it actually *saves* time to consciously listen to another person for one whole minute. Just think of how many times in a day you ask your employees to

TRY THIS

Awareness Building: Listening

Try this quick awareness exercise: the next time someone comes to you to present something, take one full minute to listen without responding verbally. Notice the nonverbal cues you are giving. Focus on the process and the content of what is being said. See if slowing down and listening is new for you.

Paraphrase back what you heard by stating the *process* instead of just the content of what you heard. See if it changes how the person you are listening to responds to you. They may feel more heard and acknowledged, particularly if they have an emotional connection to what they are talking about.

For example: "Naidre, you seemed really excited when you said you spoke with the distribution director and got his feedback on your work. It's great that he gave you specific instructions on how we can create a smoother transition between our group and his group."

Or: "Elvis, you told me that story with a big scowl on your face—is there anything else I need to understand here?"

repeat themselves because you weren't focused on the conversation at hand and you'll understand.

- *Realize that* can *doesn't mean* should. As a leader, you have a choice about how to spend every moment of your time. And one of the most important lessons to learn is that just because you *can* do something—you have the ability, the budget, the staff, the technology—doesn't necessarily mean you should do it. To be the most effective, enduring, and fulfilled leader you can be, you have to decide what is most important at a given moment. Sometimes speed is the answer—to do your job well and achieve the results you want, you have to get to market first, no matter what. In other situations (perhaps most), quality might be more important, and therefore a project might take longer to develop.

One thing I know about successful leaders is that they didn't get where they've gotten by *not* doing things. Often it's the most action-focused, delivery-conscious people who become senior executives. It is just that ability to perform, to do every job well, that can also bite you you-know-where. Once you become a leader in your organization—owner of a bakery, the principal of a school, or a senior VP in a global corporation—your job is to stop being the superstar action hero and to start being the person who sets the vision, direction, and intention behind those superstars you lead. Again, we all know you *can* do most things well, but that doesn't mean you *should*.

Here's a great illustration of this point: Henry is a former stockbroker who made a fortune on Wall Street then founded a small business, and he says of his experience, "I escaped barely with my life and sanity." A thin, wiry triathlete, Henry thrives on competition. He enjoys being the best. He runs a small technology company, just six employees, that serves brokerage houses. Henry's problem is this: he does everything well. Henry is a good salesperson. Henry is a good programmer. Henry is a good accountant and bookkeeper, and Henry is a good organizer and administrator. Unfortunately, when Henry does all the things he's good at all at once, he loses traction and goes off schedule, off balance, and starts doing what he's normally good at rather poorly. When Henry's coach started working with him, Henry didn't know why his performance was so far under par. He could not understand it. Only when he charted out just where his time was going did he realize that there were not enough hours in the day for one person to address the multiple roles he was playing.

Leaders can be tyrannized by deadlines and the feeling of "not enough time," but if you are constantly watching the clock, you cannot focus and be aware of what's going on in the moment. When you are concentrating on the most important issue at any given moment, then you are achieving at your peak level of performance. You know when something needs your utmost attention, and when it does, you will do your best work by focusing on it 100 percent.

When you are evaluating decisions such as which calls to return in which order, or which meetings to attend, you have to think about your long-term goals. Technology is often the culprit: just because you can link six sales reps into the conference, that doesn't mean you should. Just because you can research twenty-seven new vendors online, that doesn't mean you should. Just because you can be up all night talking to your client in Hong Kong, that doesn't mean you're making any sense while you're doing it.

The common assumption is that we want to do these things, but what's the point? Make this your time-saving mantra: *Just because I can, that doesn't mean I should.*

- *Set boundaries.* You can control the way you manage your time doing your work, but there is always that one undeniable x factor: other people. Namely, employees, customers, shareholders, vendors, accountants, attorneys, spouses, and so on and so on and on. These days we live in a culture of constant interruption: by phone, fax, e-mail, text message, instant message, door knocks, shoulder taps, and everything in between. How can you slow down, focus, and center when everyone around you wants an answer *right now?*

The issue in this case becomes protecting your time. Those leaders who actually start realizing how valuable their time is are the ones who have reached a new level of leadership. When you start saying no to your clients, that is a moment to celebrate as a leader. When you do this, you make it clear to others that you have to take care of yourself, otherwise you won't be as valuable to them. Most of us in wanting to perform think that we should give away our time. But as a leader you could give away all your time to other people if you are not careful. Everyone wants your time when you are a leader.

This is where boundaries become crucial. To invoke the sports metaphor once again, no one can win (or even play) a sport without clear boundaries. What is allowed and what is not? When does the game begin and end? What constitutes a foul? You need to create boundaries around your time so that the people you lead can help you succeed, not just in the moment but in the long term. Think about it: If the ethic in your organization is that the client says "Jump" and you say, "How high?" then what is the long-term outcome? Are you really serving your clients? You might jump into the stratosphere and never come back.

Clara, a coaching client of my company, was a media buyer at a major media company. She had a very difficult boss and the boss constantly demanded that she produce more and more and more.

No matter what she did, it was never perfect, never enough. At the same time, Clara also had a client who was very demanding. Between those two, she was always trying to please. Her task: boundary setting. The moment she understood that she was never going to please her boss or the client, she learned to set boundaries on her time. When faced with an impossible deadline, Clara learned to say, "I can't do that. What I can do is x, y, and z. Tell me what you would like out of these options."

This tactic led to increased respect from her boss, who was able to better understand her time lines. He understood what she was doing much more clearly because she was communicating. With the client (a trickier situation), Clara would center herself, remain very calm, and say, "Here is what we are going to do." If the client complained, she would say, "Okay, so you tell me what you'd like to replace here." This way, Clara's workload remained manageable. By setting boundaries, clearly communicating them, and sticking to her limits, Clara could slow down her own workload and ultimately achieve more effective results for her boss and her client. She was in control, and therefore her confidence increased as well. In her moments of boundary setting, Clara was truly a leader.

How can you apply Clara's strategy? A few key components must be in place for leaders to set boundaries effectively:

- *Know yourself.* Be aware of how long it takes you to do certain tasks and achieve certain results. If you aren't sure, next time you perform a certain task, time yourself and write it down for future reference.
- *Know your relationships.* Remember that much of business is based on relationships. If you want long-term, sustainable relationships, you cannot overpromise and underdeliver. If you can't be available because of pressures pulling you from multiple directions, explain that to people. Nine out of ten times they'll understand that you need to prioritize, and they will learn to take your time when it's urgent and important.
- *Learn to protect your physical space.* Physical boundaries are critical for our mental and emotional well-being. Think of the last time someone got in your physical space. Awful. The following story illustrates one step toward redefining your physical (and mental) space.

Executive coach M. Nora Klaver offers this story of a corporate executive: a young vice president, Kim, was feeling a lack of confidence as she began working with a new team. She wasn't quite sure intellectually what she was doing, and she had one team member who felt like he should be in charge. He would get in her space physically—actually come around her desk to talk to her. She would be sitting and he would be standing over her, trying to dominate the conversation and throw her off balance. She knew it would be awkward to say anything about it, so she did not confront the behavior. Nora, Kim's coach, taught her how to reclaim her confidence through physical centering.

Nora explains, "I know my clients have power to shift their focus and energy by concentrating on their physical body and not just their mind. Centering enabled my client to gain confidence, and to get a different behavior out of her direct report through her focus on their personal power and boundaries."

The next time her employee repeated his behavior, Kim closed her eyes and imagined her energy coming back into her body and centering her. She reported back that her employee was somewhat startled and set off-center by Kim's clear energetic shift. So Kim tried it again the next time he came behind the desk. He immediately pushed away, and he never tried it again. The subtle, or even not-so-subtle, change in Kim's feeling of personal power was enough to change how her employee perceived her and responded to her.

The amazing difference between these centered postures and our common unbalanced stances is the difference between centered and uncentered action. Commit to trying the following quick exercise the next time you have a decision to make, a meeting to run, a presentation to deliver. It's guaranteed to change your effectiveness, because you will be using the body's intelligence to tap into your best thinking.

TIME FOR GOOD STRESS

We need a certain amount of stress—in the form of dynamic tension that makes great things happen.

When stress and friction start burning you out and depleting your resources, that's the bad stuff. Good stress creates something new, and it replenishes. You see that in creative environments when

TRY THIS

Physical and Mental Centering

To understand the power of centering yourself, try these two exercises:

Seated Centering Exercise: Take a deep breath and set your feet firmly on the floor. Set the book down in front of you and put your hands on your knees. Feel the center of gravity in your body, and imagine a cord that grounds your feet into the earth and pulls your head up straight into the sky. From this position, imagine remaining flexible and loose, like a tree that can bend and blow in the wind but never loses its roots. From this centered position, calm your mind by taking another deep breath. This is similar to meditation, but is focused on physically grounding you to the earth, and on making your body as stable and balanced as possible, all while remaining relaxed.

Standing Centering Exercise: Take a deep breath and stand straight. Plant your feet firmly on the floor and spread them apart the width of your hips. Shift your weight around, loosen up your muscles and your mind, shake out your arms, relax, and find a comfortable standing position—a *power* position that reflects you at your most confident. Cultivate your most authoritative, comfortable pose and center yourself in it. Memorize it. Notice the position of your arms, how you are holding your neck, shoulders, and head. Are you loose and flexible? Good. Take another deep breath.

people are onto something and really working hard. It's stress that results in something positive—achievement.

Good stress is the tension held in the body and mind when something good is about to happen. It's the kind of stress that makes a dancer's performance better on stage. The kind of stress that makes us excel when something great is being launched or created. There is a Native American proverb about stress: "Good stress is when a tree is just about to unfurl its leaves, when it knows that the transformation is coming and is about to burst." That is what good stress does: it allows us to bloom.

How do you know the difference? Think back to the skill of inquiry developed in Part One. You can use inquiry to uncover your peak state of performance and "good" stress level.

When you are feeling the physical signs of a stress response (such as nervousness in the stomach, loss of appetite, or sleeplessness), ask yourself:

- Is this stress leading up to a positive event or achievement?
- Is this stress finite or will it keep going forever unless I do something different?
- How does my body feel when I complete a task?
- Am I able to focus?
- Am I functioning at optimum for the situation at hand?
- Am I centered and "in the flow"?

This is about acknowledging your great energy. It's about champing at the bit when you're still in the gate knowing this is going to be a great race, and you will cross the finish line. Good stress is exciting, energizing, and gets you ready to take off.

Good organizational stress is an echo of good individual stress. All good stress is finite. Good organizational stress is temporary. It leads up to something positive that is a shared achievement or accomplishment.

Good organizational stress ends when something is achieved and is captured in a culminating event like a project launch, a group celebration, a bonus, or a holiday. There is a finite amount of time pressure affixed to a group deadline. We may put off our "important but not urgent" items for a while, to come back to them when the pressure is off.

Good stress is also about trusting your timing. A consultant in a large global firm tells this story:

> The leaders of a consulting firm had come together for a global meeting of the practice leaders, including me. They knew they needed to come together and capitalize on the intelligence and energy of two distinct groups. I distinctly remember the morning that we came up with our "big idea" after we had been carefully

coming up with two methodologies for the work in the organization. One of the team members came up with the idea that we needed a single approach. He came up with an overarching way of looking at the work that no one else had seen. He saw the connections we had missed because we were so in the details. We had spent three months working on this, and we thought we were ready to finish it. We were proud of what we had accomplished, but there was something missing.

This guy, Eric, knew we were close to something, he felt the tension of something about to burst forth, but knew that our initial ideas weren't quite it. When he came up with the "one method" plan, we were initially upset that our work had been in vain, then we figured out that all of the hard work and late nights had resulted in this one big idea that would help the company change everything for the better.

Trust that even when something doesn't happen quickly, all the work you do will get you to the big ideas you need. When you are putting good thought into anything—testing ideas—you are not wasting time. Trust that your work will pay off, even if it takes awhile.

An Alternate Theory: Energy Management

For seriously time-challenged leaders, it can help to think more radically about your critical resources of time and energy. Are you the kind of person who has tried to-do lists, Franklin Planners, PDAs, and every other time management system out there? Then you might need to think outside the day planner. What if, instead of thinking in terms of managing our hours, minutes, and seconds, we thought instead of managing our energy? Think about your body as housing an enormous supply of human energy, as long as you take time to replenish it.

Think about what adds energy to your body and what depletes energy from your body. What gives energy (to you as an individual, to your team, to your company) versus what takes energy away? Depressed people, for instance, can take away your energy when you are with them. (Remember that pesky mood contagion idea?) It also depletes energy to work beyond your capabilities more than every once in awhile. Sleep, of course, adds energy. As we have discussed, when you look at leaders at peak performance, they exercise and go to the doctor and care about their family. They delegate. They are regularly replenishing their supply of energy.

We as individuals have energy inputs and energy outputs. If we drain our vital life energy (health, vitality, focus, ability to think, act, participate with a clear head) we are sabotaging our ability to lead, and most important, to lead with endurance.

Think for a moment about the seriousness of this issue. McDonald's Corporation has lost two CEOs in the past three years to premature death. In Britain, a recent survey showed that over half a million people have stress-related health problems associated with their work.[3] In 2001, the Japanese government reported a significant increase in heart attacks and strokes due to overwork. They even have a word for death related to overwork: *karoshi*. A common belief is that personal well-being should be sacrificed for one's company. This is ultimately creating enormous health problems, and as workers work extremely long hours without breaks (and take only 49.5 percent of their vacation time), economic problems are being created because many in the workforce have no time to spend their hard-earned money.[4]

In the United States, according to the U.S. Department of Health and Human Services report, *Healthy People 2000:*

- Considering all visits to the doctor, 70–80 percent are for stress-related and stress-induced illnesses.
- Stress contributes to 50 percent of all illness in the United States.
- The cost of job stress in the United States is estimated at $200 billion annually, including costs of absenteeism, lost productivity, and insurance claims.[5]

When we begin to replace time management with energy management, we start becoming aware not of the time we spend, which is gone, but of the energy we spend, which can be replenished. We start cultivating practices that help us sustain our own performance, not just reducing our bad stress levels but engaging the best of what we have to offer both physically and mentally.

Nina Merer, starting in the 1980s, pioneered the concept of managing one's physical, emotional, and mental energy at work.

She called this practice "Energy Management." Her innovative programs were far ahead of their time. The next "Try This" activity is based on her work.

Practices for increasing and replenishing individual energy include getting a good night's sleep, napping, meditation, breathing clean air, physical exercise, receiving a massage, eating healthy food, having a stimulating conversation, experiencing art and culture, and spending quality time with family and friends. What are your personal energy replenishers? When do you feel refreshed, reinvigorated?

Energy Management "Dos"

> *Life begets energy. Energy creates energy. It is only by*
> *spending oneself wisely that one becomes rich in life.*
> —Eleanor Roosevelt

- Invest time in people and projects that add to your energy.
- Watch your energy patterns throughout the day and the week. Start to notice what is building and depleting your energy.
- Cultivate an environment that increases and enhances your energy. This may mean putting symbols in your office of positive activity, as one of our clients did when she put up a poster-sized photograph she took in India at the Red Fort and the Taj Mahal that represent her spirit of creativity and adventure, and brings a sense of possibility to her day.
- When putting your energy into something, remember to measure ROE—return on energy.

Energy Management "Don'ts"

> *If, after having been exposed to someone's presence, you feel*
> *as if you've lost a quart of plasma, avoid that presence.*
> *You need it like you need pernicious anemia.*
> —William S. Burroughs

- Limit time with people who drain your energy.
- When mentally drained, don't answer any questions.
- When emotionally drained, don't make decisions.
- When physically drained, stop.

TRY THIS

Energy Management Exercise

Fill out the following worksheet. Revisit the worksheet each day for a week to capture patterns and gain awareness of your personal relationship to energy.

Energy Drains		**Energy Replenishers**	
Physical	_____	Physical	_____
Mental	_____	Mental	_____
Emotional	_____	Emotional	_____

Circle your highest and lowest energy times below.

High-Energy Cycles	**Low-Energy Cycles**
6 A.M.–8 A.M.	6 A.M.–8 A.M.
8 A.M.–10 A.M.	8 A.M.–10 A.M.
10 A.M.–12noon	10 A.M.–12noon
12noon–2 P.M.	12noon–2 P.M.
2 P.M.–4 P.M.	2 P.M.–4 P.M.
4 P.M.–6 P.M.	4 P.M.–6 P.M.
6 P.M.–8 P.M.	6 P.M.–8 P.M.
8 P.M.–10 P.M.	8 P.M.–10 P.M.
10 P.M.–12 midnight	10 P.M.–12 midnight
12 midnight–2 A.M.	12 midnight–2 A.M.
2 A.M.–4 A.M.	2 A.M.–4 A.M.
4 A.M.–6 A.M.	4 A.M.–6 A.M.

Notice the following in your worksheet:

What is draining your energy?

What is replenishing your energy?

What is in balance?

What is out of balance?

When are you most energetic? Least energetic?

What are other contributing factors to your energy cycles?

Are you more energetic in your office? Outside? Around certain people? By yourself?

What aspect do you need more support in?

What can you do more of?

What will enable you to sustain yourself over time?

What are the most important patterns for you to remember?

As we discussed in terms of time management, taking time to reset can be a quick, simple, and in-the-moment way to replenish energy. For you as a leader, this may mean recalibrating your energy as you are talking, working, presenting, and thinking. It may also mean preserving one day a week for yourself.

As the poet Andrei Codrescu says,

Take one day of the week and be kind to yourself. Don't drive yourself where you don't want to go, don't drive yourself insane, don't drive. Look out with half-closed lids at the tree or the building across the street, stay unfocused, unintentional, indeterminate. Let everything flow through you like it's water or wind, don't stop it with thoughts, ideas or judgments; don't try to figure out how it fits in your five-year plan. For one day a week forget pedagogy, self-incrimination, disapproval, political rage. Let it be a cliché if it has to, but just let it. It's the Sabbath.

Something or other is going on on earth, under the earth, on top of the earth; maybe it's leaves falling or new catastrophes brewing, but whatever they are you're only just a stick of flesh holding on to your Sabbath. They'll be back tomorrow, the bills, the troubles, and the work. Today you're on sabbatical and there is nothing they can do to you if you don't invite them. The sabbatical . . . doesn't have to be justified. God took his on the seventh day to be alone not because he wanted to be bothered by prayers, incense, lamentations and pleas. He was hoping that you'd do the same, that's all.

If for one day a week every creature looked after itself without worrying about anything else, creation would become instantly self-evident and there'd be no need to fix everything. All that said, there are people who don't have the luxury of a day off. They have to dig themselves out of rubble, tend to a wound, swim for life or get down from a tree. OK, but when they've dug out and haven't died they should keep the Sabbath. All suffering can wait.[6]

Always remember that your time is your choice. You can choose to take the hyperkinetic route—going faster and faster until you are like a spinning top, or the *festina lente* route—hurry up slowly. If you spin out of control, you'd better bet that others will follow. As we will discuss in the next chapter, as a leader you are constantly modeling the behavior you wish to see in others. The final stage of being faster is to bring your stakeholders along for the ride.

Summary

- When you understand and appreciate your personal time style you can start to work smarter and understand where you need to make changes if necessary.
- As the leader of a company, you can't just *say* balance is important. You have to have it yourself in your own life to some degree and understand what resources you need to provide.
- To feel that time is abundant, you can focus on present-moment time, listen more carefully so you hear and understand things the first time, realize that "can" doesn't mean "should," and set boundaries.
- Taking a moment to center yourself can change your effectiveness, because you will be using the body's intelligence to tap into your best thinking.
- Instead of time management, consider thinking in terms of energy management. When you expend energy, be sure to renew it.

CHAPTER SIX

FASTER TOGETHER
Energizing Your Team

We don't accomplish anything in this world alone . . .
and whatever happens is the result of the whole tapestry
of one's life and all the weavings of individual threads
from one to another that creates something.
—SANDRA DAY O'CONNOR

When you think about energy, Gary Erickson should be at the top of your mind. An avid cyclist, rock climber, backpacker, skier, and chef, Gary needs all the energy he can get—and did I mention he's also the founder of a company that has been on *Inc.* magazine's list of the fastest-growing companies in the United States for four years running?

Gary's brainchild, Clif Bar Inc., has won numerous awards honoring the company for its treatment of employees, commitment to the environment, and support for important causes such as the fight against breast cancer. He is the author of *Raising the Bar,* which tells the story of the development of his company and of its climb to success after a last-moment decision not to sell out to one of the corporate giants.[1]

When I asked Gary about leading an energetic culture, he had this to say:

Understanding the kind of business we are and where we are going is inspiring for people. Our vision here is to work to live rather than live to work. It's more of a long-term vision. We're not in the fast lane trying to grow this thing as fast as possible. The people here work really hard, they give themselves over and they're sharing in the profits when we meet our goals. We have different bottom lines than a traditional business does. We try to have several and they're not all money. Inspiring and taking care of our people is critical. As the shareholders, my wife and I want that to be our return on our investment. We also have a lot of the other benefits other companies have: 401(K) plans, medical and dental and so on. On top of that we try to spice things up in the atmosphere itself.

Our office is open, alive, not like a cubicle type of workplace. We're family-friendly and dog-friendly, so we have babies and dogs around. Every week we have an all-company meeting and we all eat together, very casual—we have bagels and fruit and we sit down in the auditorium and we all just meet there and we read letters from consumers, sometimes we review the financials, sometimes we just have fun and hang out together and learn what's going on in the company and the world outside.

We make a healthy product and people feel energized by that. Once when we got off track and jumped on the low-carb thing, it was really demotivating. Sticking to our food philosophy is something that gives life and energy to our group.

On the physical side, we have an on-site fitness center with yoga, spin, kickboxing, and so on. The gym is world class, with a separate dance studio, two full-time personal trainers, and instructors who have classes. We have some quirky things too: Thursdays we have a hair salon and a carwash. We have a washer-dryer here that people can use if they need to do their laundry. What we're trying to do is to free people up when they get home to have more of a life. If we can do that, people get more done in a shorter amount of time.

One other thing is, at 6 P.M. around here, it's empty. We don't encourage people to work nights and weekends. We believe the way we plan and budget, and with how many people we have, that we're able to get our work done in normal business hours. I know that's not the norm, particularly living in the Bay Area and watching the Silicon Valley boom when people were working eighty to a hundred hours a week. Our particular business is very competitive. We can't sit still, but we know this is the way to go to get the job done. Every day is like a half-marathon. We run really hard, we play really hard, and some years are better than others. We've been in business since 1992, we've remained private, and we're competing against Kraft and Nestlé and Coke. Everyone is jumping into this category. Our story is compelling, and we need to keep doing things right. We're trying to do good business, and that's working for us. I don't take anything for granted. We work very hard, and we're doing it the way we believe in.

How can you make your organization more like the energetic culture of Clif Bar?

Here are some strategies for saving time in the long run by slowing down long enough to set the tone for the entire culture of your organization:

- *Reorient toward purpose and values.* Purpose and values inspire energy. Motivation comes directly from a focus on meaning. What is your collective purpose as a team? As a company?

Recently in a strategy meeting for the board of a nonprofit arts organization, I saw the group energy waning and dissipating. We were bogged down in fundraising challenges, legal issues, and an argument between the board and the founder of the organization. The energy shifted as soon as someone said, "Remember *why* we are here: because we all care about the arts, and we all care about lifting the spirits of others through dance. These challenges are all-important because we care about our mission." It completely changed the tone of the room. In your next group meeting, take the opportunity to reorient toward purpose and values, and ask others to do so as well.

- *Do what you want to see.* As a leader, you are the model for the behavior of everyone else in your organization. The number one strategy for helping others manage time and energy more effectively is to model the behavior you want to see in others: walk the talk. I like to think of this one as the "oxygen mask" phenomenon. On an airplane, the flight attendants tell you not to cover the nose and mouth of your child with a mask until you have put on your own mask. Once you can breathe, helping others will be much easier. Are you personally motivated, enthusiastic, high-energy? What do you need to do to reenergize first and foremost? Have you taken care of your own oxygen mask first?

- *Be clear about what you want.* The more you say it, the more real it becomes. "I want us to become more energized, to believe more, to focus on what we do best." Stating your goals clearly and appreciatively as a leader has great power to effect the exact change you are seeking. There is a particular way to be clear about what you want. Don't assume that this is a direct order. Share what you want for the group, not just yourself. Note the language: the term *we* has energy. Remember, what we focus on becomes our reality. How can you help your team focus on what's working, and doing more of that? Tell them what you want to achieve together, and see how quickly it manifests.

- *Look for opportunities to include people in adding value.* Ask for their contribution. The more valued people feel, the more energy they have to contribute to the cause. Ask yourself, "Who can I tap today?"

- *Create a "play ethic."* What's useful about a work ethic? It means there's a commitment to getting things done. What if you adopted a "play ethic"—committed to enjoying your natural-born ability to create, imagine, and make working more fun? The more we play, the more energy we cultivate for our work. Remember, productivity doesn't mean drudgery.

- *Acknowledge the need for physical replenishment.* Encourage people to take an exercise class. Have someone who's trained to give

TRY THIS

Use Appreciative Inquiry to Conduct an "Energizer Meeting"[2]

Meeting #1—Mini-Energizer

Get your team together and pose the following questions:

What kind of future do we want as a team?

What kind of energy do we need in order to build that future?

What are some mechanisms we can use to build our "energy resources"?

How can we engage people at all levels to be involved in building that future?

Meeting #2—Maximum Energizer

Take the following "Appreciative Inquiry" to stakeholders from all over your company. Gather as many participants as you can to engage their full participation and excitement. The best-case scenario is to have as large a group as possible. And if you think you're looking at bringing in too many people, remember that places like Roadway trucking, the EPA, Green Mountain Coffee Roasters, and even the U.S. Navy have done inquiries such as this one with more than a thousand people in a room.

Create the inquiry: It might be something like, "What brings us the best, most productive energy? As an organization, what are our human energy inputs and outputs? How do we cultivate energy? What would it mean if all of us were completely energized and engaged in the success of our work? What mechanisms would be in place to support that?"

Step 1. Discovery. Conduct appreciative interviews: find out about the best of the past in order to replicate and build on that best practice.

Step 2. Dream. Engage the group in a brainstorming session devoted to your vision. Share stories from the Discovery phase. Ground your dreams on moments from your organization's most positive experience. Create a list of powerful ideas for what the "new" organization would look like. What is the dream that stakeholders can share? What are the most compelling future visions of being fully energized and engaged?

Step 3. Design. Create "Provocative Propositions": great ideas that will be considered for enabling the dream to happen. Those "Provocative Propositions" are captured in writing and presented to the large group.

Step 4. Destiny. This phase is ongoing. After the Design phase, a set of top "Provocative Propositions" is adopted. Each proposition that will be taken to the next level must have two champions who will take responsibility for making it happen.

neck massages available once a month. Teach people how to manage their stress effectively. Start a running team that raises money for cancer research. Serve healthy food at meetings instead of donuts and coffee.

Beyond these steps, you can develop other practical strategies for building and replenishing energy in your organization.

GOING SLOW ORGANIZATIONALLY

Redefinition: Fast (adj.)

Slowing down enough to find most efficient and effective use of one's time and energy. Getting things done right the first time. Making sure the processes used to deliver work product are smooth. Helping your organization to move faster through effective pacing and energy management.

Not all time pressure, of course, is self-imposed. What if you are a leader of a public company with quarterly earnings pressure? The demands of Wall Street and the legal responsibilities of a public company to produce greater and greater rates of return for the shareholders are very real. The rules of engagement change when you are bound by the creation of short-term wins. But what does that mean for long-term value? For the greater good? For not just the stock owners but the employees or the customers? Shareholders want to be informed about the long-term gains that come from long-term strategy. We will talk about this in much more detail in Part Three. For now, remember that thinking about short-term earnings does not have to be the sole focus of your day. You need to address both short-term and long-term profitability.

3M commits millions of dollars per annum to innovation, which has put the company at the forefront of invention in its category. Every year it has a large number of people working to come up with great ideas that are not on an urgent schedule. Again—not urgent, but important.

George Stalk, author and world-renowned strategist at Boston Consulting Group, came up with the idea of "time-defined competition." This theory, developed in the 1980s, said that in the United States we had to go faster, faster, faster to compete with the Japanese. Because Stalk's theory was all about faster, companies adopted time-defined strategies. They stopped thinking about being more efficient, unless it helped them get to market faster. But now, in a different era, Stalk is creating new strategies to propose for our current time and place.

Many ahead-of-the-curve strategists' ideas are now less in line with time and first-to-market production, and more in line with the idea of defining your own market through innovative thinking.

W. Chan Kim and Renee Mauborgne suggest in the October 2004 issue of *Harvard Business Review* that rather than competing within the confines of your existing industry or by trying to steal customers from rival organizations (what they call the "Red Ocean Strategy"), the key to success is creating new market space that makes competition unimportant (their "Blue Ocean Strategy").

If you have your own market space, time-defined competition is no longer the key to success. The bloody battlefield of the Red Ocean is overcrowded and isn't a great place to sustain high performance. The real opportunity is to create Blue Oceans—great seas of opportunity.

In Blue Oceans, demand is created. For example, eBay created a whole new industry of online auctions. Another Blue Ocean strategy is to expand one's existing market into a new area. Vans started making skateboarding shoes in the 1970s before anyone else had commercialized the sport. A whole new category was formed. How do these ideas happen? Slowing down, taking time to think, and coming up with new and innovative ways of creating market space.

Red Ocean Strategy	*Blue Ocean Strategy*
Compete in existing market space.	Create uncontested market space.
Beat the competition.	Make the competition irrelevant.
Exploit existing demand.	Create and capture new demand.
Make the value/cost trade-off.	Break the value/cost trade-off.
Align the whole system of a company's activities with its strategic choice of differentiation or low cost.	Align the whole system of a company's activities in pursuit of differentiation and low cost.

Think about your organization for a moment. Do you spend more time thinking about your competitors or your own company? Are you in a Red Ocean or a Blue Ocean? How can you define a new, uncontested market space? I would argue that the time you spend finding your Blue Ocean will save you enormous amounts of time later that you might have spent trying to beat the competitors in your Red Ocean. Finding new, innovative Blue water will make you faster in the long run.

CREATING A POSITIVE FLOW

> *Concentration is so intense that there is no attention left over to think about anything irrelevant, or to worry about problems. Self-consciousness disappears, and the sense of time becomes distorted. An activity that produces such experiences is so gratifying that people are willing to do it for its own sake, with little concern for what they will get out of it, even when it is difficult.*
> —MIHALY CSIKSZENTMIHALYI, *FLOW: THE PSYCHOLOGY OF OPTIMAL EXPERIENCE*

Another way to conceptualize organizational energy and how to affect it is to think again in terms of flow. Water is a great metaphor for flexibility. Think of water and all its attributes: it's clear; it conforms to any shape; it's completely flexible, but it wears down solid rock.

In 1990, Mihaly Csikszentmihalyi published a breakthrough book based on decades of research on "flow." He looked at the question, "When do people feel the most happy?" What he discovered was that happiness is not a random occurrence, and it's not about luck or money, power or intellect. Happiness is not determined by external experience—it springs from our internal workings. Csikszentmihalyi says that optimal experience is a kind of flow state—when we are deeply engaged and exhilarated by life.

> Flow is the way people describe their state of mind when consciousness is harmoniously ordered, and they want to pursue whatever they are doing for its own sake. In reviewing some of the activities that consistently produce flow—such as sports, games, art, and hobbies—

it becomes easier to understand what makes people happy. . . . Most people spend the largest part of their lives working and interacting with others. . . . Therefore it is crucial that one learn to transform jobs into flow-producing activities.[3]

In an assessment interview for a professional hockey team, a young goalie said to his interviewer, "When there's a huge slap shot coming at me, I can actually slow it down. I can see it rotate, and it slows down so I can see the puck and stop it." He followed by saying "please don't tell anyone else this." The goalie thought he might sound crazy, but it's common that in the flow state our perception of time shifts. Our pacing becomes fluid, and we are able to masterfully interact with the world around us from a place of confident ease.

Here are some examples:

- *When master cellist Yo Yo Ma is playing his music.* It took him hard work to get there, but once a musician achieves mastery, he is able to let go of the hours of practice and work and flow with the experience of making beautiful music for an audience.
- *When former President Bill Clinton is talking to his audience.* No matter how you feel about Bill Clinton's politics, to watch him speak is to be entranced by someone connecting and flowing with his audience. A good speaker's words seem to string themselves together. Every individual in the audience feels a direct connection to the speaker. It takes a great deal of preparation, but once excellence is achieved, then *ease* sets in and takes over.
- *When Michael Jordan played basketball.* Watching a pro athlete during a moment of focus, we are aware that nothing else exists for that person except the present moment. Michael Jordan's iconic ballet-like leaps and moves are a perfect example of graceful, elegantly paced flow.

It is impossible to think we can maintain that flow state at all times, but think if that was the goal of your work, rather than speed? How would your work change? What would work better? What would the ultimate result be?

Whassup?

Steve Conner is the chief creative officer of Burrell Communications in Chicago, and knows about creating flow and positive energy in his organizations. I met Steve a few years back when he was acting as the founder and lead creative of his own small New York advertising agency (which he called STEVE). Steve has a beautiful story of how he got his team into the creative flow state, and how they came up with big ideas for their clients.

> My working environments, the ones I've led, have always been about truth and authenticity. With that comes fun and joy in creating. At the time of this story, I was trying to figure out what was different when we were feeling happy. What was different about those days when we feel good? That's what we're here for, to feel joy. One of the things I started talking about with my team was being conscious about our decisions to be joyful. To go toward joy, there must be something we believe. The choices we make are dependent on our beliefs . . . and whether we gravitate toward what we value and believe in. What's your personal belief? If we could be in touch with that and create some expression of that truth, then how could the passion and the purity of what you achieved be a mainline of passion and purity to the person who experiences it. That's what art does: it can touch others through that direct channel.
>
> In this spirit, I passed out this assignment that everyone was involved in, from secretaries to creative directors, everyone in the company was involved. They were asked to submit the answer to "What is your personal truth?" boiled down onto one piece of paper. Examples:
>
> - "I believe that life is not what you think it is, there's always something new around the corner."
>
> - "What you say is who you are, and if I say something, then the word is the truth for me."
>
> - "If you say something negative you become that way. If you are positive you become positive."
>
> - "I am in touch with the universe and anything that comes out of me. I am a channel for the truth, it doesn't come from me."
>
> - "We are in constant evolution, breaking down the old, finding the new."

So they did that, and I said, "Now let's take these truths and see if we can condense them even further. Now come up with five ideas that would illustrate your truth somehow. The ideas would be expressive. People wrote poems, made collages, one did an installation art piece, and the person that said there was something around every corner created a mannequin, and an explosion coming out of that mannequin of everything you might need to prepare for disaster. It could fill the whole room. It was right there in the office—great self-expression. Telling these truths, these stories, was a powerful thing to share in a group. It was emotional, a bonding experience.

[One of my staff members] Charles Stone's truth was that there are codes in life, and life is built around them. "Guys don't have to say anything to say everything," was one of those codes. We started thinking about that as an idea about the truth about men and how we communicate. One of the ideas he came up with was this wonderful three-minute film of all these guys saying nothing, but saying everything. That's how he and his friends talked to one another.

Charles produced the piece, and it was truthful enough that people really responded to it. The Internet was the medium: we shared it over the net and it buzzed around the world. When brands have a truth to them that is beyond the thing they are doing or making, you see the human spirit peeking out from behind the corporate logo.

This became the seed of the famous Budweiser "Whassup" campaign. From the beginning of this exercise, it proved true that in every one of us there's a little bit of what the others were thinking. We all relate to these basic truths. Every truth has resonance. For me, I really saw that we had this opportunity to find brands that have similar DNA, and Budweiser really related to this truth. We licensed the idea to Budweiser and their agency DDB Needham, and the rest is history.

To really create a positive flow, it's most important to build a really strong relationship with the people you work with—to develop passion and shared experience. I'd take passion over pure talent any day. Loyalty, excitement, closeness, willingness to assist each other—you can't buy that. You need to encourage it, and reach out to people with your own care as a human being. If you can achieve a balance between beliefs, goals, and shared experience, you can move mountains.

Steve's cultivation of flow began with an important truth of its own: to hurry up and find a great idea was not the starting point. It took time, thoughtfulness, and creativity to find the right idea. They waited until the right idea came about.

Warren Bennis once said, "Good leaders make people feel that they're at the very heart of things, not at the periphery. Everyone feels that he or she makes a difference to the success of the organization. When that happens people feel centered and that gives their work meaning." To remain centered and model that behavior for others includes the ability to be calm in a crisis, and to demonstrate your stability, balance, and faith, and to influence others to find their own. Great leaders help to set the pace, the energy level, and the flow of the people they lead.

THE DOMINANT OSCILLATOR

The disparate fields of electronic and biological systems make use of a term that provides a great metaphor for leadership and pacing. Scientists speak of the *dominant oscillator* as the feature of a system that seems to control the rest of its cycles—a concept so abstruse as to be difficult to comprehend in the physical world, but one that fits right in when you look at human organizations. People do take the leader's measure and comport themselves accordingly, whether in happy or unhappy ways. Thus the leader is the dominant oscillator for a group, setting the pace by which the rest of the members move, and whether or not they are in a state of flow.

The best leaders I know are the ones who understand their job as the dominant oscillator. They are the willing pacesetters. Their job is to inspire, to enable others to feel passionate and committed to their work. Their success doesn't come from just their own personal actions, it also comes from the actions of others. Their satisfaction does not come from great personal fame or wealth but from the knowledge that they have enabled the success of their organization through their stewardship. They are the leaders whose ideas take on a shape of their own, who express themselves fully but don't require kudos for it. Those are the leaders who understand that their ability to deal with time pressure will enable others to do the same.

The story of Ernest Shackleton, the famed English explorer, comes to mind. His is one of the great survival stories of all time.

His ill-fated expedition to the Antarctic led his band of men to a two-year epic journey that started well, but within six months saw their ship, the *Endurance*, frozen in a field of ice and eventually crushed there. After more than a year of living on rations, consuming their animals, and fighting to survive, he and his men were able to move out when the ice broke up. With jury-rigged lifeboats, they made their way to the desolate Elephant Island, where they were again marooned.

Shackleton never let his men lose hope. He kept them moving, creating, and occupied and working as a team during the entire long ordeal. Eventually, he and two other men set out in one of their three small boats to find help. After days at sea and only three readings off their sextant, they made their way to South Georgia Island, covered in glaciers and rough terrain. When they found help three days later, they brought the men to safety. For many years after that ordeal, each and every man (all of whom survived) said that they would repeat their experience again. They would follow Shackleton anywhere because of his leadership.

Although Shackleton failed in his 1914 expedition to the South Pole, he was able to help his men remain calm and centered in the heart of crisis. He enabled them to survive. He won their loyalty for life by maintaining a pace and mood that allowed them to return to safety—every last one of them.

As the leader, the "dominant oscillator," you provide not only the rhythm that other people work by but also a source of energy—emotional, mental, and physical—that has a ripple effect. Your influence may have impact far down the road from when you did something, said something, suggested something, or even felt something. You make a difference every day in making yourself and others faster. As Martin Luther King Jr. said, "Whatever affects one directly, affects all indirectly. I can never be what I ought to be until you are what you ought to be. This is the interrelated structure of reality."

TAKING TIME FOR PEOPLE

Part of leadership is developing others around whatever you're doing, so that capability is there next time. That makes you faster. You've got to take on capacity building, which means timely mentoring, coaching, teaching—all with an eye toward creating capability.

If you are surrounded by the right people, they not only make you smarter (as described in Part One), they also make you faster. When you have the right people, you can delegate and rely on other people. You will have more time, because work shared is work halved.

This is one place to invest your time and energy. When a leader says it takes so much time to train people, what are the resources outside you? How much time does it really take to train someone and have a relationship-building conversation? It just takes an initial investment. Once you have gotten to know someone, you can have very short conversations after that. An hour or even thirty minutes is time well spent to get to know an employee. Sometimes helping others to make you faster is an investment of time up front. Do not be fooled by the seduction of doing a chore yourself. Of course it takes less time for you to do something when someone else does not know how.

Do you have an assistant or other employee that you rely upon? Developing that person (or those people, if you are so lucky) is a crucial strategy for every leader to adopt. I recommend thinking of this as developing more brains for yourself. Many successful leaders rely heavily on an assistant or other close employee for this kind of support. How do you assess if a person qualifies for the job of "additional brains"? Here are some questions to think about:

- *Values.* Does this person understand and respect your core values? What behaviors does this person need to demonstrate to correlate to those values?
- *Communication.* How do you want this person and others to communicate with you? E-mail? Face to face? Regular phone calls once a week?
- *Performance.* How will this person know that he or she is performing to your expectations? What measures will you use?

As a leader, you'll find that it is critical to determine your expectations of behavior and performance for those around you, and to communicate those things to your direct reports. The following worksheet is designed to outline your basic values, communication style, and performance expectations.

TRY THIS

Expectations Worksheet

Values and behavioral expectations	
Communication style and expectations about communication. (Include preference for voice mail, in-person conversation, e-mail, or other correspondence)	
Performance expectations	
Development expectations	

A final story of leadership excellence in helping others to go faster by slowing down comes from the terrorist attacks in New York City on September 11, 2001. Lisa Arhontes, disaster specialist for the American Red Cross, describes a powerful example of helping others maintain their energy. For nearly three months, the American Red Cross ran several Respite Centers for the workers of what was known as the "hot zone." For twenty-four hours a day, seven days a week, these centers provided meals, snacks, a place to rest, and nursing, emotional care, and spiritual care services. Upon their closure, they had provided comfort to thousands of hard-working people from around the country, many of them volunteers.

From the dedicated members of police and fire departments to the skilled tradespeople who filled Ground Zero, those responding to 9/11 had no choice but to stop worrying about the time it would take to clean up the enormous mass of debris left in the wake of the attacks. They let go of being fast and helped others to tackle the challenge ahead with pride, energy, and a sense of purpose. The work was slow going if it was to be done right.

The work that was going on was mostly debris removal. It was a gigantic deconstruction site, a slow and tedious process. Front-end loaders, cranes, and other heavy equipment methodically removed debris. Various members of different police and fire departments "escorted" each piece of equipment. They walked and watched and ultimately signaled each and every time they thought they found human remains. It was then that the bustle and beeping of equipment came to an eerily quiet standstill. Even at the periphery of the "hot zone," local utility workers moved methodically to help get the local community reconnected.

Lisa Arhontes comments,

> I was at Ground Zero during the month of November, a month and a half after the incident. The Respite Centers provided an oasis from the surreal environment of the site. It was like an ant farm— a constant movement of people. The crews worked in shifts around the clock, so we needed to support them around the clock. This was different for me. Traditionally, we at the American Red Cross respond during the initial "emergency" phase of a disaster. To be involved in something so heavily for so long was really unusual for us, but we needed to reflect our environment. If the crews moved slowly and methodically, then there was no need for their only place of solace to be filled with adrenaline. People stayed calm and focused partly because it was so surreal but also because we were so committed to getting the job done.
>
> The group of volunteers, both ours and others, at Ground Zero were energized by a common purpose: Life is short. We were all stunned by the tragedy, but also stunned by the amazing power of the human spirit. In order to do this job fast, we all had to slow down, to remember what was truly important, to stop rushing and to stick with the task at hand until it was done. It is something that I learned then, and that I continue to practice today.

What's the ultimate aim of going faster anyway? So we achieve profitability quickly, or we get a deal done quickly, but what is the *result* of going faster? What is the end goal? What is the point of "winning"? Ultimately isn't the idea to improve efficiency? Effectiveness? Revenue? Results? To change the world? Sometimes faster helps, but ultimately I believe we are all striving to be *better* . . . for ourselves, our companies, our community, and ultimately our interconnected globe. What does it mean to you to be better?

Summary

- To create an energetic company culture, reorient your company toward purpose and values, model what you want to see in your employees, and be clear about what you want your culture to be.
- Cultivate energy through good physical, mental, and emotional practices in your organization—the goal is health on all levels.
- Choose a flow state instead of a hyperkinetic state.
- As a leader you are the dominant oscillator; you're the one who sets the pace by which others around you move.
- Invest your time in developing "more brains"—a person or small group on whom you can always rely.

PART THREE

THE *BETTER* PARADOX

To be better, we need to stop focusing on our personal gain and start focusing on giving back—to our organization, to our community, and to the world as a whole.

CHAPTER SEVEN

WHAT IS BETTER?

Not all leaders are visionary and not all leaders change the world for the better. My challenge to you is to be one of the leaders who *are* visionary and *do* change the world for the better. This is the only path to truly effective, enduring, and fulfilled leadership. To create the kind of world we all wish to inhabit (and wish for our children and grandchildren to inhabit), we need to use our leadership power to envision and build the kind of organization and ultimately the world we want to be a part of.

Are we responsible for bottom-line profitability? For quarterly earnings statements? Yes, absolutely. But for what else are we truly responsible? To whom are we accountable? What kind of future do we want to create through our actions? First, think about what it means to be *better*. Does betterment mean winning a race with your competitor? Does it mean dominance over others? Does it mean dying with the most toys?

Then think about this: Leaders who are too focused on beating everyone else often don't have the impact they want, because everyone is a potential threat and because they are expending valuable energy and time on trying to assuage their competitive fears. When you focus too much on your competitors, your stress levels rise—and, as we know from Part Two, your capacity for great strategic thinking disappears.

A smart leader pays close attention to improving the bottom line, but also regards "becoming better" as building an increasingly successful business where people are excited to come to work every day. Or making the community a safer and more sustainable place to live. Or improving clients' lives and businesses. A smart leader knows that you can't achieve success alone.

Like being smarter and faster, becoming a better leader involves a paradox: To be better, we need to move away from trying to be better *than* others—our competitors, our colleagues, our predecessors. Instead, we need to engage with others, collaborate with others, and ultimately better ourselves *with* others. Leadership success does not depend on being smarter, faster, and better *than* the rest of the group you lead. Leadership success depends on being smarter, faster, and better *with* the rest of the group you lead.

To be "better with" means focusing on inspiring, not dominating or controlling. To be "better with" means focusing not just on competition but on collaboration. To be "better with" means accepting and leveraging all the strengths, challenges, and opportunities you possess as a leader, all in service of making others better.

The point is this: you can't be in this just for yourself. You must think about the greater impact of your leadership. It's about *we*, not *me*.

Attributes of "Better Than" Thinking	Attributes of "Better With" Thinking
Dominance	Empowerment
Greed and hoarding	Abundance and sharing
Fear	Confidence
Closed systems	Open systems
Competition	Collaboration and "coopetition"
Defeating the other	Having a positive impact
Short-term wins	Sustainability
Me focus	We focus

In the wise words of Sussan Skjei, director of the Authentic Leadership Program at Naropa University in Boulder, Colorado:

> Our only hope for shifting consciousness to change what's happening in the world will come from collective wisdom—from bringing people together. And leadership development is critical for this. If a leader knows how to cultivate that collective wisdom, then one

leader can have an incredible impact on many people. But doing this takes courage and vision, because it means being involved in something bigger than just one's own life.

Our current Age of Interdependence requires each and every one of us to cultivate the "better with" perspective. We need to focus not on our own self-gain but on our collective future as a global community.

Someone we've met before, Gary Erickson of Clif Bar, knows about this firsthand. He was offered $120 million for his thriving energy bar company, and had to think long and hard about what he wanted to do. Instead of taking the money, early retirement, and never having to work again, Gary chose to keep building his business. Gary knew that his business had a purpose, and that purpose was beyond shareholder returns. In his words, "I thought I was doing something good with Clif Bar. I never thought of growing the company and selling. Why was that better than owning a company, employing people, creating great products, using the power of the company for philanthropic ends and possibly making positive changes in the world?" Gary followed his beliefs and chose the path that he knew was best. His decision made it possible to build something different from a traditional organization: to be a role model for business owners who care about more than building their own financial bottom line.

> We're working to reduce our ecological footprint. As a food company, we're working on converting all our ingredients to organic. Conventional agriculture is destroying the land and contributing to global warming. Organic foods are better for you—fewer pesticides. We buy millions of pounds of raw ingredients. Over 50 percent now of what we make is organic, and that will go higher in the coming years. We've invested in a wind farm in South Dakota called Native Energy. Native Energy is building windmills that are safe for birds, because they're huge and turn slowly. That energy is fed into the grid as clean energy. We offset the energy we use by investing in that. We use post-consumer recycled paper and boxes. We have a long way to go, but we've come so far in just five years.

> I look at great leaders and they've always done it their way. Traditional capitalism was saying "grow it and sell it." Why would anyone think I could steward a company this size? Tradition was saying do

what everyone else does. I don't think that's how great things are done. I think we can make such enormous changes by making the world the way we want it. We see it happening. We're proving that it's viable and important.

David Fischman is one of my favorite examples of transformation to a "better with" leader from a "better than" leader. David is a renowned entrepreneur and author who is a founder and vice president of development at Universidad Peruana Ciencias Aplicadas in Lima, Peru. I've had the privilege of working with David and his faculty, and the energy and enthusiasm he has for his work is infectious. He has this to say about his own story of moving from "better than" to "better with":

My first business was creating a very small computer college. I had graduated, and I wanted to own the world. I was twenty-two years old with a lot of passion and entrepreneurship. We opened the college with two computers and one classroom. This was 1982–83, and people really wanted to know about this stuff. We were very successful. I was driven. I wanted more than anything to be successful, to be the best. I was basically concerned with my own self-interest. I wanted to be important, to have status. We started with $3,000.

Four years later we owned our first property, sixty computers in the labs, had a great business of about a million dollars a year. We were known in the business community—things were going great. If we got bigger we needed more education. My partner and I went to university to get our MBAs. At Boston University I had a huge ego. I wanted to be number one in the class. I wanted to ask the smartest questions, get the best grades. I was difficult to stand. I was so results driven—I ended up I think number two in my class—but I was awful to be around because I was so competitive.

I came back to Peru and grew the business really big. We grew, we owned more property, we had two thousand students at the institute. We were making five million a year. I was only thirty years old, and I had a BMW, I was single, I had any woman I wanted, it was supposedly a really happy time in my life, but it wasn't that at all. I realized I had a problem, really. My main problem was that I was always searching for something better. I needed help. I went to a psychologist, and after that I realized I had had a difficult childhood. I wanted to please my mother—as an entrepreneur, I kept trying to be *more* successful, so I could have the attention I had needed as a child. *When you have these problems, the world is for you. When I solved these problems, I was for the world.*

I immediately thought that if I had that problem, many people must have the same thing. I had a university spin-off of the computer college—I created the center for leadership there to help people become more aware of themselves. I started giving courses in self-knowledge, and I felt that I could help people grow inside as well as outside.

Besides the center for leadership, I had never done anything for other people. I found that I wanted to help beyond what I was doing. I started to visit cancer patients, and started to help them meditate, and gave them support in their illness. I was scared. Helping someone is a very scary thing in the beginning, because you don't know how they will react. I did that with a dying patient. I have never felt so happy in my whole life. Everything I had done in my life, I can't compare it with the feeling I had when I helped someone for the sake of helping. I realize that the essence of life is that we are here to serve. I decided that I needed to get enough money to be able to help my family—I have my wife, kids, and they need enough to be comfortable, and I can devote myself to service.

Another thing I have had to learn is to be patient—I can't do everything at once, but every day I can stop and give to others. It gives me such happiness. I also needed to get help to make the transition from one mind-set to another. I needed a partner—in my case a therapist—and I needed meditation, which I recommend to everyone. The path depends on the person. I believe in having someone who can make you think and realize what you're doing, someone who can be a mirror for you. In your case it may be a therapist, an executive coach, a business partner, but without other people we can't see ourselves as clearly.

I continue meditating every day. I've created an organization called Sunrise in Peru. It has twenty volunteers. We help cancer patients. I give the funds, and I am in the process of moving into doing more of that helping work. Our university is doing more than $30 million a year in business. We have now sold the university to a large conglomerate, but we still manage it. At fifty, I will have the capital and the freedom to devote myself to working part time for the university I founded and part time doing service. I really know I have done good things for others, not just myself.

HUBRIS

What if David Fischman hadn't changed? What if he were still as self-interested today as he felt at age twenty-two? His life would be very different today, and I believe his leadership experience would be far less enduring, effective, and fulfilling for him—and for those around him.

Unfortunately, we have a lot of examples of leaders who took the other path—toward total self-interest and "better than" thinking. We all have this element within us, but we each make a choice about how to handle our own feelings and desires related to competition, success, and power. We often get to become leaders because of our naturally competitive natures. There is nothing wrong with being competitive. There is something wrong with letting that competitiveness eclipse our ability to collaborate, create, and leverage relationships.

You may be familiar with the ancient Greek concept of *hubris,* literally translated as "exaggerated pride." In Greek tragedy, hubris is the fatal flaw in all of human nature. I like to think of it as the basic desire to be "better than" others.

In Shakespeare's storytelling, hubris is emblematic of having too much faith in power. For instance, the king starts off as an honorable and ethical leader, and as time goes on and the tragedy plays out, it's his pride—his hubris, his ego—that brings him down.

It's not hard to find more recent examples. Look at Kenneth Lay and Jeff Skilling of Enron. Skilling was fascinated with power and with being the best, and he had such faith in his own intellect and the power of that intellect to win that he convinced himself and many others that the Enron strategy would dominate the marketplace. They felt they were "the best." Skilling, not surprisingly, was fascinated with Social Darwinism, or the application of the concept "survival of the fittest" to human behavior. This ultimately set an engine in motion that not only brought down the leadership of the company but brought down the entire organization and others with it.

It's unfair to blame the collapse of Enron completely on Lay and Skilling; in fact, it's much more accurate to blame it on the web of corrupt leadership behaviors based solely on short-term, bottom-line wins. I think the Enron failure proves the ultimate destructiveness of "better than" thinking in leaders.

The executives at Enron, and their unethical behaviors and actions, ultimately fell apart because of their own hubris. Until they got caught, they were playing a dice game. They were adrenaline junkies and risk-takers. They might have felt thrilled at the height of the company's financial success, but I wonder if they could have felt fulfilled? That type of behavior is simply not sustainable over long periods of time. I could go on here about the complicity of so many others in the Enron scandal, but the important message here is simple: greed and self-interest may result in significant short-term gain financially, but it does not result in effective, enduring, and fulfilled leadership.

Enron represents the extreme of hubris in the business world. But all of us have experienced various levels of hubris. By understanding this fatal flaw in others and in ourselves, we can begin to act in a way that makes us better leaders.

Consider how hubris rears its head in the three areas discussed in this book:

Hubris can prevent us from being *smarter* leaders when

- We take credit for the intelligent ideas of others.
- We profess to know more than anyone else about a given topic.
- We gain political power from knowledge (or secrets) gained at the expense of team success.

Hubris can prevent us from being *faster* leaders when

- We sacrifice balance and don't take care of our health (emotional, mental, and physical).
- We do too many things at the same time and lose our ability to retain information and think clearly.

Hubris can prevent us from being *better* leaders when

- We sacrifice the best interests of our employees or other stakeholders for our own gain.
- We believe we are above the law or above compliance with ethical guidelines.

- We don't model the behaviors we wish to see. ("Do as I say, not as I do.")
- We damage our shared external environment for the short-term gain of our organization.

Perhaps you see some of your own behavior, or your past behaviors, reflected in these lists. Most people do; we're only human. And the goal of this chapter is to help us become better leaders who are more conscious of the choices we make and the actions we take on behalf of ourselves and our organizations. The goal is not perfection; it's betterment.

Let's look at one final example of the dangers of "better than" thinking and leadership hubris. It is nothing less than the fall of the Athenian empire—a classic story of "better than" thinking over-taking "better with" thinking.

Melos was a small island in the Cretan Sea. It was surrounded by several other smaller islands, all of which were members of the Athenian empire. Officially, Melos was allied with Athens' enemy in the Peloponnesian War, the Spartans, because Melos was originally a Spartan colony. The Melians, however, remained neutral during the Peloponnesian War. The Athenians arrived off the coast and demanded that the Melians become part of the Athenian empire, but the Melians asked to remain neutral.[1]

At the time, a debate took place between two factions in the Athenian senate. One believed they should invade and exercise their vast

TRY THIS

Hubris Inquiry

If you think you're beyond reproach—think again. Most of us are complicit in something we don't believe in.

Ask yourself: What am I complicit in? What do I not support that my company is doing? What personally can I change to address that issue that is in opposition to my value system? What am I gaining from *not* challenging what I don't like or believe in?

military strength over the small island: "We can crush the colony because might makes right." The other opposed the takeover: "We'll lose our moral authority if we adopt this strategy."

As it turns out, the "might is right" faction won the debate. The Athenians sent a fleet to Melos, slaughtered the men, and sold the women and children into slavery. By doing this, the Athenians, who justified this taking of Melos, lost their moral authority among their own people. The Athenian public began to see their leaders as morally bankrupt. Within fifty years, the entire Athenian empire had collapsed, partly due to the decision that sold the Athenian soul for perceived profit.[2]

In addition to the problems associated with hubris in leaders past and present, it seems that honor has been taken out of the call to leadership. I believe there is an honor that is bestowed on those who take up the mantle of leading. It is an honor and, therefore, a responsibility. What happens when "better than" takes precedence over "better with"? Honor goes out the window.

The wave of corporate accounting scandals in the early 2000s has been a frightening example of "honor-less" leadership. Enron and Arthur Andersen collapsed. Executives from Adelphia Communications were arrested for fraud. A jury convicted Tyco executive Dennis Koslowski on thirty counts of grand larceny, securities fraud, conspiracy, and falsifying documents. Fannie Mae substantially underreported its profit. Qwest Communications admitted that an internal review found that it incorrectly accounted for $1.16 billion in sales. Halliburton improperly booked $100 million in annual construction cost overruns before customers agreed to pay for them. Global Crossing engaged in network capacity "swaps" with other carriers to inflate revenue and ended up in Chapter 11. The list could go on and on, not to mention all the privately owned, smaller companies that take dishonorable actions but don't make the front page of the papers.

Where is the nobility, the self-sacrifice, the responsibility that comes with leadership? Is honor in leadership a thing of the past? Is our corporate landscape so corrupt that we should give up? Never. True leadership, which we will see demonstrated over and over again, is the ability to envision and bring about a positive change through influencing and guiding a group toward that change.

Honor is the bridge between "better than" and "better with." When you lead from a position of honor, you are taking responsibility with respect for others, even if they are your competitors. You are holding others in high esteem. You are honoring the greater good today and into the future.

WHAT LEGACY WILL YOU LEAD?

Now let's apply all these lessons of hubris and honor (or should I say warnings?) to our own roles as leaders. I believe this next question is the most important inquiry of this book:

> WHEN HISTORY LOOKS BACK ON
> YOUR LEADERSHIP, WHAT WOULD
> YOU LIKE THE BOOKS TO SAY?
> WHAT LEGACY WILL YOU LEAVE?

All of us leave a legacy. Or to be more precise to the topic at hand, we *lead* a legacy. For some people, this means an inheritance for our children or grandchildren. For others, it means an organization, program, or service we've created that we will hand over to those who come next. And for all of us, it means the difference we make in the lives of the people we encounter through the many years of our lives and our leadership.

One of the most powerful coaching exercises I've seen in action involves asking leaders to write a legacy statement. Similar to a company's mission statement, a legacy statement expresses what you value and what contribution you wish to make to the world—and how you plan to make this happen. Your legacy statement really represents the culmination, in writing, of your desires to be smarter, faster, and better: it shows what you want to learn and teach, how you want to live each day and what is most meaningful to you.

Creating a legacy statement and acting on it can be life changing. For example, Kelley Shimansky, a human resources executive at a public company with headquarters in Maine, has spent real time defining her personal legacy statement. She says she works hard to tie her daily actions at home and at work to her legacy statement. She keeps a copy of it in her daily planner for easy access. Kelley thinks of her legacy statement like this: "If I were not on this Earth anymore, what would I want to be known as?"

"You need to know what end result you want to achieve in order to move forward," Kelley says about the legacy statement. "Steve [Steve Goldberg, the coach who taught the legacy statement session Kelley attended] asked, 'What is the legacy you want to leave in your life, career, and organization? What are the things you need to be doing to sustain your legacy energy? What do you need to do to be able to make it all happen?'"

Here is Kelley's legacy statement and supporting strategy:

What Is the Legacy I Want to Leave in My Life, My Career, and My Organization?

- *A loving mother and life partner* who nurtured, supported, and learned from those she loved most.

- *A teacher and learner* who remained open and humble as she coached and mentored others. Those who worked with and for her grew into respected leaders of people, organizations, and communities.

- *A leader* who consistently created individual and collective success wherever she went and demonstrated the value of effective leadership at an individual and a collective level to every organization with which she worked.

- *One who gave back* by sharing her time and energy with a passion that demonstrated her respect for those in need and inspired those around her to give their time and talents to the issues that they felt most strongly about.

What Are the Things I Need to Be Doing to Sustain My Legacy Energy?

- Continue to give my children all of my attention and energy when we are together.

- Consciously invest in refocusing on my relationship with my husband as life partners given our new context as parents.

- Continue to balance the first two with by investing in myself physically and emotionally.

- Reinvent the Organizational Development role, create plans, and demonstrate successes that build sponsorship and support for the role.

- Focus daily on leading the team.

- Continue efforts at networking but improve the quality of those I am networking with.

- Attend two events a year that get me out of the office and shift my paradigm enough to reenergize me; share what I learn with others.

- Mentor and share with others; learn from them.

- Close my mouth, listen, ask questions.

- Do it! Start down the leadership development strategy path.

- Work with Board Network to identify the ideal nonprofit that taps into my passion and meets their needs.

Kelley says, "If you don't understand yourself, I don't know how you can lead. Effective leaders understand their strengths and weaknesses, understand themselves. That requires some level of introspection, like a legacy statement. It keeps you in touch with yourself when there are so many things pulling you. It helps you define for yourself what success and leadership look like. Writing the statement was hard, but the real challenge is referring back to it and really using it every day."

The legacy statement offers a different perspective on the act of goal setting. It achieves more meaningful results than simply asking, What do you want to achieve at work? The key question behind the legacy statement: Am I having the impact I wish to have?

LEADING A LEGACY IN YOUR ORGANIZATION: THE STATEMENT OF PURPOSE

In the best-selling business book *Built to Last,* Jim Collins and Jerry Porras outlined the differences between what they called "visionary companies," who were at the top of their industry, and their number two competitors. How did leading a legacy relate to the visionary companies? In seventeen of eighteen pairs in their analysis, the visionary companies were driven more by ideology and less

TRY THIS

Legacy Statement

Refer back to your values exercise. What do you care deeply about? Who do you wish to be? What change do you wish to see in the world?

Take time to think about this, and to refine and shift the language until it works for you as a living document you can refer to every day to make sure you are always working toward the legacy you want to leave.

Step 1. Define the top roles you play in your life. For example: husband, father, son, leader, citizen, philanthropist.

Step 2. For each role, define what it is you would like to do in your lifetime, what you would like to leave in your wake.

Step 3. To support the goals you have for each role, define how you will keep your energy alive for each one. What systems will you have in place, what commitments will you make to see that you leave the legacy you want?

Remember, this statement will change with time. As we expand our vision of what is possible, we expand our definitions of what we can and will achieve.

by pure profit motivation.[3] "Like the fundamental ideals of a great nation, church, school, or any other enduring institution, core ideology in a visionary company is a set of basic precepts that plant a fixed stake in the ground: This is who we are; this is what we stand for; this is what we're all about.

Once you know what legacy you want to leave, it's time to focus on how you can build that legacy in the here and now, in your current position at your current organization. What is the purpose of your role as a leader in your current context? What is the purpose of your organization? Just as a leader needs a legacy statement, an organization needs a statement of purpose. I am a great advocate for statements of purpose rather than mission statements. A purpose is a reason for being. It's clear, straightforward, and positive.

Most organizations have a mission statement on their wall—but do they really know how to apply them?

Case Study: The Tattered Cover

Coach and consultant Susan Spero tells this story of a legacy-driven leader she admires greatly:

> Tattered Cover is a locally owned independent bookseller in Denver, Colorado. It was started in the early 1970s by Joyce Meskis. Joyce put comfy, oversized chairs all over, and encouraged people to sit down, get comfortable, curl up, and read—even if they didn't buy the book.
>
> Today, Tattered Cover has grown to three stores, the largest is four or five floors and they have hundreds of employees. Now they have a coffee bar and restaurant too. There are still nooks, crannies, overstuffed chairs, and places to sit and read, even though it's huge.
>
> I've never met a rude employee, even at Christmastime when customers are six deep at every register. Their staff seems thrilled to help you [in a sincere way] and seems to know where every book is or know how to find out.
>
> Several years ago, I wrote Meskis, introduced myself as a management consultant, and said, "I've been your customer since you opened the first store and have watched you maintain the same culture in spite of your growth. Could I possibly have thirty minutes of your time to ask you how you've done that?" She called right back and gave me [exactly] thirty minutes in her office. She said:
>
> "I'm clear about my *purpose, and the purpose of the store:* to connect people with books. I know that many people are not comfortable with books and reading, hence the chairs, small nooks and crannies . . . now coffee and food to encourage comfort, and to encourage customers to stay in the store and see it as their own place to relax and enjoy.
>
> "I know people use us like a library . . . they call with reference questions, then don't buy the books. Some try to return books here that were bought elsewhere.
>
> "We don't worry about that . . . it makes them loyal customers."

Ask any Denverite: Tattered Cover customers are fiercely loyal . . . almost cult-like! Many of us take out-of-town visitors there as one of the points of interest, like the museums and the state capitol.

A year or two ago, they started a "Tattered Cover Gives Back" program that customers join at no charge, and get a card with a number on it. They show the card every time they shop. Then a percentage of their purchase goes to a charity. Giving back to the community is clearly another value. They also have lots and lots of events—not just book signings but readings, drama, and music. They've had a *big* Harry Potter party complete with costumes from 10 P.M. to midnight for each of the book releases, all fostering more fierce customer loyalty.

To help employees be very clear about values and priorities of an organization:

1. The purpose and values must be clear and easily [and repeatedly] communicated—not just in words but in action.
2. The team must look for ways to constantly weave those messages into every activity in the organization.
3. Top management must also find ways to reward employees for demonstrating those values and purpose-related things in all they that do.

As a result, I as a long-time customer am also fiercely loyal. I love going there, even if I don't end up buying anything. It feels nice to just be there, not to mention shop there. TC is such a wonderful, customer-focused, generous organization, and the chains are threatening TC and all the other independent bookstores in a serious way.

I especially admire and appreciate Joyce Meskis as a community leader and business owner because of how she has carefully shaped, nurtured, and maintained a very clear and values-driven culture, in spite of the phenomenal growth of her stores. In person, she comes across as a quiet, introverted person. She clearly is very bright, has very strongly held values, and has the courage and skills to help her employees live and work by those values on a daily basis.

Joyce Meskis is not concerned with competing with the big chain stores. She's focused on her purpose and that of her company. She's also focused on maintaining a culture that supports that purpose. She's focused on maintaining excellent customer experiences, from the moment you walk in the door. She's creating a community that is loyal and steadfast.

What is the purpose of your organization? What is the purpose of your leadership according to your organization? Does your organization have a statement of purpose? Tattered Cover *connects people to books*. What does your company do?

Stories like the Tattered Cover happen in big corporations, too. In true Appreciative Inquiry fashion, when Jim Collins and Jerry Porras put together the research study that would become the business best-seller *Built to Last*, they asked, "What makes the truly exceptional companies different from the other companies?" They came up with a set of powerful truths about what they call visionary companies—companies that are the leaders in their industry—and what makes them better. Their first discovery? That the companies that are indeed built to last have a purpose that is greater than the bottom line.

They name companies like Merck, Ford, Johnson & Johnson, Motorola, and Marriott for their focus on a purpose that is "more than profits."

"Contrary to business school doctrine, we did not find 'maximizing shareholder wealth' or 'profit maximization' as the dominant driving force or primary objective through the history of most of the visionary companies. They have tended to pursue a cluster of objectives, of which making money is only one—and not necessarily the primary one."[4] In visionary companies profitability is necessary but not the end game. It enables the organization to fulfill its other goals or purposes.

HOW TO CLARIFY YOUR CURRENT PURPOSE

In working with an entrepreneur I'll call Brad, I discovered the clarifying power of organizational purpose statements. Brad was at a loss about the direction of his small business. He was a minor success as a branding consultant, but he had no passion for his work. He kept comparing himself to colleagues he had worked with before whose businesses were more profitable than his. That "better than" thinking was part of a negative spiral he was beginning to fall into. He was burnt out, frustrated, and wanted to really look at his purpose as a leader. As his coach, I took him through an identity creation exercise. We decided to name five directions his company could pursue, and have him name the *purpose* he would be expressing as the leader of each direction. These were the five directions we came up with:

- Keep doing what I'm doing. My purpose = to build the business.
- Close the company and go back to school. My purpose = to discover my purpose.
- Stop working with nonprofits and keep working with entrepreneurs. My purpose = to use my creativity to help other people build their businesses.
- Close the company and get a corporate job. My purpose = to get back my equilibrium financially.
- Add video production to what I do. My purpose = to make life more interesting and spice things up.

"Well, changing my customers to entrepreneurs is the most compelling," he said, "because I have passion around it. I really enjoy getting entrepreneurs to start thinking about their brand. I get to teach them things they haven't thought about, and I get to be really creative. When I think about that one, I think it might even be fun to rebrand myself."

Brad came up with the following purpose statement for his revitalized business:

"Our purpose is to build the visibility of growing entrepreneurial businesses."

He also created a personal one: "To be a creative pragmatist," which he defined as being creative with a purpose—using his creativity outside of fine art to do something that would help him and others to be successful.

He followed with an expansion of his envisioned services: "We do this through logo development, collateral design, product packaging, and events planning, all based on a clear brand platform." Nice and clear! Creating a purpose statement was a great new start for Brad's business. He got so excited that he stopped focusing on his perceived competition and started focusing on developing his own brand—developing what was unique and special about his work that differentiated him from others. Within a year, Brad was enjoying his work more than he ever had, and his company had expanded and was growing more profitable quarterly.

SUCCESS AND POWER

Now that we have talked about purpose, let's address a pair of key terms that affect your becoming a "better with" leader: *success* and

---

TRY THIS

Writing a Statement of Purpose

To write a statement of purpose for your organization, I recommend these guidelines, which I appropriated from non-profit expert Janel M. Radke's guidelines for writing an organizational mission statement:[5]

To craft your organization's statement of purpose, answer the following questions:

1. What are the opportunities or needs that our organization exists to address? (This is the purpose of the organization.)

2. What are we doing to address these needs? (This is the business of the organization.)

3. What legacy do we want our organization to leave, or what principles or beliefs guide our work? (This represents the values of the organization.)

Radke also recommends that a mission statement or statement of purpose should . . .

- Express the organization's purpose in a way that is inspiring and positive
- Be articulated in a way that is convincing and easy to grasp (not convoluted or wordy)
- Use active verbs to describe what you do
- Be free of industry jargon

power. Few words hold as much intrigue. It is impossible to talk about leadership without addressing success and power and what they have come to mean in society, and in the business world in particular. Perhaps these words are even mentioned in your legacy statement or your organization's purpose statement.

I don't think success and power are inherently bad or good words; rather, I think they hold different meanings for every person. To be a better leader, you must come to your own decision about what success and power mean to you and how they play out in your leadership role. The rest of this chapter focuses on these two words and your relationship with them as you work toward becoming a "better with" leader.

What Does Success Mean to You?

Smarter, faster, better . . . what is the end result? Many people would answer, "Success." But what defines leadership success? This is an intensely personal inquiry, and the answer is again unique to you. If your goal in becoming smarter, faster, and better is to achieve *success,* you need to define clearly what that means.

There are two kinds of success. One is transitory: the accomplishment of a great achievement. It can include recognition by others, material rewards, and a finite sense of pride or satisfaction.

The other offers true fulfillment. That is what you've pondered in your legacy statement: Who do you want to be in your life? What impact do you want to have? That kind of success is not transitory or fleeting. It is grounded in the internal, not external, world. When we believe our success depends on the external world—external validation and external opportunities—we are missing a sense of personal power. It's the transition from an external locus of control to an internal locus of control that is the task of fulfillment.

Ralph Waldo Emerson sums it up:

> To laugh often and love much, to win the respect of intelligent persons and the affection of children, to earn the approbation of honest critics, and to endure the betrayal of false friends, to appreciate beauty; to find the best in others; to give of oneself. To leave the world a bit better, whether by a healthy child, a garden patch, or a

redeemed social condition; to have played and laughed with enthusiasm and sung with exultation; to know that one has breathed easier because you have lived—To have succeeded.

About a year ago I was delivering a speech at a Midwestern insurance company, as an opening to an off-site retreat where I was to help leaders across the company get more motivated and see ways to inspire their own teams. The head of the business unit introduced me, and in his introduction he said, "Remember, we're not here to be nice people. We're here to produce shareholder value, to make the stock more valuable. That's why corporations exist. That is the only measure by which we succeed or fail as a company, and by which we succeed or fail as leaders." His body language echoed his words. He stood hunched over, eyes drooping and sad, as if he was being crushed by the weight of this mighty responsibility.

This was not exactly the most motivating and inspiring leadership moment. This group of values-driven leaders, who had just one day earlier been talking about how to better serve people in their geographic areas, and how their work was really about helping people in desperate situations to recover their lives, began squirming in their chairs. They weren't in their jobs just to make stock more valuable—were they? Was all that other stuff just fluff?

How would you have felt in the same situation, if you had been in that audience? Do you believe organizations exist only to move the stock price up? Do you lead for that purpose alone? Don't all organizations exist to serve a need? Maybe the needs of another business that needs a widget to operate a key piece of machinery that delivers mail on time? Maybe a drug that cures cancer, or a breakfast bar that is easy to eat on the go and provides quick nutrition? There are millions of products and services, and without serving a need or desire, those products and services disappear quickly in a competitive marketplace.

I would argue that success is defined by other currencies, such as relationships, influence, survival in a challenging global environment, and most of all by our contribution to our communities and society overall.

If you don't think so, ask some of the up-and-coming generation, known as Generation Y and "Millennials," who are starting in the ranks of your employees. In *Millennials Rising,* Neil Howe and William Strauss characterize this generation (born from around 1977 to 1995) as optimistic, team players, rule followers, smart, watched over, trusting, on the cutting edge, and having a capacity for greatness.

These young people are surely the most globally aware and racially diverse generation in history. According to a study by Merrill Associates, "Diversity is a value for this generation and thus they display an incredible tolerance and a slowness to judge other people. . . . True products of the civil rights movement, these young people do not display the same prejudices that have divided earlier generations. They are great team members, ignoring gender and racial biases to work with anyone to accomplish common goals."[6]

Eric Chester, in *Employing Generation Why?,* tells us more about this group:

> Sometimes referred to as the over-achieving, over- scheduled generation, their lives have been programmed from the beginning with school, sports, arts, clubs and activities. They have never known the slow pace of life of their grandparents, when mail was delivered by the Postal Service not the Internet. In the first quarter of the century change occurred over ten to fifteen year periods. Now it occurs in months. The high tech media driven society of today has opened the world and exposed these young people to more than previous generations even dreamed of. They have been programmed to live life at a rapid pace to keep up with the constant change that is happening around them. They see life as a drop down menu of choices that can be accessed immediately with the click of a mouse. Speed, change and uncertainty are normal for Ys.[7]

We are also already starting to see this generation's volunteerism. Volunteerism is at an all-time high, thanks to the unprecedented involvement of Generation Y members, who are putting their time where their hearts are. Chester points out that it is hard to find an organized student club, sport, or activity where participants aren't involved in some type of community service. As he notes, soccer teams stick around after their games to clean up the park. Student councils visit nursing homes, paint homes for the elderly, and hold canned food drives.

According to Robert Putnam in *Bowling Alone,* America might be on the cusp of a new period of civic renewal, especially if this youthful volunteerism persists into adulthood and begins to expand beyond individual care toward a broader engagement with social and political issues. This generation is all about making their world better.

What makes this civic-minded, globally aware, well-educated, and diverse generation different? It's worth repeating the Howe and Strauss characterization: optimistic, team players, rule followers, smart, watched over, trusting, on the cutting edge, and having a capacity for greatness.

What does this mean for those who lead Generation Y and Millennial workers? According to Merrill, young people are looking for ways to make their mark and find their causes. When the match is right with an organization, they are highly committed and fiercely loyal. Keep in mind that the youngest members of your workforce are looking for purpose and something to believe in. They need to know the companies they work for have the greater good in mind, and that they will have a positive impact through their involvement.

TRY THIS

Defining Success for Yourself

Reflect back on your values.

What does success mean to you?

When do you or will you know you are a successful leader?

Write a paragraph on your personal definition of success and see if this is reflected in your legacy statement. If not, go back and revise your legacy statement to reflect your vision of success.

THE GOAL OF SHARED SUCCESS

To integrate "better with" into your definition of success, there is one last critical principle to embrace. You must want success that is not just your own. You must strive for shared success, for win-win outcomes. For your whole organization to thrive, not just the top layer. For leaders, a key function is to set an example. Do you live up to your word? Do you set the kind of example people want to follow? And in the words of a wise executive I once met: "Am I making this the kind of company I would want my kids to work for?"

At this point, I would suggest returning to your organizational purpose statement and taking it to the next level—add a sentence to your statement about what success will look like if your organization's work stays true to its purpose. What kind of success will you help build for your stakeholders—employees, board members, customers, or others whose lives you touch?

Let's return to Brad and his desire to change his client base from nonprofits to entrepreneurs. Here was Brad's organizational purpose statement:

"Our purpose is to build the visibility of growing entrepreneurial businesses. We do this through logo development, collateral design, product packaging, and events planning, all based on a clear brand platform."

To express the goal of shared success, Brad might add a sentence like this:

"Our goal is to build the success of our clients' businesses in order to build our business."

As another example, Rob Lederer, a management and operations consultant and part-owner of a factory in Connecticut, is known for caring deeply about his workforce. He says,

> There are ten employees out of four hundred in supervisory roles in the factory who have been there over ten years each. They are all very loyal, very hard workers and really nice guys, but recently they've felt in over their heads because the company has outgrown them.
>
> I'm particularly thinking of Raphael, the shipping manager, and two other employees. These are people who love the company. This is their life and their coworkers are part of each other's families. We've got a factory, in fact an entire business, that is handling

more orders than it ever has, and dropping more orders than it ever has—10 percent, which in our industry is enormous. This has to do with structural issues that a larger business could handle, but ours is really weak under the stress of all of the new work. We need people who can handle more elevated operations, who are trained in business and in shipping. We want to show employees that the things we're doing to make the company operate more efficiently are important.

We want to keep our employees' spirits up, and here we are about to fire one of our most loyal and popular people, because he isn't capable of doing what we need in this new phase. He helped us be the company we are. So what do we do for Raphael? The answer is that we are going to tell him that we have hired someone to take the position that he's been in, but we're going to keep him on in the department at the same pay rate for six months, so that he has time to find another job, because we know how much he cares about this company, and what he's done for us. We want him to succeed.

We told Raphael, anytime you get a job, you can leave. In six months we may find another position for you that our company has a need for, where you can succeed. If so, we'll pay you the pay rate for that position, but you'll be able to succeed so you'll have job security. It will be hard for him, because this job is so important to him. We need to take care of him. Our workforce is important to us. Even though he's no longer right for the job, this is how we need to take care of our own.

This comes back to the purpose of our company. We reflect a loyalty and commitment to our people, the same kind they have given to us. Also, this is demonstrating that we aren't blaming anyone for the problems that are happening—we see that it's a new phase in our corporate growth. Finally, we're sending a message that we all need to succeed and perform in our positions, and that if you don't fit, you need to find another place. We want a win-win for everyone here. And we know we attract the best people through our reputation for being great to our employees.

As you can see, definitions of success can change and evolve, but when you stay true to your purpose, values, and "better with" leadership mind-set, you can find ways to be successful even in the most challenging situations.

WHAT DOES POWER MEAN TO YOU?

What are your first memories of feeling powerful?

Really take a moment to think about that question. Where were you? How old were you? What kind of power did you feel? Was it physical? Was it achievement? Did it involve bullying someone? Manipulating your mom into giving you ice cream and cake for breakfast? Our first experiences of power are often moments of transition, where we begin to understand that we can have an impact on the world around us.

For leaders, power is one of the main ways of relating to the world. It has everything to do with how much we can leave behind "better than" and move to "better with."

Let's look at power at its most primal level. As we discussed in Part One, Abraham Maslow's hierarchy of needs, introduced in the late 1960s, is a famous model for human development (see Maslow's Hierarchy on next page). At the base of the model, organized as a triangle, is survival at the physical level (food, water). The next step is safety (shelter, comfort), then comes love, esteem, and finally at the top is "self-actualization." Self-actualization meant that people were "fully functional" and possessed a "healthy personality." It also meant the people on this level thought and acted purely of their own volition, rather than conforming to social norms, and also operated with a sense of "justice." They are willing to share power for the good of their community.

Maslow believed that people are born good, and that they are driven by needs at each level. Ethics are determined by our place in the hierarchy. If we need food, we are not yet capable of focusing our attention on our self-esteem; we must address the immediate need for survival first. All our power is placed on the need for survival. Maslow believed that people do not lie, cheat, or steal for the joy of it, but because they have an unmet need driving that behavior. While leaders today are not lacking in food or shelter or other basic needs, they may have an unmet desire for power. If a leader—no matter how wealthy, high-status, educated, and apparently successful—feels threatened, then that leader is involved in a fight for survival and may well act as unethically and selfishly as a wild animal in search of food.

What's missing from Maslow's model is something he conceived of later in his career, after the dissemination of his famous

MASLOW'S HIERARCHY.

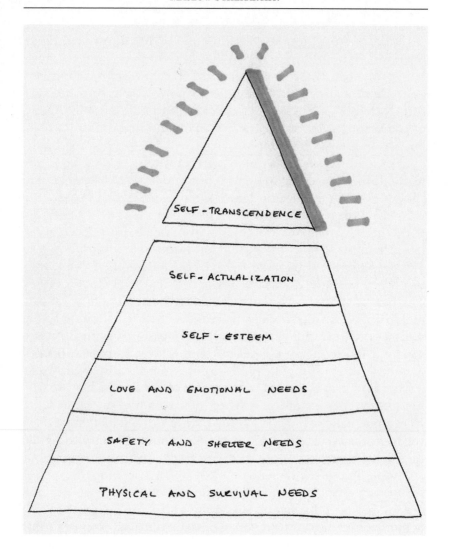

Source: Adapted from C. George Boeree, 1998.[8]

model. In his later years Maslow believed that at the top of the pyramid, above self-actualization, there was a final level, self-transcendence. At this point, human beings are able to disconnect from the self and put others first. This is the place of giving back to the community, to others, and transcending the world of ego-driven decisions. This is the top level of "better with."

What if the path of leadership turns out to mirror Maslow's hierarchy? It would mean that the greatest leaders would achieve a level of self-transcendence, and would set aside their own needs for the good of their people and the good of the external environment. They would demonstrate "power with" others rather than "power over" others. They would share their power for the greater good of their companies and communities, and not hoard it for their own survival.

Jim Collins, author of *Good to Great*, supports this belief. He demonstrates through research that leaders who have achieved self-transcendence (which he refers to as Level 5) are capable of leading organizations to greater and greater levels of achievement. "Level 5 leaders channel their ego needs away from themselves and into the larger goal of building a great company. It's not that Level 5 leaders have no ego or self-interest. Indeed, they are incredibly ambitious—but their ambition is first and foremost for the institution, not themselves."[9]

Remember the two types of success? The first, the transitory, finite experience of success, is possible at any level of Maslow's hierarchy. The second, the lasting kind, is possible only upon entry into the top two tiers of the pyramid.

When leaders work to enhance their personal standing and operate from self-interest and ego, they are trying to be "better than" others. When leaders transcend their self-interest, work toward a greater purpose—toward the greater good of others—then they are working "better with."

MOVING FROM POWER OVER TO POWER WITH: POWER GRID ASSESSMENT

You're now invited to take a brief assessment to determine your relationship with power, with the goal of developing added self-awareness. When are you operating at the top of Maslow's pyramid? What is your default style? Would your answers be different under stress?

Instructions:

Read each statement below. Circle the number (1–5) to indicate the extent (1 = least, 3 = neutral, 5 = most) that the statement reflects your beliefs, attitudes, and behaviors.

	Least Like Me		Neutral		Most Like Me
1. It is important to be seen meeting with the influential leaders in my field.	1	2	3	4	5
2. I get a strong sense of satisfaction from a job done right.	1	2	3	4	5
3. I insist that all important decisions must be made by me.	1	2	3	4	5
4. The collective wisdom of an organization provides its direction and purpose.	1	2	3	4	5
5. A leader is guided by a strong sense of purpose.	1	2	3	4	5
6. An organization is most effective when it has a clear vision that informs all decisions.	1	2	3	4	5
7. Self-confidence is a critical leadership trait.	1	2	3	4	5
8. I have often felt a strong energy in the room when we have resolved a critical issue.	1	2	3	4	5
9. Awards and recognition I have received are a testament to the effectiveness of my leadership.	1	2	3	4	5
10. My subordinates need to be available when I call them.	1	2	3	4	5
11. When something needs to be done right, I am usually the best one to do it.	1	2	3	4	5

	Least Like Me		Neutral		Most Like Me
12. Leaders' lifestyle should reflect the importance of their position.	1	2	3	4	5
13. Sometimes leaders must make decisions based on what is moral and just.	1	2	3	4	5
14. I have witnessed greatness in the people around me as they tackle the tasks of this organization.	1	2	3	4	5
15. When an employee makes a mistake, the incident must be written up and placed in the employee's personnel file.	1	2	3	4	5
16. We, in this organization, are not the same people as we were when we started down this path.	1	2	3	4	5
17. Fear is a tool I use in increasing productivity.	1	2	3	4	5
18. I wish I could clone myself so I could properly perform all the tasks for which I am responsible.	1	2	3	4	5
19. The strength of my convictions has inspired others to do great things.	1	2	3	4	5
20. I value that I am recognized as a leader in my field.	1	2	3	4	5
21. My contributions have brought me to the leadership position I now hold.	1	2	3	4	5
22. When there is a controversy within my organization, I am confident that my understanding of the situation will lead us to the solution.	1	2	3	4	5

	Least Like Me	Neutral		Most Like Me
23. Mistakes are not tolerated under my leadership.	1	2	3	4	5
24. I know that a higher power/ God has contributed to the success of our organization.	1	2	3	4	5
25. My goal is to empower others in my organization to be the best they can be.	1	2	3	4	5

KEY:

Add your scores for each question and obtain a sum for each column.

A	B	C	D	E
3. _____	1. _____	2. _____	5. _____	4. _____
10. _____	9. _____	7. _____	6. _____	8. _____
15. _____	12. _____	11. _____	13. _____	14. _____
17. _____	20. _____	18. _____	19. _____	16. _____
23. _____	21. _____	22. _____	25. _____	24. _____
Sum _____	Sum _____	Sum _____	Sum _____	Sum _____

Which sum is highest? This is your primary approach to power and leadership. The second highest sum is your secondary approach to power and leadership.

A = Power Over
B = Power from Outside
C = Power from Inside
D = Power from Meaning
E = Power With (All are one)

ASSESSMENT DEBRIEF: FIVE LEVELS OF POWER CONSCIOUSNESS

Along with Maslow's hierarchy comes a step-by-step model for understanding our personal relationship to power. Each stage offers new ways of working with power, and as you make the transition from the first stage (power over) up the ladder to the fifth state (power with) your ability to become an enduring, effective, fulfilled leader grows exponentially. By understanding your own personal relationship to power, you can determine any gaps between where you are and where you want to be. By understanding your own relationship to power, you can better understand the impact you have on others and the perceptions you create in the workplace.

What kind of power is the most effective in leadership? The answer isn't simple—until we look at what kind of leader you want to be. If you want to lead by force, what are the consequences? Power by force is the greatest risk. As we move up the ladder, the consequences of our leadership actions change.

The "Power Grid" on the next page refers to a flexible model of our personal relationships to power. We are not all consistently fixed at one point of this chart, but instead we fluctuate in our use and consciousness of leadership power. You will also see that each level of power has a "shadow side," a negative aspect associated with it. That shadow is important to be aware of. Many of us don't pay attention to the negative perceptions of our personal strengths, and this grid can be a guide to themes to look for.

Power Over

We all know those dominant leaders: alpha leaders, whether male or female, who need to be large and in charge. They don't explain their instructions, they just give them. They expect everyone to do what they say, even when they haven't established any credibility. They make tough decisions based on the idea that might makes right. They're the boss, after all!

What is the shadow side of this "power over" leadership? The dominant leader lives life from a polarized perspective. Either it's black or white, good or bad, powerful or victimized. The shadow of the leader who operates from "power over" is victimhood. Those who stay within the parameters of "power over" have two options—dominance power or complete lack of power. The "power over" leader is fighting for survival.

Abraham Maslow's view on "power over" was this:

> When the jungle view of the world prevails, enlightened management is practically impossible. If all people are divided into hammers and

POWER GRID.

Stage	Consciousness	Incentive	Maslow Stage	Life-View	Emotion	Shadow	Leadership Style
1 Power Over	Dominance or submission	Emotion	Survival	Struggle	Anger	Victimhood	Force
2 Power from Outside	Prestige	External validation	Comfort	Demanding	Desire	Gluttony, endless want and need, never satiated	Charisma
3 Power from Inside	Mastery	Internal validation	Love	Hopeful	Satisfaction	Depression when disbelieving in the self	Trust
4 Power by Meaning	Purpose	Impact	Self-Actualization	Connection	Harmony	Perceived as innocent and naive	Inspiration and empowerment
5 Power With	All-are-one	Witnessing	Self-Transcendence	Presence	Reverence	Perceived as disengaged	Transformation

anvils, lambs and wolves, etc., then brotherhood, sharing of goals, identification with team objectives becomes difficult, limited, or impossible. . . . It follows that this is another principle of selection of personnel for the enlightened organization. Authoritarians must be excluded or they must be converted.[10]

Famous "Power Over" Leader: "Chainsaw" Al Dunlap. Remember Chainsaw Al? Al Dunlap believed that you had either all the power or none of it. He was the renegade CEO of Sunbeam who instituted "slash and burn" policies including abandoning all corporate charity, firing 30 percent of the company's employees, and cutting all research and development when other American companies were heavily investing in technology. He wrote a book called *Mean Business* that extolled his philosophies, and praised . . . himself. Initially, Chainsaw Al inflated Sunbeam's stock price and built value for the shareholders—but not for long. After an investigation into "bill and hold" accounting practices, the board discovered the financial ill-health of the company and gave Chainsaw Al his own walking papers.

Power from Outside

Power from outside is just like it sounds—when we are supported by our external environment we use our relationships and our external power to lead. External power might be status, wealth, title, or having a large group of constituents willing to support our leadership. The power from outside leader is seeking comfort.

The shadow side of "power from outside"? Those who crave external praise or status may never be satiated. There is an unquenchable thirst for more, and it can create obsessive thinking and focus on pleasing various constituents rather than standing up for the good of the organization.

Famous "Power from Outside" Leader: Donald Trump. Think of "The Donald" for a moment. Every time I fly into LaGuardia airport in New York City I see his giant name emblazoned on his black and gold airplane saying, "Look at me!" Not only does "The Donald" put his name on everything, he cultivates an over-the-top, dripping-with-money brand identity, even when his operations are in dire financial shape. This focus on status as power isn't unique to Mr. Trump, but he exemplifies it on a grand scale.

Power from Inside

Internal power shows up when we achieve mastery in our role, our industry. We know our own value and are willing to take risks, even when our ideas are unpopular. The power from inside leader is able to master the flow state.

The shadow side of "power from inside"? The moments of self-doubt that come from too heavy a reliance on the self rather than the group. Power from inside leaders can live too much inside their own heads and lose touch with reality, and can forget to involve others in their ideas.

Famous "Power from Inside" Leader: Martha Stewart. Notwithstanding her legal issues, Martha has a vision. She doesn't ask her team for one—it really is hers. She has an eye for detail that shows up in everything she does, and she is the key decision maker on how her business will operate from her magazine to her TV show to her home products. Her vision isn't dictated by mass-market taste; she's the one who shapes and changes those tastes through her own mastery. Like her or not, she's deriving her power not from external forces but from sheer force of will and creativity.

Power by Meaning

Power by meaning is the point at which we activate our personal sense of purpose, our values, and our convictions as the driver of our leadership. Through our convictions, we inspire and empower others. Power by meaning leaders ask, What impact am I having, and is it the impact I wish to have?

The shadow side of "power by meaning" is being perceived as naive, or perhaps not understanding how impossible the vision really is. Often power by meaning leaders will hear from others such comments as "that's impossible" or "that's not how business works."

Famous "Power by Meaning" Leader: Anita Roddick. Anita Roddick built The Body Shop with the purpose of creating profits with principles. Roddick wanted her company to help create social and environmental change in addition to money. She applies her power by meaning leadership in every area of the business, even when her tactics are at odds with accepted business practices. For instance, The Body Shop stores use their window space to display promotional posters for environmental groups and anti-animal testing instead of their own products. The Body Shop sets an example not to exploit Third World workers by paying them comparable wages to those that are earned by British workers. In the United States, Roddick has used The Body Shop stores as voter-registration sites. The Body Shop headquarters staff are given one day a month off to work with disadvantaged children. Meaning infuses every area of the business.

Power With

This is the stage at which all power is shared. In fact, the leaders who function in this stage often reject traditional power and put it in the hands of the larger group. Their personal leadership power is granted by the people, rather than taken by the leader. They often see their work in leadership as sacred. It is virtually impossible to be in this state all the time, but leaders should aspire to moments of this purely selfless leadership—just as those of us who practice meditation cannot all be as peaceful as the Dalai Lama, but we can feel moments of that state of oneness with all things.

Famous "Power With" Leader: The Dalai Lama Tenzin Gyatso

> *His Holiness the 14th the Dalai Lama Tenzin Gyatso, is the head of state and spiritual leader of the Tibetan people. He was born Lhamo Dhondrub on 6 July 1935, in a small village called Taktser in northeastern Tibet. Born to a peasant family, His Holiness was recognized at the age of two, in accordance with Tibetan tradition, as the reincarnation of his predecessor the 13th Dalai Lama, and thus an incarnation of Avalokitesvara, the Buddha of Compassion.*
> —THE OFFICE OF TIBET

The Dalai Lama has been the head of state for the Tibetan people since 1950, right after the Chinese People's Liberation Army invaded Tibet. With more than 120,000 Tibetans in exile, the Dalai Lama has worked tirelessly to preserve the Tibetan culture and to negotiate on behalf of the Tibetan people. A Nobel Peace Prize winner, the Dalai Lama accepted his award on behalf of people who are working for peace and freedom everywhere, and spoke of the commitment to nonviolence. He is famous for his statement that despite his role as spiritual leader, he is just a simple Buddhist monk. In his Nobel lecture at the University Aula in Oslo, Norway, on December 11, 1989, he shared these thoughts:

> The realization that we are all basically the same human beings, who seek happiness and try to avoid suffering, is very helpful in developing a sense of brotherhood and sisterhood; a warm feeling of love and compassion for others. This, in turn, is essential if we are to survive in this ever-shrinking world we live in. For if we each selfishly pursue only what we believe to be in our own interest, without caring about the needs of others, we not only may end up harming others but also ourselves. This fact has become very clear during the course of this century. We know that to wage a nuclear war today for example, would be a form of suicide; or that by polluting the air or the oceans, in order to achieve some short-term benefit, we are destroying the very basis for our survival. As individuals and nations are becoming increasingly interdependent, therefore, we have no other choice than to develop what I call a sense of universal responsibility.
>
> Responsibility does not only lie with the leaders of our countries or with those who have been appointed or elected to do a particular job. It lies with each of us individually. Peace, for example, starts within each one of us. When we have inner peace, we can be at peace with those around us. When our Community is in a state of peace, it can share that peace with neighboring communities, and so on. . . . What is important is that we each make a sincere effort to take our responsibility for each other and for the natural environment we live in seriously.[11]

In *Ethics and the New Millennium,* a 2001 publication with Howard C. Cutler, the Dalai Lama speaks of "our habitual preoccupation with the self," and how we must transcend it to act out of concern for other human beings.

We need not all aspire to be exactly like the Dalai Lama, but his leadership is consistent, diplomatic, grounded in his beliefs and spirituality, representative and respectful of other traditions both religious and cultural. He has successfully built relationships with most major world powers on behalf of his people, who are less than six million in number. He is both powerful and humble, and there is much to learn from his example.

What is important about recognition of our interconnection as human beings? What is important about sharing power? The leader who practices "power with" is one who supports an enlightened organization. In the words of Jim Collins:

> Imagine if you were to build organizations designed to allow the vast majority of people to self-actualize, to discover and draw upon their true talents and creative passions, and then commit to a relentless pursuit of those activities toward a pinnacle of excellence. Then imagine if the organization were to revolve around those self-actualized individuals. The outcome would be nothing short of a Copernican revolution of work and society, catapulting us out of what future generations will look back on as the Dark Ages of management. The potential is enormous.[12]

In 1938, Maslow did summer fieldwork with the Blackfoot Indian tribe in Alberta, Canada. At the time, the Blackfoot were the only self-sustaining tribe in the region. While studying emotional security among the Blackfoot, Maslow began to learn that the Blackfoot suffered far less from self-doubt and self-consciousness than people in competitively based societies.

The Blackfoot had a leader for every important function in the tribe, and no one leader was in charge of all functions. The Blackfoot focused specifically on shared power, and their primary value was generosity, which was seen as the highest virtue. Accumulating assets or knowledge was unimpressive, but giving them away brought prestige and security within the tribe. There was a strong sense of personal responsibility from a young age. Children were expected to do many things for themselves within a loving and supportive environment. The needs of the tribe were one with the needs of the individual tribe members. Maslow's understanding of healthy teamwork, healthy organizations, and healthy leadership was vastly influenced by this culture that embodied "power with."

How do you share power? How do you empower those you lead, or tap into people with specific skill sets to lead projects with you? When we begin thinking in terms of "power with" it can remind us that we can create exponentially powerful results when power is shared. It is a level of leadership that many of us only experience on occasion, but when we do, it is truly glorious.

When I'm at my best and most appreciative, I often think about how magnificent the world could be if everyone focused on being better with others, if everyone wanted to obtain power with others and if everyone acted honorably. But my approach to the world is also realistic, so I know that these goals can be difficult to attain in the complex society in which we operate. The next chapter focuses on the actions you can take to be a legacy-focused, honorable leader in an ever-changing world. How close to your legacy statement can you live on a day-to-day basis? Let's find out.

Summary

- You can't be a better leader just for yourself. You must think about the greater impact of your leadership.
- There is nothing wrong with being competitive. There is something wrong with letting that competitiveness eclipse your ability to collaborate, create, and leverage relationships.
- Beware of hubris and "honor-less" leadership.
- Leaders should understand the legacy they want to leave behind— and how they plan to make it happen.
- A statement of purpose can help align your organization around the future results you would like to achieve.
- To be a better leader, you must come to your own decision about what success and power mean to you and how they play out in your leadership role.
- Leaders should aspire to "power with" leadership—moments of sharing, giving, collaboration, and selflessness.

CHAPTER EIGHT

GETTING BETTER ALL THE TIME

In this chapter, we will look at how you can cultivate a personal "better with" philosophy in your leadership by adding practical betterment concepts to your leadership tool kit. Integrating these concepts into your leadership can help you on the path of leading a legacy of which you can be proud. They are the tactics that will help you be better with others, from your employees to your customers to the entire world. The main concepts include the *sustainability principle*, the *path of the learner*, the *mandate of personal accountability*, the *role of the representative*, and *"coopetition."*

THE SUSTAINABILITY PRINCIPLE

> *The role the corporation needs to play in individuals' lives, the community life, and the world life is to sustain the platform upon which the corporation exists. Leaders must recognize that we live in one big system that is our planet. We can't spoil the groundwater in one area, and not expect it to show up in another area. Corporate leaders need to understand that the only way to sustain an enterprise is to pay attention to its impact on the world as a whole system.*
> —FRANKLIN JONATH

In the public, for-profit sector, it is an irrefutable truth that companies must make money in order to survive and thrive. But, as discussed in Chapter Seven, there is a second issue to address: What do corporations do with those profits? In our increasingly global, interconnected community of the twenty-first century, corporations have an additional responsibility: sustainability of our shared world. If we continue to eat up resources in order to turn a profit, eventually there will be no resources, and no profit, left.

If you want to be a better leader with the rest of the world, think about your responsibility as twofold:

- Your company must be profitable, so that your shareholders and stakeholders have some return on their work and investment.
- Your company must work in harmony with the sustainability principle: don't take what you can't replenish.

Great leaders create sustainable work practices in every attribute of their work, both individually and organizationally. The sustainability principle includes our individual and collective energy resources, our financial resources, our environmental resources, and our community resources. To be "better with" includes seeing the interconnectedness of all these things and acknowledging that we need to be better with all the resources that we tap.

Ray Anderson had his own epiphany about the sustainability principle. Let's look at his story:

Anderson, CEO of Interface, the world's largest commercial carpet manufacturer, had a serious wake-up call to his moral responsibility as a leader. In 1994, staff from Interface came together to address questions from their customers about their environmental policies. Anderson had never considered the impact of the production of his product on the environment, nor was he interested in doing so.

He was asked to come and speak to a new environmental task force about his "environmental vision." He had none. In a moment of pure synchronicity, he was given a book called *The Ecology of Commerce,* which he read with incredible focus.

In the documentary film *The Corporation* by Mark Achbar, Jennifer Abbott, and Joel Bakan,[1] Anderson says,

> It was a total change of mind-set for me, and a change of paradigm. . . . Unless we can make carpets sustainable, perhaps we don't have a place in a sustainable world. One day early in this

journey it dawned on me that the way I had been running Interface was the way of the plunderer. I had been plundering something that was not mine. It belongs to every creature on earth. I said to myself, my goodness, that the day must come, that this is illegal. That plundering is not allowed. I mean it must come, and I said, my goodness, someday people like me will end up in jail.

Currently Interface publishes a sustainability report annually and, in Anderson's words, is "climbing Mount Sustainability." As a result of Anderson's top-level commitment, Interface is at the fore-front of creating sustainability in business. The following excerpt is from their 2004 corporate sustainability report. Note the measurable data and specificity:

> "The vision is not just to change our company and eliminate our environmental footprint, but through the power of our influence on others to become restorative," said Ray Anderson, founder and chairman of Interface, Inc. "In nine years, at the end of 2003, we had progressed about one-third of the way from where we started in 1994, toward our goal of zero footprint—what we call the top of Mount Sustainability. To name a few relevant metrics:
>
> * Carbon intensity, down one-third.
>
> * Greenhouse gases down 46 percent absolute.
>
> * Number of smokestacks reduced by 33 percent, number of effluent pipes reduced by 47 percent, with water usage down 78 percent per yard of carpet tile and 40 percent per yard of broadloom.
>
> This reduced footprint is embodied in every product we produce. As we perform life cycle assessments on our products, we are moving toward evaluating our manufacturing facilities on the basis of the cumulative impact of all the products a facility produces; and we are doing this worldwide.
>
> Anderson looks to the future: "The remaining two-thirds of Mount Sustainability is twice as high as the one-third we have traversed. Looking ahead to the next 10 years at Interface if we are successful in executing our plan. . . .
>
> * Waste will be halved again.
>
> * Energy will be further reduced in relative terms by half again.

- Half the remaining energy will come from renewable sources (photovoltaics, wind, biomass).

- The number of smokestacks and effluent pipes remaining will be halved.

- Half of all materials will be post consumer recycled, including a portion from nylon 6,6, said by some to be commercially impossible.

- Interface as a whole will be climate neutral.

- The Evergreen Service Agreement will be a major factor and a big competitive advantage as we move toward selling the "service" our products deliver, while retaining ownership in the products themselves, along with responsibility for recycling them.

- "ReEntry"—our reverse logistics and closed loop recycling initiative—will become a way of life.[2]

TRY THIS

Sustainability Vision

Create your own "sustainability vision" by answering the following questions:

- What is our organization's impact on our environment?
- How can we replace what we take away from our earth?
- What are we doing well already that we can expand on?
- How can a sustainability initiative enrich the lives, and the loyalty, of the workforce?
- How can a sustainability initiative enrich the lives, and the loyalty, of the customer base?
- How can investing in sustainable practices help our bottom line to grow?

Think of who you might enroll to explore this issue in your organization. Is there a group of high-potential leaders who could be challenged with researching and developing solutions? Can you appoint a sustainability champion if you do not already have one?

THE PATH OF THE LEARNER

At this point, I invite you to return to the point raised in Part One: becoming smarter requires asking questions and being willing to let go of the need to know everything. Becoming better requires the same philosophy: embracing the path of the learner as you work on leading your legacy every day. The learner sees every bump in the road as a learning experience, every challenge as an opportunity. Instead of collapsing into despair when things go wrong, the learner takes value from all experiences and knows that such experiences help make a more effective, enduring, and fulfilled leader. Add this question to your daily tool kit:

WHAT CAN I LEARN FROM THIS EXPERIENCE,
CHALLENGE, OR MISTAKE THAT WILL MAKE
ME A BETTER LEADER IN THE FUTURE?

If we as leaders adopt the viewpoint that everything is a learning opportunity, we will constantly grow and improve—becoming better with the people around us and certainly less frustrated by setbacks. Be aware, however, that your teachers may be different from what you expect.

LEARNING FROM HEROES

Who are your heroes? What do you know about their personal success stories? What do you admire in them and why? A rich vein of learning can be obtained from our heroes in business and in life. Take Mary, whose hero is Oprah Winfrey. During a challenging period for Mary as the general manager of a company recently acquired by a large corporation, I asked her to identify the traits she admires in Oprah as a way to cope better with her transition. She identified a top five: courage, strength, business sense, humor, and heart. I pointed out to her that those attributes also describe Mary when she is at her best. I also asked Mary to talk about how Oprah has faced big challenges, and I asked her to make it into a case study she could learn from.

Mary quickly identified two "case studies" she could learn from in watching Oprah's way of handling challenge. I asked her to

Hero Identification

Make a list of your heroes in life and in business. Get creative. . . . You can tap into anyone to learn from.

Some examples of famous heroes we've heard of from the people we coach include Jeff Bezos, Andrea Jung, Albert Einstein, Henry Ford, Colin Powell, Ronald Reagan, Sandra Day O'Connor, Techumseh, Robert Evans, Queen Elizabeth I, Henry Ford, Thomas Edison, Clara Barton, Jack Welch, Hillary Clinton, Ray Charles, Benjamin Franklin, Desmond Tutu, Bruce Lee, and Picasso.

name the action Oprah took that impressed her. She came up with the following scenarios:

First, Oprah's legal battle with the beef industry. Oprah Winfrey never backed down, and she always took the high road. She behaved with dignity and courage. She also surrounded herself with friends and trusted advisers who helped her through.

Second, the failure of her pet film project, *Beloved*. Again, with the same dignity and courage, Oprah has not let that stop her from being involved with film and still doing the best talk show on TV.

When Mary saw what she had identified as Oprah's actions, she could find the application to her own challenge. Do you have any heroes you can look to for guidance in this way?

LEARNING FROM WHO YOU DON'T WANT TO BE

Part of becoming better leaders involves avoiding behaviors that would make us worse. What do you *never* want to replicate? Have you ever had an atrocious boss? What made working there so bad? How can you learn from that person's attributes and failings? What can you learn from the experience? You can identify what the boss did, and find the opposite. If you were dealing with a micromanager, do your best never to micromanage others. If you were dealing with a screamer, remember the impact that had on you and what you'd like to do differently.

When we start having kids, we sometimes think of the attributes of our own parents that we don't like. We think, "I'll never be like that!" and then we find ourselves sounding exactly like that dreaded unfeeling or overindulgent parent. Being conscious of what you don't want to do doesn't always mean you don't do it. You have an opportunity to relearn how to lead, manage, or be the boss you always wanted but never had.

THE MANDATE OF PERSONAL ACCOUNTABILITY

Accountability really means doing what you say you will do.

When we make choices as a leader, we need to take responsibility for those choices. Choice is a difficult concept. There are things

TRY THIS

Leadership Lessons Learned

Fill in the blanks below, and track what you have learned. Use this exercise much like you would do a traditional postmortem on a project—but from the perspective of your own leadership learning.

What happened	How I responded; what actions I took; what I didn't do	The outcome was	What I would do differently	Key learnings

we cannot choose—the circumstances we are born into, the opportunities handed to us. Likewise, there are things we can choose—what we do with those circumstances and opportunities.

Leadership is filled with choices: decisions that must be made, growth opportunities that can be embraced or reprioritized, people to trust or not. When we are conscious of our choices we can then take responsibility for them.

Why is this a mandate? Because a leader who lives and acts with personal accountability may ask for it from others. If you are willing to take responsibility for your own actions in all circumstances, then you can expect this in return. Remember that personal accountability also means taking responsibility for your own happiness, fulfillment, rest, mood, problems, insecurities, ego, and all the rest of your reactions. As you learned in Part One and Part Two, you set the tone for your organization. When you are honest, values-driven, and actively trying to be better with other people, your team will follow suit.

One of my coaching colleagues shares this story about an executive who didn't take personal accountability seriously:

> This executive is one of the very few I have ever run across whom I can only characterize as "an enigma." I could never figure him out, nor could anyone else. You never knew what he was going to say or do next, and he created ongoing disruption on the executive team. He was one of the top three executives in a $2 billion-a-year business. Because he was such an expert in a much-needed capacity in the company, the president kept him around.
>
> Among other difficulties people had with him is that he would never truly take responsibility for anything. At some point, he realized he had to say he was responsible when something went awry, but he would then go back and blame someone else for it later.
>
> He was a master at getting a manufacturing plant running well, but mostly he did it all himself. He would take on a plant, within some period of time have it running smoothly and efficiently, and then move on. After he left, the plant performance would go downhill. He continually blamed plant personnel for this phenomenon.
>
> Needless to say, line employees became very resigned and disenchanted about their work. While the company was trying to improve employee engagement and morale through a variety

of methods, it was not working because of the influence of this one executive. Efforts to improve overall performance across the company would take three steps forward and two back, and, although a good trajectory of improvement was established over time, it began to reverse itself as the employee morale grew worse.

Eventually, the executive was given his walking papers. Almost immediately, you could feel the difference on the executive team and in the manufacturing plants. People were coming alive again. And the possibility for dramatic improvement in performance became a reality.

As you can see, one bad apple really can spoil the barrel—and will most definitely do so if left in a position of leadership. Better leaders take responsibility for the work of their teams, both good and bad. Remember that once you start deflecting criticism and lose the respect of your colleagues and staff, it is extremely difficult to regain their trust and loyalty. Check in with yourself periodically to make sure you are taking responsibility for all aspects of your leadership—you're the model for what you'd like to see others do.

Gary Erickson's big choice not to sell Clif Bar required him to be accountable to his own system of values, and it required something else: self-sacrifice. (Millions of dollars' worth of self-sacrifice, as he had to buy out a partner who did want to sell.) All of us who take on a leadership role are committing to represent something greater than our own interests, to be stewards of something bigger than ourselves. It's all part of the job. Winston Churchill, the night he was ushered into the role of prime minister, was awakened from a deep sleep to the announcement that France had been invaded by the Nazis. Welcome to power. Now here's the tough part: you're now responsible and now you'll have to make the big decisions. The truth about leadership is that you're in charge, for better or worse.

THE ROLE OF THE REPRESENTATIVE

Another key philosophy of "better with" leadership is the belief that leaders are not just in it for themselves. When you are in a leadership position, you are representing the needs, desires, values, and interests of a larger group. And thus, when you become

TRY THIS

Personal Accountability Inquiry

Step 1. Suspend your judgment and self-criticism.

Step 2. Think of an area of your life that you are tolerating rather than enjoying. Now ask yourself the following questions:

What do you complain about in this circumstance?

Who is responsible for your being in this situation or circumstance? What do you blame on others?

What is the gain you are getting from being in this situation or circumstance?

What choices are you making (or not making)?

What actions or omissions on your part are contributing to the situation or circumstance?

What could you change to take on full accountability for the situation?

---

better, you have a positive effect on the people you lead. For better or worse, all leaders are role models.

Leaders who are true representatives are listeners, thinkers, visionaries, and influencers. They are constantly acknowledging the power of relationships of all kinds, and they represent the multiple interests of all parties that make up the organizations they lead: customers, employees, and investors. But there is one more constituency that leaders sometimes forget to consider, although it is mentioned often: the external community.

We cannot afford to lose the external community in the leadership equation. We need to step back and acknowledge that leadership means shaping culture, getting results, and being a steward of change for people we may never meet. That change must include our greater communities, because we need the external world to survive. We are all connected. Market forces will not in themselves preserve the environmental and social systems that we depend

TRY THIS

Try a Valued Customer Survey

Customer surveys, while impersonal, can get you incredibly valuable data, depending on how you frame your questions. Ask for complaints, and that's what you'll get! Ask for what's working well, and you'll get a very different type of information, and you will get it from your satisfied customers, who are the ones who will most likely stick around. The more you keep a dialog with your happy customers, the more you solidify the relationship over time.

Valued Customer Survey

What makes our product or service valuable to you? (Circle all that apply.)

Quality, Customer Service, Economical Pricing, Product

Design, Maintenance Services, Ease of Use, Availability, Other _____.

What makes our product or service unique?

Why do you trust our brand?

When are we at our best?

What else are you looking for that we might provide?

How can we best keep in touch with you? (Circle one.)

E-mail   Phone   Mail

upon to provide our products and services. We need to acknowledge and take part in the stewardship of the whole picture.

How can you tell if you are acting as an effective representative? Seek answers from your team. And remember to seek answers with a group of people who are invested in your success but are not physically in your office or on your payroll: your customers.

An alternative (or addition) to surveying your customers is to ask your employees to role-play the part of customers. This may sound silly, but it is very effective. Electing some representative consumers can be a great way to brainstorm customer wants and needs. Instead of guessing, ask the people assigned to play the customer role what they think. You'll be surprised what you learn from employees who really get inside the customer mind-set.

Barry Cunningham, in his capacity as founder and publisher of Bloomsbury Children's Books, was the editor who discovered Harry Potter. Regarding the importance of understanding the customer mind-set and how this relates to the greater community, Cunningham says, "I choose books purely based on what I believe children will react to. If you carry the child within you, that's what works."[3] What a fantastic example of taking on the customer mind and representing their wants and needs. And what an excellent outcome: one of the best-selling children's series of all time was recognized and published after a dozen publishers had already turned it down. Most children would say that Barry Cunningham has done his part to make the world a better place—and his company would wholeheartedly agree!

COOPETITION

> *The nature of work is fundamentally changing for today's information workers. We've moved from an era of personal productivity to one of joint productivity. From tightly coupled systems and organizations, to loosely coupled interconnections between people, business processes, and work groups.*
> —RAY OZZIE, CTO, MICROSOFT, MARCH 10, 2005

> *Do not hold the delusion that your advancement is accomplished by crushing others.*
> —MARCUS TULLIUS CICERO

When you release the idea that everything in leadership and business is about being "better than," you may find yourself wondering: What about healthy competition? Competitors are always out there and must be addressed.

My answer is this: In the new era of open-system organizations and shared information, running a company needs to involve a more *cooperative competitiveness*. Better leaders understand that as humans we have a competitive aspect to us. But when we're talking about cooperation, we are really harnessing the competitive spirit of the human animal *and* the collaborative.

Think about it. When leaders create a cooperative environment, they are really invoking some form of competition: what you do with people when you ask them to cooperate is to *accentuate their differences,* and you recognize that the differences create a dynamic tension that results in greater creativity. As people are going through the cooperative process, they experience themselves and their individuality at the same time that they experience identification with the group. They understand their individual importance by seeing themselves as different and unique. Difference and uniqueness are what makes them critical to the marketplace.

The most successful team players are the ones who do not steal, cheat, or exploit; instead, they inspire others not through force but through positive example, and they *collaborate* effectively, particularly inside their own affinity group.

More than business precedent supports the need for cooperative competition. Just look at nature. Robert Wright's books on evolutionary psychology, *The Moral Animal* and *Nonzero,* demonstrate that in ecosystems, collaboration is what assists species to survive rather than become extinct. In a biological sphere—man to man, ape to ape—overly selfish behavior will lead to its own extinction. The group ends up eradicating the bad behavior. For example, think about a chimpanzee who takes too much food, picks fights, and ignores the needs of the rest of the chimp peer group. Observations have shown that the next time that chimp is starving or hurt, the group will deny access to food and help. It's a biological way to stave off chaos and disruption in a society.[4]

In evolutionary terms, the strategy of cheating, exploiting others and resources, and not transcending our selfishness is a losing game. And these days, with rampant mergers and acquisitions, you never know when your competitor may be sitting in the next office tomorrow.

The traditional view of business is that our competition is everywhere: we compete for rank inside our organization and we compete in the marketplace with other providers of the same product or service. The predominant mental model is that we in business are at war. That idea is changing.

If we look at history and give ourselves to the war model, even Sun Tzu, author of the ancient classic *The Art of War,* does not see war or conflict as good or as a desirable means to an end. He sees the highest form of warfare as avoiding it.

Sun Tzu also goes on to show that the epitome of war fighting isn't "prolonged operations, however brilliantly executed." Instead, the general who can avoid war and ironically by so doing receives no glory or acclaim is the true hero of the people and the state.[5]

Science also tells us that fighting and competing for business doesn't always work to our advantage. When we use only that mode of thinking, we're cheating ourselves of some excellent opportunities to innovate, collaborate, and focus not on beating someone but on our own unique value to our consumers. Remember from our discussion in Part One that the military general is not the right model for everyday leadership in the twenty-first century.

We need to start focusing less on fighting for small slices and more on creating a bigger pie. There are some great thinkers out there coming up with new ways to play the game of business . . . and their ideas are firmly linked to a relatively new branch of mathematics: Game Theory.

GAME THEORY AND "COOPETITION"

Game theory is a branch of mathematics with direct applications to psychology, economics, and sociology. The theory was first developed by John von Neumann. Later contributions were made by John Nash (of *A Beautiful Mind* fame), A. W. Tucker, and others.

Game theory research involves studies of the interactions among people or groups of people. Because people make use of an ever-increasing number and variety of technologies to achieve desired ends, game theory can be indirectly applied in practical pursuits such as engineering, information technology, and computer science.

Game theory enables us to model complex social interactions—like markets and capitalist-based business—through computer simulation. What game theorists have found about behavior is that cooperation is often the backbone of a well-played game.

Here's an example. In a tournament set up by R. Axelrod, computer programs were submitted that were then allowed to interact with each other as a simulated society. Upon each interaction, the programs would decide whether to cheat or cooperate. Each program would then get a score. Anatol Rapaport's winning program was called "Tit for Tat," and its strategy was very simple. On its first encounter with any program, it would cooperate. On any subsequent encounters, it would replicate what the other program had done on the previous occasion. Tit for Tat would reward cooperative behavior with its own cooperation, and would punish cheating with cheating. Finally, after many iterations of the game, Tit for Tat ended up creating the most stable, cooperative relationships in the simulated society.[6]

> *Some people see business entirely as competition. They think doing business is waging war and assume they can't win unless somebody else loses. Other people see business entirely as cooperative teams and partnerships. But business is both cooperation and competition. It's coopetition.*
> —ADAM BRANDENBURGER AND BARRY NALEBUFF

Adam Brandenburger and Barry Nalebuff's best-seller *Coopetition* takes recent developments in game theory and applies the thinking to business. The key take-away? "Better with" is a more viable strategy than "better than." There are new ways of thinking about the marketplace, particularly as an opportunity to cooperate, even with our competition. This doesn't mean that we lose our competitive genes along the way—just that we are collaborating to acquire resources (capital, customers, employees, or whatever) and competitive when we divide them up! Test out their thinking with your own game play at http://mayet.som.yale.edu/coopetition/index2.html, a companion site to their book.

How do great organizational leaders enact this principle of coopetition? Consider two simple strategies for connection and collaboration:

- Develop and cultivate external relationships.
- Embrace differences.

DEVELOP AND CULTIVATE
EXTERNAL RELATIONSHIPS

When we are actively working to be "better with," we see the opportunities to align with other organizations to make our work stronger for both parties. How can it help you to collaborate with competitors? Maybe it's sharing best practices at an industry forum. Maybe together you can create new industry standards that attract a whole new market to your product or service. Maybe a competitor is a company you might want to acquire someday.

Complementary services and products are a critical part of business success. A real estate agent might align with a mortgage broker, a real estate attorney, a general contractor—any company that could increase the value of the real estate agent's services.

Strategic alliances take many forms depending on the level of interdependence and the ownership of the outcomes. For example, my leadership development consulting firm has a very simple and straightforward alliance with an executive recruiter. We refer clients who need a recruiter's help to fill a position to this firm. Should we start to develop programs and materials together, our alliance would become more complex, and our agreements would include issues of ownership, client management, brand representation, and so on. The strength of the idea is its uniqueness, and the way it gives both organizations an advantage.

TRY THIS

Listing Your Opportunities for "Coopetition"

Ask yourself the following questions:

What are our opportunities for aligning with our competition?

What possibilities are we not yet seeing?

How could coopetition help us leverage what we are best at?

In the technology sector, strategic alliances are a mainstay of the industry. Think of Intel and manufacturers of desktop PCs, laptop computers, and wireless devices: "On 9/18/97, Compaq Computer Corp. and Intel Corp. entered into a strategic alliance to develop 100-megabit Ethernet equipment. Under the terms of the agreement, Compaq and Intel shared engineers and marketing resources in the development of the Ethernet network equipment."[7]

In this example, both Compaq and Intel provided employees—each possessing a great deal of tacit knowledge—to develop Ethernet equipment. Most likely, these engineers will draw on their past experiences in product development projects to assist them in this alliance. Since this alliance involves tacit resources (engineering know-how), it will be difficult to imitate and will therefore provide both Compaq Computer Corporation and Intel Corporation with a distinct advantage.[8]

On a different scale, here's a small business example: Toni leads Sage & Onion, a creative catering company that markets various companies offering related services under one umbrella. Toni, the president, is the master chef, and can bring in other small business resources to help her clients get what they're looking for. She works with event planners, florists, even a professional gift wrapper. Toni's strong relationships help her boost client satisfaction and also develop additional revenue streams through reciprocal referral fee arrangements with her chosen providers. The entire alliance is made stronger through a simple win-win premise.

EMBRACE DIFFERENCES

> *Whatever the topic, you have been challenged to resist the tendency—so prevalent in the public sphere, and so dangerous too, at times—to accept one point of view, and then simply forge alliances with those who agree with you.*
> —LEE BOLLINGER

Herrmann International has spent years doing extensive research into diversity of thinking style and the way high-performance teams work. The findings have been consistent across cultures and continents. The highest-performing teams leverage diverse perspectives—meaning that diversity makes groups stronger.

Creative tension comes from diverse opinions, responses to questions, and perspectives. When we all think the same, what comes out of it? The same old ideas. No creativity. No Socratic questioning and meaningful dialogue. We forget to question our assumptions because they are shared in a like-minded group. In the Age of Interdependence, diversity becomes ever more important as we work across continents and cultures. We bring different viewpoints, skills, expertise, and histories—and they are all valuable.

Challenging Discrimination

To challenge discrimination is a critical part of embracing differences. Unfortunately, discrimination is all too common, and is the enemy of cooperative competition.

First things first. Let's take the word *diversity*. Diversity in a business context doesn't just mean race representation. The idea that diversity means that there's a balance of skin color in a group is quite offensive and small-minded. True diversity is about more than race. It's about differences in our human experience.

Valuing diversity means creating a workplace that respects differences, recognizing the unique contributions that people with many types of differences can make, and creating a work environment that maximizes the potential of all employees, viewing diverse perspectives as opportunities for better thinking and ultimately better business.

> *DIVERSITY*: (N) DIVERSENESS, VARIETY
> (NOTICEABLE HETEROGENEITY): "A DIVERSITY
> OF POSSIBILITIES"; "THE DIVERSITY (RANGE AND
> VARIETY) OF HIS WORK IS AMAZING."

All of the "isms" we experience on a daily basis—racism, classism, ageism—where do they come from? Why is it important to bring out these undiscussables in the context of being "better with"? *Because our differences make us powerful together.* We are all born with a fear instinct. It's activated when we're taught to fear something, and often we're taught to fear the different. When someone is different from our small sphere of experiences, we don't know what to assume—what to expect—and our basic fear of the unknown kicks into gear. To truly leverage our diversity, the conversation needs to happen: we need to acknowledge our differences, our similarities, our perspectives that can help us *think more effectively together.*

Leaders who can confront their own biases and can embrace the uniqueness of others and the differences from their own experience offer the best of the curious, appreciative mind-set.

Lance, a sixty-something white executive from California, was shocked when his organization required him to attend a diversity awareness program that was specifically geared toward understanding discrimination in the workplace. He had always thought of himself as an enlightened guy. "We're all really the same. I don't see what this bullshit seminar is supposed to do except provoke a lot of upset in people that doesn't need to be there. I consider myself color-blind."

Lance's words betrayed his lack of understanding and awareness. As a white guy with an Ivy League education, Lance was a man of privilege. He had never experienced racism or sexism. He had also never endeavored to understand the differences between himself and other people, because it was never forced on him that he was different. Popular media images look like him. Leaders in other organizations look like him. Growing up, he never questioned his ability to adapt to the dominant culture—he *was* the dominant culture in his community. Boy was he shocked when he became a "minority" in an experiential exercise, namely Jane Elliott's Blue Eyes/Brown Eyes exercise, the subject of the famous Peabody Award–winning documentary, *Eye of the Storm.*[9]

The exercise works like this: In a large room, the facilitators divide the groups into two sets of people. The people with brown eyes are told they are the superior group. The people with blue eyes are told they are inferior. The blue-eyes are sent out of the room, and the brown-eyes are instructed to behave in a discriminatory way toward the blues when they return. In a very short amount of time, the group begins to see the impact of discrimination on the blues. They are given a history lesson told from the perspective of the brown-eyes, with no mention of the blues. The debrief of the exercise is often very powerful, and was definitely so for Lance.

I feel like that exercise changed my life forever. I really don't know what other people have been through. I've never even been curious about it. It's a completely different experience. I still believe that we're all equal, but I don't think I'll ever believe we're all the same again. I'm also appalled at myself for not thinking this was important. I have said things that could be really offensive, and I was convinced I was being enlightened and accepting. I have always thought of myself as a respectful person, and now I think I need some work.

Lance's pledge at that point forward? To become more curious, more inquisitive, and more excited to understand and appreciate differences.

Leaders who embrace differences build on the following kinds of differences:

- Differences of opinion; using conflict positively
- Differences in culture, background; using awareness positively
- Differences in skills and thinking style; compensating for each other
- Differences in age and experience; accepting and valuing different perspectives

In recognizing ourselves in others, we form bonds and shared understanding. We also need to cultivate our understanding of the inherent value of difference. Think of all the ways we differ from each other, and how exciting those differences of experience, culture, gender, age, race, religion, birth order, language, education really are. Every person is truly a window into another world.

Once we start thinking of our collaborators and our competitors all adding value to our business, we've broken through a barrier to great thinking, and we find ourselves able to use that spirit of competition and the spirit of collaboration all at the same time.

Getting better all the time requires an open, creative mind that is constantly thinking of new ways to be better with others, from your staff members to your competition to your customers to the entire global community. We really are all in this together, and as a leader you can only become better (and make your company better) by working on making the entire world better. If we all do our part, we can all achieve unprecedented—not to mention effective, enduring, and fulfilling—success.

Summary

- If companies eat up resources in order to turn a profit, eventually there will be no resources—and no profit—left. Don't take what you can't replenish.
- The learner sees every bump in the road as a learning experience, every challenge as an opportunity. Instead of collapsing into despair when things go wrong, the learner takes value from all experiences and knows that such experiences are what make people better leaders.
- There is a rich vein of learning to be obtained from our heroes in business and in life—and from the people we *don't* admire.
- If you are willing to take responsibility for your own actions in all circumstances, then you can expect accountability in return.
- For better or worse, all leaders are role models. Leaders who are true representatives are listeners, thinkers, visionaries, and influencers.
- In the Age of Interdependence, running a company needs to involve a more *cooperative competitiveness.*
- Developing positive relationships isn't just for inside of your organization.
- Challenge yourself to embrace a diversity of people, ideas, and opinions.

CHAPTER NINE

BETTER LEADERS MAKE A BETTER WORLD

As we reach the end of this book, I invite you to take a moment to feel the beauty, the wonder, the fragility, and the power of your existence on this earth. I believe you were put in your current leadership position for a reason: to make change for the better. That is the gift of leadership in all its forms. As corporations become powerful global culture builders, as more people from radically different backgrounds come together, we understand more and more deeply every day how connected we all are as a living system on this planet. We depend on one another to survive. As we allow ourselves to open our thoughts to larger and larger circles of influence, we can see that our personal legacy intersects with the greater world, and we feel both the weight and the joy of our personal responsibility for creating positive change that we wish to see.

Understanding your personal legacy, your purpose, your values, and your strengths, what do you do when the world continually changes around you? How do you change and adapt and still lead your legacy? What are some guidelines others have used? Ask Greg Steltenpohl, founder, former CEO, and chair emeritus, Odwalla, Inc.

As a panelist at the World Future Society in July 2005, Greg gave this overview of his experience in leading his legacy:

> A group of friends and myself decided that we were tired of being broke musicians, so we borrowed a couple hundred dollars and starting squeezing orange juice in the backyard, which was com-

pletely different from the typical beverage product, which is mostly water and some flavoring.

We were vegan juiceheads at that time and vegetarianism and healthy diets were a strong part of our personal value system. But we existed in a world where those types of products were almost unseen in the marketplace. Now there is a real confluence between what was fringe and futuristic years ago and what is mainstream. And the fact that Coca-Cola paid quite a premium for our company obviously exhibits either their desire to either hold something back, or own part of a success. . . . So that's an American story. . . .

But in 1996, our company experienced a food safety contamination problem and we had to make a decision whether we would try to get by without a big stir or whether we wanted to plan for the worst possible scenario that might be true and recall all of our products off the shelf. At that point the company was publicly held, and we were doing about $80 million in sales, so there were at least 25 million bottles on the shelves at that time in about seven or eight states.

We decided to voluntarily institute a recall and pulled all of the bottles off the shelf and alerted all our consumers through the media. Our sales went down to about 10 percent of their former levels, the stock dropped in half and we had to get emergency financing on some unsavory terms.

The stock was owned by a lot of institutional investors, but as it started to drop, an amazing thing happened. It hit a point at which people started to buy stock who had drunk the juice for all those years and really liked the company, but could never afford the stock. In about three weeks, we achieved a complete shift in the ownership structure of the company from large investors to very small investors. In fact after the recall, the average holding of shares in the company was only 100 shares. (At $10/share, the average holding was $1,000.)

That was a very eye-opening experience for me. I learned about the power of connectivity between authentic products and their consumer or user base.

I think one of the misunderstandings around socially responsible businesses is that it seems like an obligation . . . when in reality it changes the engine of a company. When you embody a strong values structure inside an organization, it actually drives innovation, it drives commitment, it drives performance. In my experience, there's really no conflict other than an old mental model that says doing good is an expense instead of an asset.

To put it in business terms, we should be thinking of social responsibility and accountability in creating a business as a balance sheet issue, instead of as an income statement problem. But nowadays I think there's more a sinister side to a lot of it as well that I would characterize as a commoditization and monetization of human values. And really it all boils down to, in economic terms, how we act in the marketplace—to monetary capital and what is called "socially responsible investment" strategies.

The next project that I've been working on with Dee Hock (creator of the Visa credit card) is about purchasing and consumption and how to transform the power that citizens, as consumers, really have. My work with Coca-Cola has shown me how sensitized the very largest corporations are to the tenuous threads that hold them to their brand names and their brand values.

This is not a matter of just shifting your investments over into good stocks and then sleeping softly at night. It's not a question of just having a company with a new mission statement and a new set of values and then everything starts to change. All of it boils down to, in my experience, how we are day to day in every type of activity.

Hundreds of millions of people really want to stop being part of the problems, such as the widening gap between rich and poor, environmental degradation, etc. I believe that, just as in the sixties there was a consciousness revolution, there is today in potential a new revolution underneath what we see in the marketplace. So community development and social justice are really part of the new commerce.[1]

INSPIRATION

Think about the word *inspire*—made up of *in* meaning internal and *spire* from the Greek word for breath. To inspire means to breathe life in. Inspiration is our connection to life itself. Without inspiration, we can't move forward and be better. To inspire others is to breathe life into them.

Many leaders talk about wanting to motivate their teams, but I prefer to use the word *inspire*. Why? You can't really motivate someone else. Motivation is internal. You can do all kinds of things to tap into motivation, but if you have someone who doesn't have the talent for selling and you try to motivate them with financial incentives, it still won't work. Salespeople need their own drive and their own talent to be great. Great leaders know that people are motivated by different things, all based on their core values—be they freedom, family, financial achievement, or positive impact.

Motivating others is about your needs. It's about trying to get someone to do what you want them to do. Inspiration is about being in service to others, through giving them a valuable infusion of positive energy, of belief, of belonging, of connection to a greater purpose.

Take a look at excerpts from one of the best-known speeches in recent history, and one of the most inspiring:

> I have a dream that one day this nation will rise up and live out the true meaning of its creed: "We hold these truths to be self-evident: that all men are created equal." I have a dream that one day on the red hills of Georgia the sons of former slaves and the sons of former slave owners will be able to sit down together at a table of brotherhood. I have a dream that one day even the state of Mississippi, a desert state, sweltering with the heat of injustice and oppression, will be transformed into an oasis of freedom and justice. I have a dream that my four children will one day live in a nation where they will not be judged by the color of their skin but by the content of their character. I have a dream today. . . . We will be able to work together, to pray together, to struggle together, to go to jail together, to stand up for freedom together, knowing that we will be free one day. . . .

> This will be the day when all of God's children will be able to sing with a new meaning, "My country, 'tis of thee, sweet land of liberty, of thee I sing. Land where my fathers died, land of the pilgrim's pride, from every mountainside, let freedom ring." And if America is to be a great nation, this must become true. So let freedom ring from the prodigious hilltops of New Hampshire. Let freedom ring from the mighty mountains of New York. Let freedom ring from the heightening Alleghenies of Pennsylvania! Let freedom ring from the snowcapped Rockies of Colorado! Let freedom ring from the curvaceous peaks of California! But not only that; let freedom ring from Stone Mountain of Georgia! Let freedom ring from

Lookout Mountain of Tennessee! Let freedom ring from every hill and every molehill of Mississippi. From every mountainside, let freedom ring.

When we let freedom ring, when we let it ring from every village and every hamlet, from every state and every city, we will be able to speed up that day when all of God's children, black men and white men, Jews and Gentiles, Protestants and Catholics, will be able to join hands and sing in the words of the old Negro spiritual, "Free at last! Free at last! Thank God Almighty, we are free at last!"[2]

Dr. Martin Luther King Jr. exemplifies a "better with" leader. Dr. King did not change the world alone; he did so by creating powerful resonance in his followers, in the world at large, and even with his enemies. His values were clear, and his approach was appreciative, asking: how good could this world be?

How did he execute his leadership vision? How did he lead his legacy? He risked everything—ultimately even his life—for what he knew his community deserved and needed. He addressed the best in people—that which makes us put aside our anger—and he addressed the parts of us that understand that every human being is connected. In the words of a consultant friend of mine, "Martin Luther King Jr. didn't say he had a strategic plan—he had a dream!" Think about that when you are attempting to inspire the people around you to strive for greatness.

There is one other element of Dr. King's speech I want to draw your attention to: Nowhere in the "I Have a Dream" speech does Dr. King say, "Here's what's in this for you."

Think of another inspirational speech from this time period, John F. Kennedy's, "Ask not what your country can do for you; ask what you can do for your country." You need not become a world-famous orator to think about how inspiring a leader you can be. When you are deeply interested in making your organization and the world a better place, your passion will likely shine through in all your words and actions and inspire others—all your various stakeholders—to want to be better, too.

What is inspiring? The following concepts are key to legacy-driven leaders and help them achieve the success they desire for themselves and their organizations. Think about these topics,

> ## TRY THIS
>
> ### Sharing What Inspires You
>
> Take the time to think about these questions, and to share what inspires you with your company. Do you have "town hall" meetings? A blog you can write? A regular newsletter? A podcast? Take time to share your inspiration, and to watch it inspire others.
>
> What inspires you about your company?
>
> Your work? Your industry?
>
> The customers you support?
>
> The people in your organization?
>
> How can you inspire others with that personal story?

and incorporate them into your communications with your stakeholders:

- Vision
- Belief in a positive future
- Shared gain
- Being a citizen with a voice
- Living our values and purpose
- Being great at what we do
- Having an impact on the greater community in a positive way

A New Focus: "Better With" Business Is Coming

Martin Luther King Jr., John F. Kennedy, and the Dalai Lama may seem like nice but irrelevant role models when it comes to the world of business in the twenty-first century. Okay, then I will give you some more contemporary corporate examples of "better with" thinking. I would argue that there is a new movement afoot, and the companies that do not embrace "better" practices will be left behind. Consider the following:

- *BP* is promoting a better understanding of climate change and leading efforts to control greenhouse gas emissions.
- *British Airways* produces an annual corporate responsibility report that details its commitment to best practices regarding the environmental impact in areas of noise, local air quality, climate change, and waste and resource use—with figures on progress to date.[3]
- *The Body Shop* now publishes an annual "Values Report," which, in the company's own words, "is about the future, not the past. It focuses on the challenges facing us as a values-based company . . . and the action we are taking to address them."[4]
- *General Motors* has reduced its CO_2 emissions by more than 1.1 million metric tons, to date. According to the company, the decrease is on par with the annual emissions from the power consumed by 143,000 U.S. households.[5]
- *Green Mountain Coffee* pays fair trade prices for coffee beans from farmer cooperatives in Peru, Mexico, and Sumatra.[6]
- *John Deere* recently decided to forgo selling prime real estate to a developer, instead donating $1.5 million in land and facilities to Western Illinois University, allowing the university to better serve the community, including Deere's employees.[7]
- *Patagonia* explains that its corporate definition of quality "includes a mandate for building products and working with processes that cause the least harm to the environment. We evaluate raw materials, invest in innovative technologies, rigorously police our waste and use a portion of our profits to support groups working to make a real difference. We acknowledge that the wild world we love best is disappearing. . . . We believe in using business to inspire solutions to the environmental crisis."[8]
- *Starbucks* claims as one of the company's guiding principles, "to contribute positively to our communities and our environment." The company makes community investments in three areas: literacy, environment, and coffee origin communities. A large portion of its giving supports local organizations. In its

hometown of Seattle, Washington, the company provides grants for parks and the local library system.[9]

Many other companies are also using more than Wall Street numbers to determine and measure their success. They are following a growing trend by reporting on economic, environmental, and social dimensions of their activities, products, and services. One catchphrase for this new way of looking at corporate success is the "triple bottom line," and I think we can all use a dose of it to prompt great thinking about how we benefit the world through our leadership.

The triple bottom line measures impact on three levels:

- *Economic:* Measuring the bottom line financially
- *Social:* Measuring impact on people in the external community
- *Environmental:* Measuring environmental impact

When you think about your own life and work, how would your contribution to your organization measure up in each of these three areas? How have you helped the organization to grow economically? How have you helped the organization to serve the community and environment for the greater good?

Often the answers to those questions are something like, "I help the company grow economically every day, and how am I going to take time out of doing that to grow trees or tutor inner-city kids?!" I want to challenge that idea for you. Think of a time when you were extremely successful at a given job. My guess is that you succeeded because you were giving of yourself in some way—you were fully engaged, focused, and ready to deliver. When you were calm and centered, and you knew what you were doing was important in some way. When community and environmental involvement are part of your corporate purpose and values, they become ingrained in your culture and no longer feel like extras. They become essentials.

Here are ten suggestions for developing and reinforcing corporate good citizenship in your organization:

1. Act as you say you believe. Your team is looking to you as a role model.

2. Appoint a dedicated person or a team to head your "good citizenship" efforts. This person will be the main point of contact and accountable for reporting results.
3. Engage everyone with the values of the organization.
4. Create opportunities for community volunteerism within team-building or management development programs.
5. Match employee donations to favorite charities.
6. Support volunteering in the community.
7. Establish and support a formal corporate social responsibility program.
8. Set goals around sustainability and reward those who contribute ideas and labor to make the goals a reality.
9. Ask your employees, "How can we do well by doing good?" and use their ideas.
10. Identify behaviors that exemplify the values of your organization, and use those behaviors in performance evaluation.

At Eileen Fisher, a women's clothing company, I spoke with Susan Schor, whose title is chief culture officer. She told me:

We believe deeply in our values, and by your definition we are much more "better with" than "better than." It's really who we are, from an employee's point of view it's what she learns about the company when she's hired. Our interview process is collaborative. People begin to feel the extent of the collaboration we do as soon as they're interviewed. Leadership is important—everyone is a leader. Everyone from supervisor up goes through our leadership development program.

Our leaders at every level have a responsibility to others, inclusion, follow-through, contribution, collaboration. It's about leading from our values and honoring our values. They are responsible for individual growth and well-being, collaboration and teamwork, encouraging a joyful atmosphere, and social consciousness.

In order to support our beliefs, we have a social consciousness department. In our everyday work we are involved in human rights work in factories, philanthropy, wellness, and the environment. That work is integrated into all aspects of our company. Whether it's an environment project around recycling, or a big endeavor around sourcing our fabrics—we have an organic cotton line—we're trying to expand that.

The social consciousness department is responsible for action on the following commitments:

- To support women through social initiatives that address their well-being

- To practice business responsibly with absolute regard for human rights

- To guide our product and practice toward sustaining our environment

The social consciousness staff meets with all of the retail store staff so they feel knowledgeable about how our factories operate, and how our business enacts each of our commitments. We hear very positive things from our customers about our social consciousness, but that's not why we have that department. It's just part of us almost since the get-go. We care about people, product, the planet, and profits.

A Growing Movement

> *What if these gargantuan entities, filled with the creative potential of thousands of human beings, were to awaken to this new global reality? . . . If business were to awaken, and then to change, it would have unprecedented impact— transforming the world in ways we cannot even imagine.*
> —Elizabeth Debold, in *What Is Enlightenment?* magazine

In our Age of Interdependence, "better with" thinking is also infiltrating universities, business schools, and nongovernmental organizations (NGOs). We are teaching tomorrow's leaders to be appreciative, inspirational, and legacy-driven. Take a look at what's popping up around the globe: a master's program in positive organizational scholarship at the University of Michigan, Case Western Reserve University's "Business as Agent of World Benefit" Center, U.C. Berkeley's Haas School of Business Center for Responsible Business, Social Venture Network, and the World Business Council for Sustainable Development, to name only a few.

"Better with" leadership is a growing movement of great power and with enormous momentum. It is no less than an international movement toward focusing our business leadership on the greater good. This is not just about organic farms and yoga retreat centers;

this is about big corporate business changing the way it works. Leaders who are not aware of this movement and do not get on board will be left behind, just like those leaders who ignored the rise of technology and the personal computer only a few decades ago. Soon every leader will be charged with maintaining and building a triple bottom line.

As consumers and shareholders begin to vote with their dollars, more companies are becoming aware that their bottom line depends on their focus on other types of corporate and leadership responsibility. Investors are demanding to see more than an annual report, and many companies are creating annual corporate social responsibility reporting statements.

How can you begin to adopt similar practices personally and organizationally? Just refer back to the three themes of this book:

- By being *smarter*—asking questions, engaging your curiosity, and embracing adaptation and flexibility.
- By moving *faster*—slowing down, focusing and balancing, and creating a healthy, life-sustaining platform from which to work.
- By getting *better with*—focusing on others—your colleagues, your community, and your world, instead of just yourself.

FINAL THOUGHTS: WHY DO YOU LEAD?

A main theme throughout this book is the fact that your leadership is bigger than you. When you are in the flow of leadership, you are engaging in a calling, an obsession, a duty, and a privilege. Leadership requires self-sacrifice and a dedication to serving something greater than you are. So why do you do it? Why do you lead? What idea are you fighting for? Why are you willing to sacrifice? How will you sustain yourself and your organization through thick and thin?

For me, the answer is clear. I lead because I feel I am called to do so. I enjoy the challenge of creating a vision, collaborating with others, and staying true to a set of values that can make a difference in how my team makes decisions. I believe in people, and in their capacity to grow and change. I believe in the power of thinking partnerships, and that great things happen when people commit to taking positive action. I believe in working for our global good and, in Mohandas Gandhi's words, that we must "be the change we wish to see in the world." It is a daily practice to stay true to my values in my actions, and a commitment to smarter, faster, better leadership requires me to do so. I believe in leadership at every level: we are all leaders when we are willing to step up for what we believe, to rally support behind it, and take action in collaboration with others. When I am the best leader I can be, I am contributing to the smarter, faster, better leadership of others. That is why I lead.

I know there is a reason that you chose the path of leadership. No one gets here by mistake. It's not easy. It involves commitment and faith in the stewardship of an idea that is larger than ourselves. It's a process of continually becoming smarter, faster, and better, and of realizing that, in many ways, you're already moving toward all of your goals, simply by taking on the challenge of being a leader. But every day is a new opportunity to improve, achieve, contribute, and enjoy yourself a little more than the day before.

Enjoy the journey.

Summary

- Focus on inspiring your team rather than motivating them.
- The "triple bottom line" concept of corporate responsibility measures a company's impact on three levels: economic, social (community), and environmental.
- "Better with" leadership is a growing trend. Those who do not embrace this model will be left behind.
- "Better with" thinking is also infiltrating universities, business schools, and NGOs. We are teaching tomorrow's leaders to be appreciative, inspirational, and legacy-driven.
- Take time every so often to stop and think about why you lead. You have the opportunity to make a positive difference every day.

NOTES

Chapter One

1. David Cooperrider, Diana Whitney, and Jaqueline Stavors, *The Appreciative Inquiry Handbook,* San Francisco: Berrett-Koehler, 2003, p. 1.
2. Cooperrider, Whitney, and Stavors, p. 3.

Chapter Two

1. David Cooperrider, Diana Whitney, and Jaqueline Stavors, *The Appreciative Inquiry Handbook,* San Francisco: Berrett-Koehler, 2003.
2. Ann Herrmann, telephone interview with Karlin Sloan, July 25, 2005.
3. Abraham Maslow with Deborah Stephens and Gary Heil, *Maslow on Management,* New York: Wiley, 1998, p. 28.
4. Lee C. Bollinger, "Remarks for 2005 Commencement Exercises," Columbia University, New York, NY, May 18, 2005. Available online: http://www.columbia.edu/cu/president/communications%20files/commencement2005.htm. Access date: Mar. 24, 2006.
5. Susan Dunn, "When All Else Fails, Use Your Intuition," n.d. (available online: http://barvin.com/print.aspx?ID=411; access date: Jan. 20, 2006); and Jagdish Parikh, *Intuition: The New Frontier of Management,* New York: Blackwell Business, 1994.
6. Daniel Goleman, Richard Boyatzis, and Annie McKee, "Primal Leadership: The Hidden Driver of Great Performance," *Harvard Business Review* (special issue on breakthrough leadership), Dec. 2001, pp. 42–51.
7. Daniel Goleman, Richard Boyatzis, and Annie McKee, *Primal Leadership: Learning to Lead with Emotional Intelligence,* Boston: Harvard Business School Press, 2004.
8. Martin Seligman, *Helplessness: On Development, Depression, and Death,* New York: Freeman, 1992.
9. Barbara L. Fredrickson, "What Good Are Positive Emotions?" *Review of General Psychology,* 1998, *2*(3), 300–319.
10. Joseph Jaworski, *Synchronicity: The Inner Path of Leadership,* San Francisco: Berrett-Koehler, 1996. p. ix.

Chapter Three

1. David Cooperrider, Diana Whitney, and Jaqueline Stavors, *The Appreciative Inquiry Handbook,* San Francisco: Berrett-Koehler, 2003, p. 8.
2. Abraham Maslow with Deborah Stephens and Gary Heil, *Maslow on Management,* New York: Wiley, 1998, p. 20.
3. R. Rosenthal, *Pygmalion in the Classroom,* New York: Holt, Rinehart & Winston, 1969.
4. Judith Glaser, *Creating We: Change I-Thinking to WE-Thinking and Build a Healthy, Thriving Organization,* Avon, Mass.: Platinum Press, 2005.

Chapter Four

1. Brainwave discussion is based on http://www.immrama.org/brainwave/brainwave1.html. Access date: Nov. 18, 2005.
2. Stephen Covey, *First Things First* (reprint ed.), New York: Free Press, 1996.
3. Joshua S. Rubinstein, David E. Meyer, and Jeffrey E. Evans, "Executive Control of Cognitive Processes in Task Switching," *Journal of Experimental Psychology—Human Perception and Performance,* 2004, 27(4). Rubinstein works for the Federal Aviation Administration, while Meyer and Evans are at the University of Michigan.
4. For more information on Women for Women International, please visit http://www.womenforwomen.org. Access date: Nov. 18, 2005.

Chapter Five

1. Michael Ray, *The Highest Goal: The Secret that Sustains You in Every Moment,* San Francisco: Berrett-Koehler, 2004.
2. Evan Robinson, "Why Crunch Mode Doesn't Work," 2005. Available online: http://www.igda.org/articles/erobinson_crunch.php. Access date: Nov. 20, 2005.
3. J. R. Jones, C. S. Huxtable, and J. T. Hodgson, *Self-Reported Work-Related Illness in 2003/04: Results from the Labour Force Survey,* Suffolk, United Kingdom: HSE Books, 2005.
4. J. Watts, "In a Climate of Overwork, Japan Tries to Chill Out," *Lancet,* Sept. 21, 2003, p. 932.
5. Michael A. Stoto, Ruth Behrens, and Connie Rosemont, eds., *Healthy People 2000: Citizens Chart the Course,* Washington, D.C.: National Academy Press, 1990. Available online: http://books.nap.edu/catalog/1627.html. Access date: Nov. 20, 2005.
6. Andre Codrescu, "Sabbath: Good for Non-Believers Too," broadcast in the "Poet on Call" segment of *All Things Considered,* National Public Radio, Oct. 21, 2005.

Chapter Six

1. Gary Erickson, *Raising the Bar: Integrity and Passion in Life and Business: The Story of Clif Bar Inc.,* San Francisco: Jossey-Bass, 2004. Background

info is from the "Clif Bar" corporate Web site, www.clifbar.com. Access date: Nov. 20, 2005.

2. David Cooperrider, Diana Whitney, and Jaqueline Stavors, *The Appreciative Inquiry Handbook,* San Francisco: Berrett-Koehler, 2003, pp. 38–42.

3. Mihaly Csikszentmihalyi, *Flow: The Psychology of Optimal Experience,* New York: Harper Perennial, 1990, p. 6.

Chapter Seven

1. The discussion of Athens and Melos comes primarily from Thucydides, *The History of the Peloponnesian War* (Richard Crawley, trans.), *Great Books of the Western World 5,* Chicago: Encyclopaedia Britannica, 1991.

2. See also Donald Kagan, *The Fall of the Athenian Empire,* Ithaca, N.Y.: Cornell University Press, 1987.

3. Jim Collins and Jerry Porras, *Built to Last,* New York: HarperBusiness, 1994, p. 55.

4. Collins and Porras, 1994, p. 55.

5. From Janel M. Radke, *Strategic Communications for Nonprofit Organizations: Seven Steps to Creating a Successful Plan,* New York: Wiley, 1998.

6. Merrill Associates, "Generation Y: The New Global Citizens," June 2004. Available online: http://www.merrillassociates.net/topic/2004/06/generation-y-the-new-global-citizens/. Access date: Jan. 19, 2006.

7. Eric Chester, *Employing Generation Why?* N.J.: Chess Press, 2002.

8. C. George Boeree, "Personality Theories: Abraham Maslow, 1980–1970," 1998. Available online: http://www.ship.edu/~cgboeree/maslow.html. Access date: Nov. 21, 2005.

9. Jim Collins, "Laboratory: Level 5 Leadership," n.d. Available online: http://www.jimcollins.com/lab/level5/p2.html. Access date: Jan. 22, 2006.

10. Abraham Maslow with Deborah Stephens and Gary Heil, *Maslow on Management,* New York: Wiley, 1998, pp. 20–42.

11. His Holiness the Dalai Lama's Nobel Prize acceptance speech, University Aula, Oslo, Dec. 10, 1989. Available online: http://www.tibet.com/DL/nobelaccept.html. Access date: Jan. 19, 2006.

12. Jim Collins, "Foreword," in Maslow with Stephens and Heil, 1998. Available online: http://eqi.org/maslow.htm. Access date: Jan. 20, 2006.

Chapter Eight

1. For more on the film and the movement surrounding it, see http://www.thecorporation.com/. Access date: Nov. 21, 2005.

2. Interface Sustainability Report, Aug. 31, 2004. Available online: http://www.interfacesustainability.com/. Access date: Jan. 20, 2006.

3. Interview included in Kate Bonamici, "How I Make Decisions," *Fortune,* June 20, 2005, p. 123. Available online: http://www.fortune.com/fortune/print/0,15935,1070964,00.html. Access date: Nov. 21, 2005.

4. Robert Wright, *The Moral Animal: Why We Are the Way We Are,* New York: Vintage, 1994; and *Nonzero: The Logic of Human Destiny,* New York: Pantheon, 2000.

5. Samuel B. Griffith (trans.), *Sun Tzu's The Art of War,* Oxford, England: Oxford University Press, 1963.

6. Paraphrased from Wright, 2000.

7. S. Parise and J. C. Henderson, "Knowledge Resource Exchange in Strategic Alliances," *Knowledge Management,* 2001, *40*(4). Available online: http://www.research.ibm.com/journal/sj/404/parise.html. Access date: Jan. 20, 2006.

8. S. Parise and J. C. Henderson, "Knowledge Resource Exchange in Strategic Alliances," *IBM Systems Journal,* 2001, *40*(4).

9. ABC News, *Eye of the Storm,* Video, 1970.

Chapter Nine

1. Reprinted with permission from The Center for Visionary Leadership, http://www.visionarylead.org.

2. Martin Luther King Jr., "I Have a Dream," speech delivered Aug. 28, 1963, in Washington, D.C. Available online: http://americanrhetoric.com/speeches/Ihaveadream.htm. Access date: Mar. 29, 2006.

3. See, for example, the 2004/2005 Corporate Responsibility Report. Available online: http://www.britishairways.com/travel/corpresp05env/public/en_gb. Access date: Nov. 22, 2005.

4. The Body Shop Web site, "The Body Shop Values Report 2005." Available online: http://valuesreport.thebodyshop.net. Access date: Mar. 20, 2006.

5. GM Web site, News & Issues, "GM to Reduce Stationary CO_2 Emissions 8 Percent by 2005," Dec. 7, 2004. Available online: http://www.gm.com/company/gmability/environment/news_issues/news/co2_120604.html. Access date Nov. 22, 2005.

6. Peter Asmus, "100 Best Corporate Citizens for 2004: Companies That Serve a Variety of Stakeholders Well," *Business Ethics,* Spring 2004. Available online: http://www.business-ethics.com/100best.htm#Article. Access date: Nov. 22, 2005.

7. Asmus, 2004.

8. Patagonia Web site, "Environmental Action," n.d. Available online: http://www.patagonia.com/enviro/main_enviro_action.shtml. Access date: Nov. 22, 2005.

9. Starbucks Web site, "Building Community," 2005. Available online: http://www.starbucks.com/aboutus/community.asp. Access date: Nov. 22, 2005.

RESOURCES

For corporate leadership and management programs based on this book, contact http://www.smarterfasterbetter.com and http://www.karlinsloan.com for more information.

Smarter Online Resources

Appreciative Inquiry Commons: http://appreciativeinquiry.cwru.edu

Herrmann International: http://www.hbdi.com

Ode magazine: http://www.odemagazine.com

Martin Seligman: http://www.authentichappiness.org

Abraham Maslow Publications: http://www.maslow.com

Faster Online Resources

The Wild Divine Project: http://www.wilddivine.com

Heartmath: http://www.heartmath.com

Harvard Health Publications: http://www.health.harvard.edu/special_health_reports/Stress_Control.htm

Better Online Resources

Global Reporting Initiative: http://www.globalreporting.org

The Global Business for Social Responsibility homepage: http://www.bsr.org

What Is Enlightenment? magazine: http://www.wie.org

Social Venture Network: http://www.svn.org

The Caux Round Table Principles: http://www.cauxroundtable.org

The Investor Responsibility Research Center: http://www.irrc.org

The International Business Leaders Forum: http://www.iblf.org

The Aspen Institute: http://www.aspeninstitute.org

ACKNOWLEDGMENTS

As with all big efforts, the process of creating this book was joyful, stressful, and impossible without the contribution of innumerable wise people.

My first thanks must go to Lindsey Pollak, the midwife, wordsmith, and transformer of these ideas, and to Kathe Sweeney at Jossey-Bass for convincing the team that a new author could actually sell books. Also to Julie Huss, my first writing coach, and Barbara Johnson, who both let me know this path was really for me.

As for the contributors to this book, there are too many to count and list, but great thanks go to the wonderful consulting team and extended network I'm privileged to work with, including those listed here who's stories I've used in these pages: Christina Barr, Elizabeth Cahill, Noah Blumenthal, Steve Buttner, Ben Dattner, Laurel Donnellan, Ann Fisher, Judith Glaser, Steve Goldberg, Alan Graham, John Griffith, Nicey Hilton, Sharon Horowitz, Ken Kesslin, Miles Kierson, Starr McCaffery, Elizabeth Moran, Suzi Pomerantz, Jeremy Robinson, Michael Sanson, Ethan Schutz, Deborah Shea, Lionel Shockness, Susan Spero, Susan Spritz-Myers, Robyn Stratton-Berkessel, Karen Szymanski, and Jeff Ward. Also to the wonderful members of the International Consortium for Coaching in Organizations and the Executive Coaching Summit who offered ideas, case studies, and support.

I want to give particular thanks to those who contributed not just stories and insights but edits, commentary, research, and many extra hours of loving work to this project, just because you believed in it. Thank you Kevin Cuthbert, Alan Graham, Franklin Jonath, M. Nora Klaver, and Sandra Reynolds.

To the many leaders I have had the privilege to work with and learn from, who are too many to mention here. You know who you are, and I am truly grateful for our collaboration, conversation, and mutual growth. To the coaches I've worked with both personally and professionally, thank you so much for your support, wisdom, and thinking partnership.

To my wonderful family—Kathy, Sue, Michael, Pegi, Pat, Barbara, Jay, Meghan, Erin, Baird, Steven, Julie, Jackson, Susan, Steve, Justin, Hannah, Clarence, and Hardie—I am grateful for all your love and support. And to friends near and far, thank you for keeping the flame alive.

To my partner in life, Charles Isaac, thank you for everything.

K.S.

THE AUTHORS

KARLIN SLOAN, founder and president of Karlin Sloan & Company, provides organization development consulting, leadership development programs, and executive coaching program coordination to clients in the United States, Europe, South America, and Asia. She has helped organizations develop clearer, more effective communication, enhanced teamwork, and powerful leadership in times of growth and change.

An impassioned teacher and learner, Sloan is a frequent orator on the topic of coaching and leadership development. She has been featured on ABC News Network's *Moneyscope,* Fox Channel Five's *Good Day New York,* and Boston Cable Network's series *The Art of Coaching.*

Considered a thought leader in executive coaching, Sloan is a founding member of the International Consortium for Coaching in Organizations, giving her access to a worldwide network of top coaching talent. She has published articles in *OD Practitioner,* ASTD's *Leadership and Organization Development Newsletter,* and the *International Journal of Coaching in Organizations.* In addition, she writes a quarterly column titled "Executive Coach" for *Executive Travel Magazine.* She has been featured in the *Los Angeles Times,* the *Christian Science Monitor,* and numerous other publications as an expert in workplace behavior. *Fortune Small Business* magazine recognized her for her consulting work with organizations in New York City following the terrorist attacks of September 11, 2001.

She holds a B.A. from Mills College, an M.A. in clinical psychology from the San Francisco School of Psychology, and executive coach certification through the William James Institute's Center for Executive Coaching. She is currently an adjunct faculty member at Wharton Executive Education.

Her client list includes Accenture, Allstate, Citibank, Leo Burnett, Starcom Mediavest Group, Interbrand, MTV Networks, Pennsylvania Life, Jose Cuervo International, GM Planworks, P&G Productions, Rodale, and Knight Ridder.

LINDSEY POLLAK is a writer and editor with a range of experience in books and magazines. She is a coauthor of *Women for Hire: The Ultimate Guide to Getting a Job* (Penguin Putnam, 2002) and a contributor to *Women's Studies on Its Own: A Next Wave Reader in Institutional Change* (Duke University Press, 2002). She has served as editor or collaborator for five additional business books.

Pollak is also the newsletter editor for the Downtown Women's Club and has published career advice articles in *Metro New York* newspaper, *New York Moves* magazine, and the Girl Scouts' *Leader* magazine. She speaks frequently about career issues at universities and professional associations across the country.

Pollak is a graduate of Yale University and received a master's degree in women's studies from Monash University in Melbourne, Australia. She is a member of the American Society of Journalists and Authors.

INDEX